# WALL
# STREET
# POTHOLES

# WALL STREET POTHOLES

## INSIGHTS FROM TOP MONEY MANAGERS ON AVOIDING DANGEROUS PRODUCTS

SIMON LACK

WILEY

Published by John Wiley & Sons, Inc., Hoboken, New Jersey.
Published simultaneously in Canada.

For general information on our other products and services or for technical support, please contact our Customer Care Department within the United States at (800) 762-2974, outside the United States at (317) 572-3993 or fax (317) 572-4002.

Wiley publishes in a variety of print and electronic formats and by print-on-demand. Some material included with standard print versions of this book may not be included in e-books or in print-on-demand. If this book refers to media such as a CD or DVD that is not included in the version you purchased, you may download this material at http://booksupport.wiley.com. For more information about Wiley products, visit www.wiley.com.

*Library of Congress Cataloging-in-Publication Data*
Lack, Simon, 1962- author.
  Wall Street potholes : insights from top money managers on avoiding dangerous products / Simon Lack.
    pages cm
  Includes bibliographical references and index.
  ISBN 978-1-119-09327-5 (cloth) – ISBN 978-1-119-09329-9 (ePDF) –
ISBN 978-1-119-09325-1 (epub)
  1. Investments. 2. Portfolio management. 3. Finance, Personal. I. Title.
  HG4521.L25 2016
  332.6 – dc23

                                                          2015029534

Cover Design: Wiley
Cover Image: © iStock.com/Mlenny

Printed in the United States of America

10  9  8  7  6  5  4  3  2  1

*This book is dedicated to the anonymous retail investor trying to navigate a complex financial world.*

# CONTENTS

# PREFACE

Financiers were never especially well liked prior to the financial crisis of 2008. The bank bailouts compounded a general belief that bankers always make money regardless of the outcomes for their clients. This popular view had never sat easily with me as one who had made his career first in London and then on Wall Street. Although there were inevitably bad actors, I clung to the idea that part of the reputational challenge was the result of poor understanding by the general public.

Then I met Penelope, as described in Chapter 1, and was prompted to learn about non-traded REITs (real estate investment trusts), a murky corner of the securities markets that can only damage the reputation of anybody involved in the sale of these instruments to the general public. The fees, conflicts of interest, disingenuous marketing, and more fees were breathtaking. That it was all legal, because of its disclosure via a thick, densely written prospectus, was astonishing.

Discussions with industry colleagues found like-minded practitioners with their own examples of shoddy, self-interested advice provided to trusting clients. It soon became clear that a collection of advice from people on the inside would fill a needed gap in the education available to people simply trying to save for retirement.

The CFA Institute's efforts to shape the "Future of Finance," and especially the Putting Investors First initiative, provided further impetus to promote better outcomes by warning against the wrong types of advice and products. Too often, the financial salesperson's interests are placed well ahead of the client's.

It is with this goal in mind, of Putting Investors First and thereby aiding better outcomes, that the five authors of this book have come together. The few we may offend are far less important than the many we hope to help.

# ACKNOWLEDGMENTS

Inspiration for this book came from my contributing authors Kevin Brolley, John Burke, Bob Centrella, and David Pasi. We all share a common vision that investing should be simpler, cheaper, and devoid of fee-laden traps. Further encouragement was provided by many other finance professionals, including Rich Covington and Tony Loviscek.

In my career I have had the good fortune to work repeatedly for people in banking for whom integrity was priceless, notably Don Layton, Don Wilson III, David Puth, and Jeffery Larsen. They represent the best of finance and what I still believe is the vast majority of financiers, notwithstanding the visible transgressions of some. Their values became mine.

The CFA Institute with its "Future of Finance" initiative, including Putting Investors First, promotes financial ethics as a cornerstone of investment competence, providing an institutional confirmation of the importance of doing the right thing.

The wonderful editing staff at John Wiley once again both shared our vision on an important topic and immeasurably improved the final result.

# CHAPTER 1

# NON-TRADED REITs: A SECURITY THAT SHOULDN'T EXIST

## POOR ADVICE

"I'm afraid you've been poorly advised," I told the new client as she sat in my office. That was certainly an understatement—in fact, she'd been ripped off by the advisor at the brokerage firm that invested her money.

We had just finished reviewing the investments in her portfolio, which she had brought to me out of dissatisfaction with her existing advisor. It was a familiar discussion for me. I have worked in finance my entire life, mostly in New York, but early in my career I was in London. Since 2009 I've run my own investment business helping clients from individuals to institutions invest their money. The 23 years I spent at JPMorgan and the banks that preceded its many mergers was great preparation. During that time, I managed derivatives trading through enormous growth and at times high volatility; oversaw traders handling risks across multiple products and currencies; and more recently, led a business that helped new hedge funds get off the ground. I had seen Wall Street and "The City" (London's financial district) from the inside. It had been a great career, but by 2009, I was ready for a new challenge. The daily commute was increasingly a mind-numbing grind, and big financial companies were likely to face ever-greater constraints on their activities. The politics of financial reform understandably reflected public abhorrence at the required level of support from the US government following the 2008 financial crisis.

I was and remain very proud of my career at JPMorgan. The company emerged from 2008 in better shape than any of its peers. While it's true that it has had to concede substantial settlements to regulators since then, it's impossible for any big company to be immune from poor decisions or bad behavior somewhere in its ranks. The culture and the people with whom I worked overwhelmingly reflected the best in terms of values and integrity.

So I'd left the huge company where I'd spent almost my entire adult life to run something far smaller but also completely devoid of bureaucracy. My firm would reflect the values of the best people I'd worked with over the years as it sought attractive long-term investments in a format that treated clients' money as if it was mine. Many firms, and many people, do the same thing. But as I've found out since 2009, they don't *all* do the right thing. There's plenty of room for improvement in the quality of financial advice that is given to investors.

We all have to trust professionals when we need help with something that is not what we do for a living, whether it's medical treatment, legal advice, or auto repair. We generally buy products and services with the knowledge of an amateur, and we are often vulnerable to an unscrupulous provider. We look for honesty; when we don't find it, sometimes we discover in time to protect ourselves and sometimes we don't.

The world of investment advice can be dauntingly confusing. Saving for retirement is increasingly the responsibility of the individual, as defined benefit pension plans are phased out in favor of defined contribution plans, 401(k)s, and IRAs. Unless you're a public-sector employee where pensions are still based on your salary just prior to retirement, the money you have when you stop working will largely be the result of decisions you made (or failed to make) during your decades in the work force.

My client, whom we'll call Penelope (not her real name), sat across from me waiting for an explanation as to precisely what poor advice she had received. She was here with her husband, and we had met through a mutual friend. Like many investors, Penelope and her husband are smart people who have enjoyed professional success without having to understand the intricacies of investment products. Penelope is in the pharmaceutical industry (not uncommon in New Jersey) and her husband works for an information technology company.

Penelope had bought into a very common investment called a Real Estate Investment Trust (REIT). REITs typically own income-generating commercial property, including office buildings, warehouses, shopping centers, rental apartments, and so on. They can be a great way for individuals to own real estate managed by a professional company. Many REITs are publicly traded, allowing investors to sell their holding at the market price, and there are mutual funds and exchange traded funds (ETFs) that provide exposure to REITs. Used properly, they can be a legitimate component of an investor's portfolio providing income and some protection against inflation.

However, not all REITs are good, and a particular class of them called "non-traded REITs" is generally to be avoided. Penelope had unwittingly invested some of her savings in the wrong kind of REIT, one that provides substantial guaranteed fees to the broker selling it while often generating disappointing returns for the investor.

Public securities are registered with the SEC under the 1940 Investment Company Act. Registering a security requires the company to meet various tests for accounting standards, transparency, and so on. The advantage of registering is that the security can be sold to the general public. Unregistered securities have a far more restricted set of potential buyers. The investors have to be "sophisticated" (meaning wealthy, in this case), and the seller of such securities has to adopt a targeted marketing approach, going directly to people he thinks may be interested. You won't often see an unregistered security advertised, because the laws are designed to prevent that.

Hedge funds are another example of an unregistered security. Their sale is restricted to "sophisticated" investors deemed able to carry out their own research. It's a sensible way to divide up the world of available investments. Retail investors are offered securities that are registered and usually those securities are publicly traded, enabling the investor to sell if they wish. Sophisticated investors including high-net-worth individuals and institutions don't need the same type of investor protection, which allows them to consider unregistered investments that have higher return potential and also higher risk.

Non-traded (also known as unlisted) registered REITs fall in between these two classes of investment. By being registered, they are available to be sold to the general public. Having gone to the effort of registering, it's a reasonable question to ask why they don't also seek a public listing. It would clearly seem to be in the interests of the investors to have the liquidity of a public market listing so that they can choose to sell in the future. In fact, non-traded REITs have highly limited liquidity and often none at all. They can only be sold back to the issuing REIT itself, and the REIT is under no obligation to make any offer to repurchase its shares. They are a hybrid security—no public market liquidity and yet available to be sold to the public.

Generally, companies that need to raise capital, whether equity or debt, desire liquid markets in which to issue their securities. Liquid markets are widely believed to reduce a company's cost of finance. This is because investors require an illiquidity premium, or higher return, if they have limited opportunities to sell. Private equity investors expect to earn a higher return than if they had invested their capital in public equity markets. Small-cap stocks similarly need to generate higher returns than large-cap stocks to compensate for their more limited liquidity.

Although monthly income is the main selling point, the illiquidity can mean that your holding period exceeds the lease term on the properties. For example, if the non-traded REIT in which you're invested has five-year leases on its properties but you hold the investment for ten years, you have much more at risk than just your exposure to the monthly income.

Bond issuers care a great deal about the liquidity in the bonds they issue, and the selection of bond underwriter is based in part on the firm's commitment and ability to subsequently act as market maker after the bonds are issued. The ability to sell bonds at a later date induces buyers to accept a lower yield than they would otherwise, thereby reducing the bond issuer's interest cost.

To cite a third example, the justification for high-frequency traders (HFTs) with their lightning-fast algorithms in the equity markets is that their activities improve liquidity. Michael Lewis in *Flash Boys* provided a fascinating perspective on how HFT firms have been able to extract substantial profits from investors through using their speed to front run orders. I'm not going to examine HFT firms here, but suffice it to say that their existence reflects the overwhelming public interest in the most liquid capital markets possible.

## WHY NOT GET A LISTING?

So now we return to non-traded REITs, and consider why a company that is qualified to seek a public listing because its securities are registered nonetheless chooses not to. Generally, you want to raise money at the cheapest possible cost, so why do these companies deliberately operate in a way that raises their cost of financing?

I think the answer is, they don't wish to attract any Wall Street research. Brokerage firms routinely publish research on stocks and bonds, and they look to get paid for their research through commissions. Good research gets investors to act on it, and the commissions generated by this activity are what pay for the analysts. Companies want positive research because it will push up their stock price, making the owners richer as well as making it easier to raise more money later on.

But suppose you run a company that is designed primarily to enrich the sponsors at the expense of the buyers? What if you know that drawing the interest of research analysts is likely to result in reports that are critical of fees charged to investors and the conflicts of interest in your business model? Then you would conclude that the higher cost of financing caused by the absence of a public listing is a reasonable price to pay for the higher fees you can charge away from the glare of investment research. Because if there's no public listing, there are no commissions to be earned from trading in the stock, and no commissions means there is little incentive to produce research coverage.

It is into this regulatory gap that the sponsors and underwriters of non-traded REITs have built their business. Illiquid securities are normally only sold to sophisticated investors, but since the securities are registered they can be sold to anybody. This means millions of unsophisticated investors can be induced to make investments that they'd be better off avoiding.

Inland American Real Estate Trust, Inc. (IAR) was the non-traded REIT that drew my attention to this sector. Penelope held an investment in the REIT that had been recommended by her broker at Ameriprise. Disclosure is a great defense. It turns out you can do some pretty egregious things to your clients if you tell them you'll do so in a document. IAR's prospectus discloses many of the unattractive features that characterize how they run their business. Because they are registered, their registration and many other documents are publicly available. They don't necessarily represent either the worst or the best of the sector, but they are one of the biggest non-traded REITs, so it's useful to examine their public filings.

For example, underwriting fees on the issuance consisted of a 7.5% "Selling Commission," a 2.5% "Marketing Commission" and a further 0.5% "Due Diligence Expense Allowance," adding up to a fairly stiff 10.5% of proceeds. But it didn't stop there. In some cleverly crafted prose, the document goes on to explain that "... our Business Manager has agreed to pay ... expenses that exceed 15% of the gross offering proceeds." In other words, up to 15% of the investor's money could be taken in fees.

The registration statement is full of tricky English language such as this. The entire document is 132,192 words, approximately twice the length of this book. It's absurd to think that any investor who's not employed in the industry will read and digest such a thing. The 15% in fees were disclosed around 20% of the way through the document, so in a legal sense the client was informed, but not in a way that represents a partnership between the advisor and the individual.

There are other little gems, too. The company will invest in property that will then be managed by an affiliate. So in other words, the sponsors of IAR will make money from managing the assets owned by IAR as well as for running IAR itself. "Management Fee" occurs 45 times throughout the document, and includes fees on the gross income (i.e., rent). There's also a 1% management fee on the assets. The investors do have to receive a 5% return first, but that return is "non-cumulative, non-compounded," which means that if they didn't earn the 5% return for investors in one year, they don't have to make it up the next year in order to earn their management fee. There are fees of 2.5% to the business manager if they buy a controlling interest in a real estate business. There's also a 15% incentive fee, basically a profit share, after investors have earned 10% (although it's not on the excess profit over 10%, but on the whole profit). The simple word *fee* occurs 528 times.

There are 40 matches for "conflict of interest," including most basically that the buildings owned by IAR will be managed by an affiliate of the sponsor with whom they do *not* have an arm's-length agreement. Said plainly, don't expect that the management of properties is done at a fair price, but be warned that it may be unfairly high.

Now, to be fair, whenever companies issue securities to the public they hire lawyers to construct documents whose purpose is to protect the company from the slightest possibility of being sued after the fact. Glance through the annual report (known as a 10K) of almost any company and you'll find a whole list of "risk factors" telling you why you might lose money on your investment. Even Warren Buffett's Berkshire Hathaway, as honest a company as you'll find, includes a list of risk factors in its 10K that seem fairly obvious, such as, "Deterioration of general economic conditions may significantly reduce our operating earnings and impair our ability to access capital markets at a reasonable cost." You'd think any investor would be aware of this, but it's in there anyway just so they can say they warned you.

IAR mentions "risk factors" 44 times. It warns the investor that it is operating a "blind pool," in that they don't yet know (at the time of the offering) what real estate assets they're going to buy. They go on to warn that there may be little or no liquidity for investors to sell (how true *that* turned out to be).

Another common problem with non-traded REITs is that the high dividends that attract investors may not be backed up by profits. Interest rates have been low now for years and are likely to remain historically low for a good while longer, as I wrote in my last book, *Bonds Are Not Forever: The Crisis Facing Fixed Income Investors*. Low rates benefit people and governments who have borrowed too much, which applies widely in the United States as well as other countries. The low yields on bonds mean investors are starved of opportunities to earn a reliable, fair return with relatively low risk.

Non-traded REITs are sold because of their high dividend yields. However, there's no requirement that the dividends they pay are backed up by profits. They can simply be paid out of capital. This issue isn't limited to REITs, of course. Any company can pay out dividends in excess of its profits, at least for a while. Many companies follow a policy of paying stable dividends even while their profits fluctuate, recognizing the value investors place on such stability. As long as their profits are sufficient to pay dividends and reinvest back in their business for growth over the long term, paying dividends in excess of profits in the short run may not do any harm.

But non-traded REITs can pay a dividend that's higher than they can sustain even in the long run. It's like having a savings account that pays 2%, taking out 3% of it every year, and calling it a dividend. Part of the dividend is your own money coming back to you. Calling it a dividend misleads investors into thinking it's from money earned, which it's not. On top of that, non-traded REITs can often invest in properties that pay high rent but depreciate. An example might be a drug store such as Walgreen's, which could hold a ten-year lease on a property that has no obvious alternative tenants should Walgreen's decide not to renew the lease at its termination. It will pay above-market rent to compensate the building owner (i.e., the REIT) for the possibility that in ten years the building will have to be expensively reconfigured or even torn down in order to find a new tenant. As such, the building may well depreciate during the term of the lease, given the specialized nature of its construction. The depreciation often won't show up in the REIT's financials, leading to a delayed day of reckoning.

In fact, non-traded REITs are notorious for maintaining an unrealistically stable net asset value (NAV). They simply don't update the value of their holdings, and because their securities are not traded there's no way for investors to know if the value of their holding has fluctuated.

## DISINGENUOUS ADVICE

Some advocates of the sector, with utterly no shame, argue that the absence of a public market is a good thing. Sameer Jain, chief economist and managing director of American Realty Capital and someone who really ought to know better, praises "illiquidity that favors the long-term investor" (Jain 2013) as a benefit. Sameer Jain surely must know that illiquidity *never* favors any investor, long term or otherwise. This is why illiquid investments always require an *illiquidity premium,* a higher return than their more liquid cousins, to appropriately reward investors for the greater risk they're taking. Inability to sell what you own is never a good thing. He adds that non-traded REITs are "not subject to public market volatility," as if that's a further benefit. That's like arguing that closing the stock market is good for investors so they can't see their investments fluctuate. Sameer Jain is a graduate of both Massachusetts Institute of Technology (MIT) *and* Harvard University, so I know he *must* be smarter than these statements make him sound. If you don't want to know what your portfolio's worth, don't look! In any case, as long as you haven't borrowed money to invest (rarely a smart move), fluctuating prices need not compel you to do anything you'd rather not do. Looking at an old valuation that's wrong and not updated should not provide comfort to anyone. It's head-in-the-sand, ostrich investing.

For example, in July, 2014 Strategic Realty Trust, another non-traded REIT, reduced the valuation of their REIT by 29% (InvestmentNews 2014), from $10 per share to $7.11. The previous $10 value had remained unchanged since it was launched in August 2009, at what should have been a great time to be investing in anything. It's doubtful any of the hapless investors in Strategic Realty would agree with Sameer Jain that five years of no reported changes in valuation had been helpful.

The reality is that the value of the underlying assets fluctuates depending on the economy, shifts in demand for real estate, location of properties, competition, successful retention of tenants and other reasons. Failing to change the NAV of the security in no way shields investors from their exposure to all these factors, it simply shields them from the knowledge of how their investment's value may have shifted. Publicly traded REITs provide a market perspective on these factors every day through their fluctuating prices.

The true value of Strategic Realty Trust didn't suddenly fall by 29%; that move reflected the cumulative effect of not updating the value over the prior five years. This is why investors normally seek higher returns on illiquid investments, notwithstanding the sales pitch for NTRs.

The point of this is to show how much important information can be buried in the lengthy legal agreements that accompany almost any investment. The challenge for the investor is how to navigate this territory. Penelope's experience is emblematic of an all-too-common problem for individuals trying to invest their money. They often find themselves sitting down with someone who calls themselves a financial advisor, when really they're talking to a salesperson.

In fact, the illiquidity doesn't benefit the "long-term investor" as Sameer Jain misleadingly asserts, but the issuer. For it turns out that, if you want to sell your regrettable investment in a non-traded REIT, without a stock market listing the only realistic buyer is the NTR itself. Persuading investors that they should prefer illiquid securities, and then being positioned to be the only plausible buyer when a hapless investor wants out is the essence of the sales pitch described above.

Penelope made this investment on the recommendation of the person who covered her at Ameriprise, a large brokerage firm (known as a broker-dealer from a regulatory perspective). Ameriprise, like other large brokerage firms, calls the people who deal with clients financial advisors. It's true they provide financial advice to Penelope and millions of others, but it doesn't mean they have a legal obligation to put their clients' interests first. The US regulatory structure recognizes two types of firm facing investors—broker-dealers and investment advisory firms. The difference is a subtle one, especially because many big firms operate as both. Broker-dealers generally charge commissions on trades you do, or in the case of bonds charge a price mark-up if they're selling you a bond they already own. Investment advisors charge a fee for their advice. The crucial difference is the broker profits when you do a transaction. They earn a commission, or a mark-up (or sometimes both). This can present a conflict of interest, in that a transaction may not be good for the client but is always good for the broker. Brokers are not required by law to put the clients' interests first, whereas investment advisors have a legal, fiduciary obligation to put their clients' interests ahead of their own.

One of the confusing things is that a broker can employ people it calls financial advisors, but they are not the same as investment advisors, a term that's legally defined to mean someone advising you as a fiduciary.

Who on earth wants to study the intricacies of US financial regulations? People just want access to honest advice. Calling someone a financial advisor places them in the same category as a doctor or lawyer, two professions that have a legal obligation to put the interests of their client (or patient) first. It's a bit like calling a car salesperson a transport advisor, or a real estate broker a housing advisor. Both will provide you advice, and the recipient of that advice will assess it with the knowledge that it's proffered by someone whose objectives are different than your own. There's nothing wrong with that as long as you know what type of relationship you're getting into.

I should at this point note that many financial advisors at brokerage firms are honest people truly putting the interests of their clients first. I have friends who do just that, and I'm not trying to criticize a whole industry. But they're not all good, and the bad ones create a problem for their clients as well as for the rest of us.

Some feel it would make a lot of sense for the people who work at brokerage firms and call themselves financial advisors to adopt a fiduciary standard, the same as investment advisors. (Yes, I know it's confusing. Financial advisors sound like investment advisors, but they're not.) If financial advisors had to meet a fiduciary standard it would make life far simpler for investors who choose not to become regulatory experts as they look for investment advice. But the brokerage industry recently lobbied successfully against such a move so it's unlikely to happen. I think that as long as a client understands their advisor's actual responsibilities they need not be a fiduciary.

Penelope misunderstood the type of relationship she had with her financial advisor at Ameriprise. Penelope thought she was dealing with someone who was required to consider her interests first and foremost (like a doctor or lawyer) whereas in fact she was dealing with the equivalent of a realtor, someone who would get paid out of the transaction fees extracted from Penelope.

This is where Inland American Real Estate Trust came in. The 10.5% of fees (and potentially up to 15%) that was to come out of the client's money the moment it was invested would typically be shared substantially with Penelope's "advisor." So when Penelope was "advised" to make the investment, the advisor clearly had a conflict of interest. It's no different than a doctor prescribing medication to a patient and receiving a payment from the drug company that provided it.

## WHOSE SIDE IS YOUR FINANCIAL ADVISOR ON?

Some people who call themselves financial advisors sit on your side of the table acting on your behalf. These are Registered Investment Advisors (RIAs). They act as your agent and they're legally obligated to put your interests before theirs. Other financial advisors sit across the table from you, and their interest in the client's well-being is similar to that of any other salesperson. They generally work for brokerage firms (as opposed to investment advisory firms). Yes, they want you to invest your money in something worthwhile, but they also earn a transaction-based fee so products with higher fees benefit this type of advisor and inaction rarely makes them any money.

Many if not most of the financial advisors who work for brokerage firms genuinely put the interests of their clients first. I have friends in the industry about whom I feel comfortable making this statement. And clients who invest through an RIA are charged an advisory fee as well as having to incur commissions on the investments they buy. This can make the use of a financial advisor who works for a brokerage firm appealing in that there are only commissions to be charged. However, I believe the potential for conflict of interest can represent a negative for the client. The protections for clients against being marketed a poor investment can be weak (which was why Penelope was persuaded to invest in the non-traded REIT). The brokerage industry successfully fought attempts to impose a fiduciary standard on their salespeople (who often refer to themselves as financial advisors) so the client is basically reliant on the quality of the person with whom they're dealing.

My own business is a Registered Investment Advisor (RIA) and I am an Investment Advisor Representative (IAR). I'm pretty comfortable that although we charge a fee to manage money, the commissions charged on transactions by the brokerage firms through which we trade are low enough to not make much difference. If you trade online and infrequently, you minimize transactions cost, taxes, and the irrational impulse to try and profit from short-term market moves. The RIA has an obligation to put the client's long-term interests first. The financial advisor at a brokerage firm may put your interests first if he's so moved, but he may not be legally obliged to. As long as his recommendations are suitable and appropriately disclosed, then he's fine. He'll be paid based on his revenue production, and that production is often driven by transaction volume rather than the size of the accounts on which he's providing advice.

So let's return to Penelope and the non-traded REIT, Inland American Real Estate Trust, which she unfortunately owned. It had no public market valuation and therefore no way for Penelope to sell her holding. It had performed very poorly since being initially launched, and the fees charged were shockingly high. In fact, even more surprising than the level of fees was the fact that they weren't actually illegal. You would think being charged 15% of your investment would trigger some kind of securities violation, but it does not. I guess if it's there in the documentation you're expected to have read it.

Nonetheless, I suggested to Penelope that she go back to Ameriprise, who had sold her this investment, and ask them to buy it back from her at the original price. She clearly had not understood what she was getting into, and in my opinion it should never have been sold to her. At first, Penelope was unwilling to do this. She felt the advisor she'd been dealing with was a nice person (albeit evidently not that good at providing financial advice), so Penelope decided to move on and hope that somewhere down the road the REIT might buy back her shares.

A few months later, Massachusetts announced a settlement with the same firm on the same security. William C. Galvin is the Secretary of the Commonwealth of Massachusetts. In this role, he often pursues financial firms for wrongdoing in his state. No doubt many of these firms think he's overly aggressive, but it seems to me he's protecting the citizens of the state he represents. In early 2013, Massachusetts announced a settlement with Ameriprise over the improper selling of Inland American securities, which included an $11 million fine. Although the security itself was clearly designed so as to generate healthy commissions to the brokers that sold it, Ameriprise was merely guilty of selling the REIT to investors who were deemed unsuitable in that they didn't meet the minimum income or wealth standards Ameriprise had set. In other words, some brokers at Ameriprise violated their own standards, a lesser sin than if those standards themselves had been too lax.

Nonetheless it illustrated the conflict of interest that can face financial advisors at a brokerage firm. They may want to sell a security to an investor because of the fees they'll generate, whereas if they were truly an investment advisor not paid on commissions and legally obliged to put the client first, they wouldn't be in that position.

When this news broke, I was able to persuade Penelope to submit an official letter of complaint to Ameriprise. The settlement in Massachusetts was due to a regulator who saw it as his mandate to aggressively protect the citizens of his state. The absence of a similar settlement in New Jersey didn't vindicate Ameriprise in that state; it could simply be that the New Jersey regulator hadn't pursued the company on the same issue.

Penelope hadn't understood the risks and costs of the investment when she'd made it, but it's pretty hard for an individual to achieve redress in such situations. The prospectus (all 132,192 words of it) had spelled out the risks and Penelope was assumed to have read it. Ameriprise declined to do anything. Soon after, a private equity fund offered to buy investors out at a 35% discount to the original offering price. Penelope reasonably enough decided to take the cash offered, and move on. Caveat emptor ("Buyer beware") ought to be on every non-traded REIT prospectus.

Penelope had been poorly served by the financial advisor assigned to her account. While Penelope had treated the relationship as one in which she was receiving advice tailored to her best interests, in reality she was involved in a buyer/seller relationship with misaligned interests. Of course there's nothing necessarily wrong with buying something from a salesman. You just need to approach the relationship with the right perspective. Penelope treated the relationship with her financial advisor the same way she would with a doctor, assuming that the advice offered was devoid of any conflict of interest and was with her best interests first and foremost. Really, she was dealing with a used car salesman.

## WHERE ARE THE REGULATORS?

At this stage, you might ask yourself, where are the regulators? If investors are being sold securities with ridiculously high fees and no liquidity, how come the government isn't doing something about it? There's certainly no shortage of laws and regulations that apply to finance. It is a highly regulated industry, and becoming more so every year. Fortunately, though, the Securities and Exchange Commission (SEC) is not responsible for offering a view on whether an investment is good or not. That's obviously as it should be. Reasonable people disagree all the time on the relative merits of one investment versus another. There's little benefit to the government having a view as well.

But the regulators can warn investors against certain types of investment. FINRA (the Financial Industry Regulatory Authority) has, to its credit, done this. Its website (FINRA 2012) offers warnings about the most adverse features of non-traded REITs, including the fees, lack of liquidity, and the fact that it operates as blind pools (you invest before any properties have been bought so you don't know what you'll own). The website notes that fees can be up to 15% of your invested capital (15% is the legal maximum—probably not coincidentally what Inland American set as its maximum).

FINRA's "Investor Alerts" section of its website includes warnings about several investments that should be approached with a high degree of skepticism, including certain types of annuity, structured notes, and some exchange-traded funds (ETFs). These and other pitfalls are all covered elsewhere in this book. I wasn't even aware of this website myself until I started looking for it—FINRA should find ways to publicize its existence, but it's not the kind of topic that's going to get TV producers lining up to book you on their business show. Nonetheless, at least the regulators are trying to do *something* to warn investors.

If a security is on FINRA's "Investor Alert" page, why would any self-respecting firm even get involved? Shouldn't that be enough to persuade firms that truly put the client first to stay away from such a security? I think that's part of the problem. Too few retail investors are aware of the warnings and potential problems. The brokerage firms involved like the fees and hardly ever find themselves in conversations explaining why they're selling something that, in effect, carries a government warning. It's why finance earns itself a poor reputation. Anybody who's bought a non-traded REIT and after regretting it subsequently found FINRA's website has every reason to be outraged at being offered the security in the first place. There's not enough good judgment being exercised. Maybe there ought to be a requirement that if you're recommending a security that is the subject of one of FINRA's Investor Alert pages, you have to provide a copy of the alert to the clients before they make a decision. Non-traded REITS' warning should be prominent, like that on cigarettes. The warning is already out there, just not well publicized. Doesn't the regulator want the retail investors they're charged with protecting to be aware of the dangers the regulator has identified? Isn't FINRA doing more than just expressing a research view?

I've chatted to some in the industry who disagree with me on non-traded REITs. One in particular thought my criticisms were unjustified and based on a poor understanding of the merits of the product. His argument relied on the fact that he'd had some very positive experiences for his clients with non-traded REITs, in that they'd made money. In other words, he'd found some that worked, so as long as you invested through someone like him possessing the insight to tell the wheat from the chaff, you'd be in good shape.

It's a common argument, and a weak one. First of all, just because some people have made money doesn't mean that on average they will. You can make the same case for casinos or the lottery. There are always some winners, but most gamblers understand that the odds are against them. These people gamble because the excitement of potentially winning overwhelms any understanding they may have of probability theory. Casino owners aren't poor, and publicly run lotteries augment tax revenues in many states. I avoid casinos and don't buy lottery tickets, but the people who do bet on lotteries save the rest of us from even higher taxes so they're performing a selfless public service.

Of course, using the fact of one good non-traded REIT as support for the overall investment sector isn't exactly careful research, any more than the bells ringing on a slot machine should persuade you to sit down with a bucket full of tokens. The correct question is, how have non-traded REITs done in aggregate? It turns out there's no reliable answer to this question. There's no non-traded REIT index. For the brokers who make fees selling them, such an index would probably hurt business. They certainly wouldn't want clients who knew enough to ask for the returns on such an index—the less sophisticated the better. And the existence of an index would also allow the performance on a specific non-traded REIT to be compared against its peers, revealing whether the profitable return was simply a result of a good market for similar securities rather than value-added security selection by the broker.

## OVERALL RETURNS ARE POOR

There is a 2012 study (Reuters 2014) by Blue Vault Partners and the University of Texas that analyzed the start-to-finish returns on 17 non-traded REITs. They found that the internal rate of return (a type of investment return that reflects inflows and outflows on multiple dates) was just over 10%. That sounds good, except that over the same time, publicly traded REITs performed 1% or so better.

Another study carried out by Securities Litigation and Consulting Group (Wall Street Journal 2014), a research company based in Fairfax, Virginia, compared 27 non-traded REITs that had gone through a full cycle from raising capital to returning the proceeds to investors. Their study covered a period of more than 20 years, from June 1990 to October 2013. They found that after fees investors earned 5.2%, compared with the Vanguard REIT Index Fund (a mutual fund) of 11.9%. So in exchange for no liquidity, higher fees, and generally fewer safeguards, investors earned a lower return. Private equity investors expect returns above those available in the public equity market, as compensation for the additional risks involved. An additional return of 3% to 5% is not an uncommon requirement, meaning that if a chosen equity index such as the Russell 2000 returns 10% during the time period that the private equity investor held his investments, he would expect to have earned 13% to 15% or more. Otherwise, the choice of private equity was not worth the risk compared to its more liquid publicly traded equivalent.

There's a saying on Wall Street that certain investments are sold, not bought, in that they require a salesman to push them on a willing investor rather than the buyer actively seeking them out. This would certainly apply to non-traded REITS. Because the first question any investor, or for that matter well-intentioned advisor, should ask before considering non-traded REITs is how the sector is likely to perform going forward. Asset allocation, the choice of how much an investor should put in stocks, investment grade bonds, REITs, high-yield bonds, commodities, or any other asset class generally drives 80% to 90% of the investor's overall return. In other words, assuming you hold a reasonably diversified portfolio and don't bet heavily on just a few investments, if stocks are up 10% you should be up by a similar amount. Of course it's a generalization, but the point is that the biggest decision an investor makes is how much to allocate to an asset class.

So before even considering an individual non-traded REIT, you need to consider how the sector is likely to perform and how this compares with the other assets available to you. This is how institutional investors start their investment process. Given the limited amount of data available for non-traded REITs and the unsophisticated investor base, it's unlikely this basic question receives any attention. It also means that investors are unlikely to properly evaluate the performance of a non-traded REIT once they've bought it. Unless you're in finance for a living, comparing results with a benchmark won't come naturally.

## THE IMPORTANCE OF BENCHMARKING

Non-benchmarked returns are great for the broker, though. You'd think that because numbers are the very essence of investing, they'd be used in discussing performance. It's really quite incredible how often results are presented without comparison to the alternative choice, or the relevant benchmark. A 5% return can only be evaluated if you can compare it with what else you could have done with your money. In the case of non-traded REITs, the upfront fees and ongoing expenses represent a substantial impediment to outperforming or even matching any relevant benchmark. That's why the results are not usually compared with anything. Brokers love nothing more than to use adjectives rather than numbers to characterize the results they've achieved for their clients. It's so much easier to tell a client they were "up 7%, which was good." However, if the investment has lost money, the advisor may well resort to a comparison with a benchmark, such as, "you were down 9% which wasn't bad considering equities were down 11%." It may or may not be a valid comparison. A balanced account with 50/50 stocks and bonds shouldn't be compared simply with equities.

Clients should always ask how a strategy will be evaluated. It's as simple as asking at the beginning of the relationship, "What should we both look at in order to correctly evaluate the performance of my account once you're managing it?" Ideally, it should be compared with a relevant benchmark. An equity strategy should be compared with the S&P 500 if the underlying stocks are large cap US equities. The Russell 2000 might be more appropriate if smaller stocks will predominate. A fixed-income strategy should be compared with a bond index, such as the Barclays Aggregate Index. It should be possible to agree on an index at the outset. If the advisor is any good, he shouldn't mind having his performance benchmarked. Many will try to argue that their strategy doesn't fit easily against a benchmark, or that a previously agreed benchmark is not relevant "for this type of market." As the client, your response should be simple. Tell the advisor that if we can't agree on how to evaluate you, we'll never know if you're doing a good job. And if we can't tell how you're doing, why are we bothering with you in the first place?

Obfuscation of performance is the mediocre financial advisor's friend. Non-traded REITs are the perfect product for a salesperson who doesn't want to be evaluated other than on the fees he generates. There's no accepted benchmark and hardly any investment research. These factors work against the interests of the client.

## PUTS AND CALLS

Recently, I was asked by a new client to evaluate an IRA that was being managed by his former advisor. It included a selection of dividend-paying stocks combined with some options positions. Many people like what are called "covered call" strategies, in which they write call options on stocks they already own with a strike price above current market levels. It's often described as a way to generate additional income through earning option premium, and if the stock that's owned does get called away well, it'll be at a price at which you were in any case happy to sell.

There are a couple of problems with this. One is that if you own XYZ stock and you write a call option against it, you have created the exact same position as if you had simply sold a put option. It's called "put-call conversion." Like a mathematical equation, the profit/loss on your covered call trade can be shown to be identical to that of a simple, short put option with the same strike price and expiry as the call option. Although a covered call strategy doesn't sound that risky, many people would find shorting put options to be very risky. You've got all the downside associated with owning the stock, and have only limited upside. I've run interest rate options trading in the past, ranging from plain vanilla to complex and exotic options. Exploiting put–call conversions to manage risk was one of the basic elements in our toolkit, and this remains so for today's options traders.

I once met a hedge fund manager who claimed to run a covered call strategy. I asked him why he didn't just sell put options instead, since it required fewer trades to execute and so would be a cheaper way of achieving the same result. For a brief moment, his honesty exceeded his marketing skill as he admitted that no investor would seriously consider investing in a hedge fund that simply shorted put options. Naturally, we didn't invest with this manager.

Covered call strategies are also very appealing for managers who would prefer that their results are not easily compared with a benchmark. Covered call strategies will generally underperform a rising market, as the winners get called away and cash has to be reinvested. They can outperform in a down market if the premium income offsets some of the losses on stocks that have fallen in price. But it's impossible for the typical investor to figure out if the returns were good or not. If stocks are +10% one year, is +6% good for the covered call strategy? Should it be +8%? There's no really good answer. Similarly on the downside, is losing 15% when stocks are down 20% good, or should you only be down 8%? Because it's not clear and therefore open to judgment, the broker managing the account can use terms like "good" or "acceptable under the circumstances" when reviewing performance with his client. Therefore, it's often very hard for the client to know if the return he earned was commensurate with the risk he took. It can be great for the broker, yet bad for the client. And the commissions can add up, too.

## FINANCIAL ADVISORS NEED TO DO BETTER

While the financial services industry is full of good people, Penelope is representative of thousands of clients who have received less than a fair deal. Non-traded REITs are by no means the only investment designed with hefty fees. As I learned what she'd gone through, it deepened my conviction that, while the system isn't broken, it sure could use some improvement. Public opinion routinely reports an unfavorable view of Wall Street. The banking bailouts of 2008 contribute to this, although my personal reading of history is that while the government deserves a lot of blame for getting us into the crisis, they made the right decisions to get us out. Government subsidized mortgages were made available to people who weren't equipped for home ownership; regulatory oversight was too relaxed; there was too much leverage, most especially among the investment banks.

But having created the stage for the excesses that led to the financial crisis, I don't think there was any serious alternative to the series of bailouts that were undertaken.

As traumatic as that period of time was for so many, it doesn't fully explain current negative views more than six years on. One poll (Wall Street Journal 2014) noted that Congress was even more unpopular than Wall Street. Neither should feel good about the comparison.

Managing people's savings is a serious subject. Preserving the purchasing power of your retirement pool so it can provide you with what you need when you're no longer working is, for most people, up there alongside physical wellbeing in terms of importance. It ought to be that the professionals advising you on your financial health can be relied upon with the same confidence with which the medical profession is trusted to help you live gracefully to a ripe old age. Through my own business I see too many cases of misplaced trust by investors in individuals or firms that they believe will guide them to fairly priced, good investments whereas they wind up paying too much for something inferior. The individual investor mistakes a sales relationship for an advisory one. Financial salespeople often understand this subtle difference and present themselves as advisors while behaving like salespeople.

Penelope's experience got me thinking about the perception problem that finance has, and what causes it. As I talked to friends of mine in the industry the response was invariably the same. "Oh yes, I just picked up a new client who had been sold a lousy investment." It might be an annuity, a closed end fund IPO, or a municipal bond with too high a mark-up. But it was clear that others were seeing the same thing I was.

I had one client who showed me the asset allocation recommendation he'd received from a large, global bank. Typically, such an analysis will include forecast returns for each asset class. As I reviewed the presentation my friend had received, I noticed that the expected return on bonds was 6%, because that was what they had done in the past. Quite apart from the fact that every investment document you ever see is required by law to warn you, "Past performance in not indicative of future returns," interest rates are no longer 6%. What you earn on a bond is heavily impacted by the yield when you buy it. Given current interest rates of 1% to 4% depending on maturity and credit risk, using a 6% return assumption was just stupid.

Another friend showed me a trust fund that her late father had created for her. The trust company holding the assets was responsible for selecting appropriate investments. They had a chunk in fixed income with a yield of 1.5%. The fees on the account were also 1.5% annually, and on top of that the account was taxable. So my friend was owning bonds, paying away fully 100% of the return to the trust company in fees, and on top of that had to pay tax to the federal government. So the trust company and Uncle Sam were making money out of this arrangement while my friend was losing money. Although there was nothing illegal in this set up, you'd think the trust company would feel some obligation to come up with a different arrangement (perhaps including lower fees) that could at least ensure that the trust for which they had responsibility wasn't being depleted to pay themselves and taxes. It just seems common sense.

It is with the belief that sunlight is the best disinfectant that my colleagues and I have written this book. We hope that by telling you what we avoid for ourselves and our clients, we'll help you, the investor, and perhaps in some modest way raise the standards of financial advice along the way. There is certainly room for improvement.

# CHAPTER 2

---

# WHY INVESTORS PAY TOO MUCH FOR YIELD

## THE MYSTERIES OF CLOSED-END FUNDS

One of the persistent curiosities of investing is the inefficiency of the closed-end fund business. Closed-end funds have been around for decades. One of the very oldest, Adams Express (NYSE:ADX), claims it has been in continuous operation (Adams Express Company n.d.) since 1929, one of only five funds able to make such a claim. Nowadays, individuals trading their personal brokerage account can access the kind of technology and real-time analytics that used to be limited to large banks and brokerage firms. In so many ways, the financial markets are more efficient. And yet, closed-end funds continue to demonstrate inefficiencies as investors routinely do things that are widely recognized to cost them money.

Closed-end funds (CEFs) are similar to mutual funds in that they are specialized companies (Registered Investment Companies is the legal term) that own securities issued by other companies. Whereas mutual funds continuously issue and redeem shares to investors to balance supply and demand, CEFs have a fixed share count. When you invest in a mutual fund, you're issued new shares in the mutual fund company, which then goes into the market and invests your cash in more of the securities it already owns. By contrast, investing in a CEF means that you're buying some of the outstanding CEF shares in the open market from someone who already owns them.

This is why mutual fund transactions are done at the net asset value (NAV) of the fund, whereas CEF transactions take place at whatever is the prevailing market price for the shares. CEFs often trade at a discount to NAV, meaning that the CEF shares can be bought for less than the portfolio of investments it owns are actually worth. It's a very appealing concept to buy something for less than it is really worth. Of course, stocks can often be found trading at cheaper than their fundamental valuation, although there's almost always a fair degree of judgment involved in assessing that value. Since CEFs own other publicly traded securities, there isn't much room for disagreement about their NAV. Consequently, the opportunity to buy a CEF at, say, a 10% discount to its NAV has attracted legions of investors for decades and will no doubt continue to do so.

We'll return to CEF discounts later on, because there can often be attractive opportunities. The area where investors routinely get duped is when a CEF does an initial public offering (IPO). It's a testament to the ability of Wall Street to spin a good story that CEF IPOs still get done.

For most companies making their initial public offering of stock the underwriters seek to create as much excitement as possible around the event. All the positive features of the new company are emphasized; their new technology, revolutionary business model and breathtaking growth prospects. Sometimes a stock never looks back after its IPO (such as Google), and trades forever higher. At other times, it's a bust (as it was initially with Facebook). But invariably, there's something novel about the investment opportunity, and there's probably no other part of Wall Street that generates as much anticipation as an IPO.

It's harder to justify the same hype with a CEF IPO. After all, the new CEF is simply going to invest the cash proceeds it receives from its new investors in a portfolio of publicly traded securities. There's no new technology or revolutionary business model involved, simply the purchase of some stocks and bonds that were available before the

IPO and will be available afterward. And yet, amazingly, underwriters routinely charge 6% of the proceeds as an underwriting fee, which is readily paid by the investors. So quite literally, if you participate in a CEF IPO, the new security you buy at $20 a share (most CEF IPOs are priced at $20) is immediately worth 6% less, or $18.80.

I can see why it might be worth it for the CEF manager to pay 6%. After all, CEFs represent what's called *permanent capital*. That is, once the money's been raised, the manager can earn fees from investing it pretty much forever, unless he does such a horrendous job that the investors rise up and vote him out (very rare). If a CEF is going to pay management fees to the manager running it of, say, 1.5% annually for many years, paying 6% up front may make sense.

But it's not the manager that pays the 6% fee, but the investors. It's generally the dumb money that buys a CEF IPO at $20. The smarter money waits until the next day, when its price reflects the 6% underwriting fee the initial buyers paid, and invests at 18.80.

Of course brokerage firms (who receive the 6%) will argue that the NAV will rise after the IPO because the stocks the CEF buys will be pushed up its buying. Or that the skill of this particular CEF manager will warrant its shares trading at a solid premium to its NAV, rendering the IPO price an attractive entry point. There may be the odd instance where this is the case, but if you avoid buying CEF IPOs completely, odds are you'll be richer for it.

I once had a conversation with a Wall Street analyst at a very big firm about an upcoming CEF IPO. She had briefly forgotten about my background in finance and must have been thinking of me as another one of the patsies who willingly part with 6% of their investment for no good reason. She was attempting to get me interested in becoming a Day One investor, and I pointed out that many investors know to avoid CEF IPOs and wait for the secondary market price to buy 6% cheaper. Quickly recognizing her mistake, she breezily acknowledged the correctness of my view! Even though her job was to write research that would help persuade investors to overpay for the securities, she understood the fallacy in the message she was pushing.

In fact, it's not dissimilar to the issues that Henry Blodget and others had back in the late 1990s during the dot.com bubble. Blodget, then at Merrill Lynch, was found to have been publicly promoting Internet stocks that he privately acknowledged to be duds. Elliot Spitzer, then New York State attorney general, made his reputation by successfully prosecuting Blodget and his employer Merrill Lynch for not believing what they were saying. Spitzer, of course, later experienced his own reputational undoing with a hooker, but that's another story.

It turns out that Wall Street analysts are supposed to believe what they say in public. Even though this would seem to be obvious, rules were subsequently imposed that require *accrediting analysts* to add an assertion to any report they issue, stating their belief in what they've written. It is symptomatic of the cynicism of some in the industry that such a rule is necessary. The analyst mentioned above was clearly guilty of not conforming to that rule. In fact, it's hard to understand how *any* analyst recommending *any* CEF IPO could truthfully add the "I believe" assertion at the end. They understand the math just described as well as anyone. And they're simply not that dumb to believe that most CEF IPOs are anything other than an opportunity to pay 6% too much.

If you avoid the IPOs, CEFs can offer some interesting opportunities for personal trading. Managing $100 million or more is hard, though not impossible—I know of a few firms that do so. But with anywhere from $100,000 to a few million to invest, along with the ability to devote many hours of analysis, you can find some genuine mispricings. CEFs usually trade at a discount, so you need to assume you'll eventually sell at a discount when buying. Occasionally, activists get involved and press for a stock buyback or even conversion to mutual fund (which eliminates the discount), so being involved in one of those situations can be profitable. Some funds trade at a premium, notably master limited partnership (MLP) CEFs where the tax reporting of a 1099 draws investors who like MLPs but don't like the K-1s that form the tax reporting. Owning MLPs through CEFs is a dreadfully inefficient way to do so unless you're investing relatively small sums and don't wish to do the research necessary to hold individual MLPs.

Yields are commonly misunderstood by investors. If a $100 bank deposit provided you with a $1 quarterly check, even though it was only earning 0.25%, you wouldn't confuse the 4% payout with a

4% yield; you'd recognize that most of the distribution was a return of your own money. Yet CEFs routinely do this, and even though your 1099 will correctly show the composition of your distribution between return of capital and investment return, many investors generally just consider cash returned to them as being the source of the yield. Many non-traded REITs do the same thing, and even though they tell you in the prospectus, the growth in recent years of the market shows the information fails to register with most buyers.

## INVESTORS CAN OVERPAY TO SIMPLIFY THEIR TAXES

There are several closed-end funds that invest in Master Limited Partnerships (MLPs). MLPs are a great asset class. They are energy infrastructure businesses that run pipelines, storage facilities, gathering and processing assets, transportation and logistics—basically, all the plumbing that moves fossil fuels from where they originate to the final consumer. For many years it was a relatively undiscovered yet lucrative area of the public equity markets. Midstream MLPs (those that operate anywhere between the exploration and production companies that extract oil, gas or coal and the retail distribution) are like toll roads, in that they mostly care about the volumes passing through their system. Although not immune to the economic cycle and commodity prices, they are less sensitive than many other traditional energy businesses.

MLPs are organized as partnerships rather than corporations, which creates some attractive tax deferral features for their investors. The practical result is that in many cases the distributions (which is what MLP dividends are called) are mostly taxed when the investor sells the security. In effect, this pushes away the tax bill into the future which can be as much as a decade or more for buy-and-hold investors. They are the most obvious investment for any reasonably wealthy, tax-paying US investor. Of course there's a catch, which is the dreaded K-1 for tax reporting instead of the far more common 1099. It turns out that getting that tax deferral requires a bit of extra work at tax filing time. This is why MLPs tend to be held by well-heeled investors, because most people need a tax accountant to handle them. Many individuals will not consider investments that fail to provide 1099s.

Back in 2004–2005 I met a very smart young fellow named Gabriel Hammond. "Gabe" had just left Goldman Sachs, where he'd been an MLP analyst. He got me very interested in MLPs as he explained all the operating advantages they possess, and at JPMorgan where at the time I ran a hedge-fund seeding business we decided to finance Gabe's new hedge fund, called Alerian. Gabe was under 30 years old at the time, which was young to be launching a hedge fund. In fact, our first meeting took place at the suggestion of someone else and I was initially quite skeptical that anything would come of it. But Gabe had a well-thought-out business plan that included greatly expanding the universe of potential investors by simplifying the tax reporting. Gabe also recognized the glaring absence of an appropriate benchmark for MLPs, and so he created the Alerian MLP Index, which remains today the most widely used index for its sector.

The tax analysis of limited partnerships and how to recharacterize the income they generate into a form that involved less onerous tax reporting is a fairly obscure area. However, during many months that followed, a substantial amount of expensive legal and tax talent was brought to bear on precisely this issue. The fundamental problem is that a partnership's income has to pass through a corporation and be taxed before it can emerge out the other side as 1099-eligible. You can own MLPs with their tax deferral and deal with a K-1, or you can invest in a corporation (such as a mutual fund), which in turn invests in MLPs and you get a 1099. On its way through the corporation, the income from the MLPs is taxed and you get what's left, around 65%. What everybody wanted was the income from an MLP without the tax filter of a corporation and with a 1099 for simple tax reporting.

Some interesting possibilities were discussed that held the potential to solve this problem, but none of them could ultimately withstand the careful legal and tax analysis to which they were subjected. Perhaps unusually, expensive legal talent was unable to identify a tax loophole. The 1987 Tax Reform Act passed under Ronald Reagan, which created the legal framework for the subsequent development of MLPs, turned out to be secure against tax arbitrage, at least in this case.

The US corporate tax rate is 35%, which is why having the corporation sit in between you and the MLPs leaves you with 65% of the return. For many years, this knowledge was sufficient to stifle the development of any 1099-type MLP investments. I mean, who would seriously give up a third of the return in order to simplify taxes? Surely any investment that has to forgo 35% of its normal return would, as a result, become quite unattractive?

Well, surprisingly, there are a great number of investors for whom 65% of MLPs remains sufficiently attractive to get their money. As a result, a plethora of products has been launched that give you two thirds of MLPs with a 1099 and money flows into them. Striving for the returns of the Alerian Index, my friend Gabe's now ubiquitous benchmark, retail investors buy products that can't possibly achieve the same return, as they make plain in their prospectuses. The biggest of them all is the Alerian MLP ETF, with over $9 billion in assets (ALPS 2015). It routinely underperforms its benchmark (the Alerian MLP Infrastructure Index) by several percentage points, because the benchmark doesn't suffer the 35% tax bite that the ETF does. In theory, the holders could be hundreds of thousands of $10,000 accounts for whom the K-1s are prohibitively expensive. There may even be a case that at this size investment it's a great product, although because of the tax hit its performance has fallen well short of the S&P 500 and REITs (Real Estate Investment Trusts), two plausibly better choices. Or it could be that most investors simply don't understand the issue.

Ron Rowland, a blogger on SeekingAlpha.com, pointed out the tax consequences back in 2010 when AMLP first launched. He's been a tireless critic ever since, during which AMLP has continued its relentless growth. Based on the flows, you might concede that AMLP has been wildly successful and that investors voting with their wallets have decided Rowland is wrong. Alternatively, it may simply show that many investors put far more effort into choosing a fridge than a security (Kennon 2015), as lamented by many including Joshua Kennon, who writes a column aimed at retail investors. AMLP boasts a yield comparable to the index, but then adjusts down its net asset value by the amount of the taxes owed. Just looking at the yield doesn't present the whole story.

Jerry Swank runs Cushing Asset Management and has been investing in MLPs as long as anyone. I once saw him speaking at a conference about the tax inefficiencies of products like AMLP. Not long afterward, he must have concluded that if you can't beat them you might as well join them because his firm launched a similarly tax-inefficient fund.

## THE HFT TAX

There are quite a few books available on closed-end funds, which aim to educate investors about the pitfalls and opportunities. Yet the market continues to confound those who believe that markets are efficient. The relative illiquidity limits the amount of capital that can be usefully deployed to exploit the inefficiencies, as well as representing an additional source of risk. Many closed-end funds fell far more than the broad equity indices in 2008 as their small market capitalizations and use of leverage caused their discounts to widen sharply.

It's not only for new issues of securities that investors overpay. Although secondary trading in US public equities is superficially incredibly cheap (based on commissions) the high-frequency trading (HFT) trolls take an imperceptible toll on the rest of us. Michael Lewis deserves great credit for explaining in plain English how HFT works in his 2013 book *Flash Boys*. Lewis is a great writer and I've enjoyed every one of his books. I even read *Moneyball*. Since I primarily watch English football on TV and have never developed any passion for American sports since moving here from England in 1982, that a baseball book was able to command my attention is about the highest praise I can offer.

*Flash Boys* illustrated quite elegantly how the current equity market structure and its regulation is several steps behind the abilities of software engineers. Some high-speed trading has its place. Legend has it that Nathan Rothschild learned earlier than most of the English battlefield victory over the French at Waterloo in 1815 and was able to profit through early purchases on UK gilts (government bonds). It's believed to be apocryphal (Kay 2013) but still makes a good story. Speed of information has always been sought.

But some HFT trading is clearly destructive and represents a tax on investors. Imagine you were able to view the electronic routing of orders slowed down by a factor of a thousand, so that you could watch an order travel from New York to Chicago and back in 15 seconds (versus the approximately 15 milliseconds it really takes (Lewis 2013)). You'd see your order leave New York first but then be passed on its way to Chicago by an algorithm-dispatched competing order that had seen your order originate and knew a faster way to reach the cheapest sell order before yours could get there. Lewis memorably describes how Brad Katsuyama, a trader at Royal Bank of Canada in New York, engages in some high-tech sleuthing to figure this out.

Free markets allow innovation, but most of us comprehending the example above would regard it as a sophisticated form of front-running. If a broker buys stock for himself before executing your order, that's illegal. You'd think that designing an algorithm to do the same thing would expose the designer to a similar charge, but life is rarely as simple as it should be. The same desire for speed has led to HFT servers being placed in close physical proximity to the New York Stock Exchange (Trugman 2014) and payment for order flow. This is the odious practice of paying a broker to send its orders to your "dark pool" of liquidity because you deem those orders to be sufficiently poorly handled that taking the other side will be profitable.

The public outcry, regulatory and Congressional hearings that followed Lewis's book may ultimately lead to fixes that help restore some balance and the public's belief in the integrity of financial markets. As with so many of these types of issue though, since it fails the "front page of the *New York Times*" test, why was it ever taking place? Too many people were facilitating exploitative behavior and modifications required its public exposure. If the victim is invisible to you, harming them seems less morally wrong. It is a consequence of our interconnected world that affords anonymous human interaction.

How is the investor to protect himself? Most obviously is to enter orders into the equity markets that are limit orders. This certainly doesn't shield you from the HFT tax, but it does at least prevent your order from being front-run by an algorithm. If you're not trying to lift an offer in the market, there's no incentive for an HFT program to beat you to it. But you'll still be exploited, as algorithms place orders a penny in front of yours with the objective of buying in front of you and profiting by selling when you increase your bid (which you may). And if the market falls, the HFT will simply turn around and hit your bid for a one-penny loss just as the market drops sharply.

In our business, we are not active traders and have no intention to compete with the speed of HFTs. We simply try and transact our business in a way that at least limits our payment of the HFT tax as far as possible. Most large stocks change price multiple times a second as HFTs compete and probe to identify what the "real-money" investors (i.e., humans) intend to do. It looks like a great deal of price "noise," and often patience can work. If you pick a price at which you'd like to execute that's close to the current market and simply leave your order there, you will at least represent the most boring type of market participant to the HFTs and the high speed oscillations in price that they cause just might result in you getting done at your price. It's the best defense we can devise for the world we're in. I think that allowing the New York Stock Exchange to become a profit-seeking entity opened the door to the abuses described and possibly many others with little discernible benefit to the rest of us. A stock exchange ought to be run as a public utility. It defies common sense that the current structure of competing pools of liquidity all with a profit motive is really in the common interest.

## WHEN MANAGERS RUN A COMPANY FOR THEMSELVES

Public companies are largely run so as to maximize returns for stockholders, but there are of course exceptions. Companies like Enron, Worldcom, and Tyco cost their investors money by committing fraud, and naturally jail terms followed for the perpetrators. Under such circumstances, an equity investor may still conclude that they should have carried out more careful research but such losses can never the less be understandable. But there are some companies who by their actions and public filings make very clear that their objective is to maximize management's compensation at the expense of shareholders. They use full disclosure to stay within the law and go ahead and loot the company. A case in point that we followed some years back is Coeur d'Alene (NYSE:CDE), a silver mining company.

Silver is a fascinating commodity to research. Most silver in the world is mined not directly from silver mines but as a byproduct of other metals such as gold or nickel. Pure silver mines are not the chief source of silver production. Consequently, the supply of silver is more sensitive to the price of the more valuable gold or more abundant nickel with which it's mined. Price moves in silver don't translate into shifts in supply. On the demand side, roughly half the silver consumed is used in "industrial fabrication" (Silver Institute 2015) and it typically represents a very small percentage of the input costs for consumer electronics items such as smartphones (Ferré 2015). Its superior conductivity qualities render substitutes less attractive, and therefore shifts in price don't have much impact on demand, either.

As a result, silver is that unusual commodity for which changes in price have very little impact on demand or supply. Both the production and consumption of silver continue with little response to price. Therefore, small actual shifts in supply or demand, caused by traders for example, result in quite dramatic price fluctuations. It's what attracts traders and speculators, because it can move a lot. Silver's volatility didn't especially draw us to research CDE, but I found the fundamentals of the silver business to be quite interesting.

When we first began researching CDE in 2010, we were attracted to gold and silver miners as a cheap way to invest in precious metals, since some of the miners were available for purchase at less than their net asset value (i.e., less than the value of the reserves they held). As we did further research, we grew concerned that the interests of management and investors weren't as closely aligned as we'd like. By 2012, we'd concluded that such companies were in fact often just a legal transmission mechanism of wealth from investors to management.

There's always a core group of "goldbugs" who believe that ultimately gold and silver will prove to be a better investment than anything else. It's a form of religion, which is to say it's completely immune to contrary evidence such as falling gold prices. Like religion, there's never any point in debating the issue with believers. Faith need never acknowledge facts; there's always more time for the disciple to be proven correct.

I have been writing a blog for several years. I find it a helpful discipline to formulate my thoughts such that they can be read by others. As we concluded that CDE had been a successful management enrichment scheme at the expense of investors, I explained this on my blog and it was published by Seeking Alpha (Lack 2012).

I noted the stark contrast between the path followed by the company's stock and the compensation of its longtime CEO Dennis Wheeler (since retired). Unusually, the company's compensation plan rewarded growth in production and not shareholder returns. This would cause any rational CEO (and Dennis Wheeler may have had many faults as a CEO but irrationality was not one of them) to seek growth at any price funded through dilutive equity issuance so as to maximize his incentive compensation. Wheeler had responded splendidly to these misguided incentives, and had further shown his smarts by owning derisively little stock.

The Internet has no barriers to entry for those who wish to write. There is no screening mechanism or quality control unless you limit your reading to well-run websites that review what's posted. Consequently, when you write a story that is critical of a company, you'll quickly stimulate the underemployed to run to its defense. When such criticism is targeted at a precious metals miner, you can quickly observe a virtual crusade of believers rush to defend their faith. It convinced me that no matter how much inefficiency and bad schemes are exposed, there will always be a steady supply of poorly managed capital susceptible to exploitation. Meanwhile, I could write the same story about CDE today, because the current CEO has continued what his predecessor did so ably, to the ongoing cost of investors.

There are plenty of other examples of public companies where management places their interests ahead of the owners. Running your own firm, as I do, creates a wonderful freedom to call things as you see them. It's hard for big financial firms to be openly critical of public companies because they're likely to be seeking to do business with one another.

So Hertz, for example, moved its headquarters from New Jersey to Naples, Florida. As a beleaguered New Jersey taxpayer and a Naples homeowner, I can completely understand the dynamic that renders Florida's zero state income tax highly attractive. However, if you're relocating a global company's HQ to Florida, at least get close to an easily accessible airport such as Orlando, Miami, or Tampa. I can attest that Naples has many attractive qualities, but direct commercial flights to a wide variety of US cities is not among them. It wasn't difficult to find that the (now former) CEO Mark Frissora belonged to a very exclusive Naples golf club, and at the risk of appearing cynical, I suspect that playing nine holes on the way home from work just might have been a consideration.

## THE HAM SANDWICH TEST

ADT, the alarm company, embarked on an aggressive share buyback program in 2013 financed with additional debt at the urging of activist hedge fund Corvex, run by Keith Meister. Management was so convinced of the rightness of this effort to return value to shareholders that when Meister suddenly decided little unrealized value was left, he availed himself of the very buyback program he had championed to sell Corvex's stock back to the company in a transaction executed one weekend. The sheer ineptitude of ADT management buying stock from the buyback proponent unsurprisingly caused ADT to drop 30% in the weeks following the release of this information. The reaction was compounded by the subsequent release of weak earnings, advance knowledge of which was held both by Meister and ADT's CEO Naren Gursahaney at the time of ADT's purchase of Corvex's ADT stock. Meister had decided internal management reports showed a deterioration in the business while for some reason Gursahaney, armed with the same information, had interpreted differently. ADT's hapless CEO subsequently defended his humiliation at the hands of a far more wily operator, but it was a hollow and barely credible stance since the original proponent, Corvex, had pivoted 180 degrees by selling into the buyback. Thus it is that the independent money manager unencumbered by any possibility of losing any ADT–related capital markets business can write about the ham sandwich test. This is the admonition of Charlie Munger (of Berkshire Hathaway) that you'd better invest in companies that can be run by a ham sandwich, since one day they most assuredly will. Writing that ADT is clearly taking the ham sandwich test isn't as much fun as making money but it can be a temporarily satisfying diversion.

The lesson for the investor is that when you invest in a company, thereby becoming an owner, assess the management as you would any other agent responsible for managing some of your assets.

Expect them to behave as the fiduciary they are and to place your interests first. But don't assume they will, and in such cases it can make sense to rearrange your portfolio accordingly. In the case of Hertz, we regarded the HQ move as one of several major missteps that the many activist hedge funds who also owned the stock would put right by agitating for new management. This duly happened. In the case of ADT, we were less optimistic and voted with our feet.

Activist hedge funds were present in both episodes. By gaining board representation, activists can agitate for all kinds of value-enhancing steps. They can press for improved operating performance, better asset utilization, the sale of underperforming units, stock buybacks, or even putting the company up for sale. By definition, their involvement follows the identification of an undervalued stock combined with ideas on how to correct this. The growing role of activists has certainly commanded the attention of most public company CEOs. Carl Icahn has evolved into a wonderfully pugnacious investor whose website warns, "A lot of people died fighting tyranny. The least I can do is vote against it." (Shareholders Square Table 2015), drawing on a statement Icahn made at Texaco's annual meeting in 1988.

Although I believe the engagement of an activist is typically positive for the shareholders because of their focus on many value-enhancing moves, investing alongside an activist does constitute a two-edged sword. While a company's management owes its investors a fiduciary obligation, the activist hedge fund isn't similarly obligated (although once they achieve a board seat this can change). Corvex showed how they were able to shift from operating in favor of the public shareholders of ADT to quickly discarding their interests. Not every activist can be relied on to make money for the shareholders of a target company.

## IF THE PROSPECTUS SAYS YOU'LL BE RIPPED OFF, IT MUST BE LEGAL

Most of the ways investors are unfairly relieved of their money are quite legal and occur in broad daylight. One of the biggest challenges for investors is ensuring an alignment of interests, whether it's in the company whose equity you own or with the financial advisor who is overseeing your portfolio. The most effective way to avoid being blindsided is to confront the Principal-Agent problem. You're the principal; your agent, whether it's a company CEO or advisor, needs to share your financial ups and downs. If they don't own the stock, or invest in what they'd have you buy, you're in a weaker position to ensure your best interests are foremost.

When investors overpay for a security, accept outrageous fees or align themselves with unscrupulous management bent on self-enrichment, how much of the blame lies with the investors themselves? The analysis in this book is largely drawn from public sources, and while it's true that the authors are all finance professionals, the information is available for those with the time and willingness to do the research. One problem is that it's so time consuming. Take the prospectus for a typical non-traded REIT. The basic document can easily run to 200 pages and then there are supplements of additional information that can add much more. Non-traded REITs provide abundant information about their planned operations that reveal just how costly they will be. For example, the Phillips Edison ARC Grocery Center REIT II, Inc. (November 25, 2013) consists of 250 numbered pages plus probably another 50 of appendices.

The front cover shows that the initial fees are 10% of proceeds. Page 14 reveals further "Other Organization Expenses" of 2%. But the list goes on from there. Although you might think that buying properties is the basic business of a REIT, they'll charge a 1% acquisition fee. If they reach their target leverage of 75%, $100 invested will eventually buy $175 of properties generating $1.75 in fees, or 1.75% of your invested amount. Other expenses related to buying properties can add up to 0.65% of their value or a further 1% of the invested amount. This all adds up to 14.75% of your initial investment.

The REIT manager receives additional shares equal to 1% of the value of the REIT annually. It reimburses affiliate expenses at up to 2% annually. There's a 0.75% payment for organizing financing; 4.5% of monthly gross receipts in property management fees; leasing and construction management fees (not determinable in the prospectus). There's a 15% share of the profits that goes to the manager and a further 15% share of the increase in value if the REIT goes public.

There are also 13 pages devoted to conflicts of interest. All the people involved in the REIT have other demands on their time. But they also benefit from fees paid to service providers, fees that, " ... have not been negotiated at arm's length." The prospectus notes that the *dealer manager,* otherwise known as the underwriter, is not independent of the REIT. We know the firm recommending the investment isn't objective because it is receiving so much in fees, but in addition, it is not independent of the REIT, further compromising its advice. The firm managing the properties is also an affiliate. And the value of the portfolio is not arrived at independently, but by the REIT manager.

It's all there in the prospectus, and frankly, an acceptable investment return to the retail buyers after all these fees and conflicts is nothing short of miraculous. There's no way that an advisor with a fiduciary obligation to a client could possibly recommend such an investment. And they don't. Non-traded REITs are sold on the basis of suitability and disclosure. Clearly, suitability is a far lower standard than a fiduciary one since this is all going on perfectly legally. And there is obviously disclosure since I've just recounted all the fees, relying on a public document.

But is there understanding? Do the buyers truly comprehend what they're getting into? My friend Penelope in Chapter 1 most certainly did not. If an abundance of information is provided such that digesting it requires the same effort as reading a very dry book, was any information really provided? If you poll finance types about non-traded REITs, it doesn't take long before you find people acknowledging that they're an accident waiting to happen. In fact, I've found extremely few people who understand the product with anything other than a highly negative, cynical view. Suppose a minority of doctors was prescribing medication known to be harmful? Would the rest remain silent? There would (or most certainly, should) be all kinds of consequences. There would be public criticism and debate. Our industry needs to take greater collective responsibility for its overall behavior. I don't believe I have any friends who are making a living from these toxic instruments, but I'm willing to risk acquaintance with a few people in order to expose utterly self-seeking actions by those who traffic in them. Others shouldn't be so afraid to criticize.

Individual investors (and often institutions, too) commit enormous errors of omission and commission in their use of financial services. At the most fundamental level, finance as a percentage of GDP roughly doubled from 1980 to 2007 without any commensurate increase in social welfare (defined as median real household income or net worth). At a more granular level, countless examples exist of investment products being bought that create far more value for the broker than the client; of investors behaving more as gamblers than investors; of only the most cursory review of important disclosures in documents. The free market most definitely provides the products and services people want, but it also provides what they ought not to want if more thoughtfully considered. When you assess how efficiently capitalism produces countless successful products that are truly worthwhile, why hasn't finance done a better job? Why doesn't it live to a higher standard?

## TIMING IS EVERYTHING

The single most sought-after advice must be timing. Of all the activities in which consumers engage, and especially all the purchase decisions, rarely do they have to consider whether what they're committing their funds to will benefit from opportune timing. Even the purchase of a house, the most analogous decision to making personal investment decisions, is driven as much by need and the availability of financial resources as it is by an assessment of the real estate market's near-term direction.

It's understandable, because before and after the moment of making an investment, it's easy to recalculate how different it might have been if bought yesterday or a month later. It's the most common question I'm asked in an infinite variety of forms. Like everyone else, I follow the market's direction. But much as I'd like to hold a strong, correct opinion on its next move, years of experience have taught me that over the short run it's almost impossible to do much better than chance.

Yet money managers, banks, and brokerage firms routinely imply that they have some methodology that will help you get the timing right. They use econometric models, proprietary tools, and even (perish the thought) technical analysis. Charting, the divining of patterns in past market actions so as to forecast future swings, has been around as long as anybody can remember. Although there are a small minority of purists who make their market decisions solely based on technical analysis, most investment professionals use a wide range of fundamental and technical tools. Personally, I'm skeptical that letting any pattern of past performance drive today's investment decision is going to make you wealthy. But charts do tell a story far more elegantly than a table of daily closing prices and so they're useful in that fashion.

One investor I know will solemnly note that the chart for a particular stock his investment committee is considering "looks great" or "looks bad." What it reveals is that he's a momentum investor. Although not all chartists are trend followers, trends show up most easily on a chart, and a stock that's been falling is not going to attract trend followers to buy it—or many people at all, which is why it's falling. I always chuckle to myself when I hear this guy's opinion, because if you're an investor you're generally trying to buy while other people are selling. You absolutely want the chart to look bad; you want to be buying from the short-term, technically driven traders since as soon as the selling is exhausted they'll quickly turn around and make the chart look good.

Overall, it's a form of alchemy. In finance, those whose entire view of a security is formed by its chart pattern are regarded somewhat quizzically by their colleagues. There is, of course, no reason for it to work. I've always thought the possible basis for it was as a visual representation of behavioral biases that investors hold collectively. Momentum investing, which is a form of trend following, has been shown to be a source of long-term returns, reflecting the comfort we humans derive from buying what our peers are buying since it confirms our beliefs. On its own, it's an insufficient tool, but occasionally and in conjunction with other forms of analysis (such as examining financial statements) it can help, or at least feel as if it helps. Because that's just the problem: if charts represent one part of a decision-making process, it's mighty difficult to figure out just how important they were to the decision. Since they might have helped, in some unquantifiable way, you ignore technical analysis at your peril. Although I've never read a definitive research paper showing that technical analysis produces reliably attractive returns, its adherents are many and passionate.

I remember one *technician* (for this is what they're called, evoking the notion of insight into the market's wiring) whose daily prognostications could often be summed up by stating that if it goes up it'll keep going up, and if it starts falling it'll keep falling. He sounded very knowledgeable while he was saying this, and often published specific trade recommendations. Such forecasts bask in the luxury of not being burdened with the requirement to actually make money. The business model is one of popularity—if a sufficient number of people are interested in the technician's views, the name exposure his firm receives as a result justifies the compensation expense he represents.

I once had a foreign exchange trader who worked for me who was an unabashed chartist. He truly believed that all the information you needed was reflected in the past history of a currency. Now it's true there can be less to consider in trading currencies than individual equities, since at least for developed country currencies it's typically not necessary to pore over their financial statements every quarter. And in my experience, currencies do exhibit sustainable trends more reliably than, say, bonds or commodities. Imbalances caused by, for example, interest rate differentials that favor one currency over another (by making it more profitable to invest in the higher-yielding one) can persist for years. Of course, another appeal of charting can be that it provides a convenient excuse to avoid having to analyze financial statements or other fundamental data. Technical analysts take their work seriously and apply themselves to it diligently, but it's also possible for a part-time technician to do his market analysis in ten minutes over coffee and a bagel. This can create the false illusion of being a very efficient worker.

The FX trader I mentioned was quite happy to engage in an experiment whereby he did the trades recommended by our in-house market technician. Both shared the same commitment to charts as an under-appreciated path to market success, a belief clearly at odds with the in-house technician's avoidance of trading any actual positions so as to provide empirical proof of his insights with trading profits. When challenged, he invariably countered that managing trading positions would challenge his objectivity, as if holding a losing position would induce him to continue recommending it in spite of the chart's contrary insight. But then, why hold a losing position if it's not what the chart said? I always found debating such tortured logic a brief but entertaining use of time when lining up to get lunch in the trader's cafeteria.

To the surprise of my FX trader if not to me, the technical analysis trading account was unprofitable. In explaining the result, my Kool-Aid drinking trader even accepted partial responsibility for at times misinterpreting the very information he was analyzing. It was along the lines of that he ought to have recognized the type of pattern that was evolving but stupidly interpreted the wrong shape. It was almost as if the results were not the result of the faulty religion but of the less than completely faithful practice of one of its adherents. So what use to a profit-oriented trading room is a fully committed chartist who can't be trusted even to follow the charts? At this stage I must confess that we had found ourselves in this position as a last-ditch effort on my part to salvage some profitability out of a trader I'd hired who had to this point been consistently losing money. His own market views expressed in the form of trading positions had been singularly unprofitable, so all that remained was to see how he did with somebody else's views. The experiment wasn't just intended to provide a "live ammunition" record of our in-house technician's market insights, it was my last best effort to prove that my recent hiring decision hadn't been a bad one. Sadly, his failure confirmed my earlier one and I had to fire him. All was not lost though, because he was able to transfer his unsuccessful experience as a proprietary trader into a new business advising clients on their hedge fund investments.

In trading, timing is everything because of the use of leverage. Whether it's explicit leverage through the use of borrowed money to finance assets or implicit leverage through the use of off-balance-sheet instruments such as derivatives, once you introduce leverage you care about the path a security takes on its way from here to there. While I can't claim to have anticipated the 2008 crisis and the collapse in equity markets, I did at least organize my affairs with sufficient conservatism (meaning no debt) that I never faced any financial pressure to sell. For me, the failure of Lehman and subsequent nadir of markets saw me glumly contemplate paper losses that I believed must ultimately recover, but by pondering my worst-plausible outcome long before we got there I avoided being hostage to events way beyond anybody's control.

The huge advantage an investor has over a trader is that the investor has the luxury of time whereas a trader may not. Warren Buffett, source of endless wonderful quotes and sage advice, often counsels that investing with borrowed money is a dumb idea. Now one can point out that Berkshire's use of its insurance "float" to invest in stocks amounts to the same thing, and Buffett himself often notes that he loves the insurance business because people pay you to hold their money. He means that insurance premiums paid by customers earn no immediate return and only have to be paid for in the future through insurance claims. But putting aside this advantageous business model that has worked for decades, for millions of individual investors it remains sound advice to limit your exposure to what you actually possess and not increase it with borrowings.

The same thing is true for leveraged companies. The more cyclical their business, the less debt they should have so that a sudden downturn doesn't see the equity holders wiped out in favor of the bondholders.

While investors using just their own money aren't as vulnerable to poorly timing the market, they quite reasonably care as much as anybody else about buying at a good time.

# CHAPTER 3

# WHY STRUCTURED NOTES ARE RARELY THE BEST CHOICE

## Kevin Brolley

### CAVEAT EMPTOR!

Today's investment markets have not been easy to navigate. The painful memory of 2008 still hangs over us and has made us reluctant to allocate much money to the stock and bond markets, and many of us are sitting on too much cash that is earning next to nothing. We worry if today's markets are really on solid footing or if they have been artificially supported by the accommodative policies of the Federal Reserve. Scaremongers have railed for years about the onset of higher inflation and a collapsing dollar, while we have watched inflation fall and the dollar strengthen. These uncertainties have left most of us underinvested in the rally that began in March of 2009 and, what's more, now we are reluctant to commit at these higher prices. As the pundits are fond of saying, this has been one of the most hated bull markets in memory.

Amidst these challenges, chances are your broker has brought up the idea of investing in structured notes. Notes with high coupons well in excess of what you are earning on cash, or notes that promise you, say, 90% of the market's upside while guaranteeing that your principal will be returned if the market falls, are pretty attractive in this environment and you will do well to consider them. You will also do well to bear in mind that with those potentially attractive returns come potentially unattractive risks and drawbacks.

This chapter will discuss some of those drawbacks and hopefully leave you better informed. These notes are expensive, totally illiquid, and often overly complex. We will discuss these negative features in some detail and look at a few specific structures that highlight them. Whatever your own conclusions, you will be armed with good questions for your broker about liquidity, commissions, cost of funds for the issuing bank, and the in-built profits to the structuring subsidiaries of the big banks. Before getting into the details, first a few words about the trading floors where structured notes are produced.

Banks and investment banks have been hiring a lot of smart people over the years. Everything from engineers and science graduates to MBAs in finance and PhDs in mathematics. Many of these have wound up on the trading floors of the big banks where they are taught the finer points of financial engineering and where they are encouraged to develop sharp commercial instincts. The smartest and the most commercial will often wind up working in the sophisticated derivatives business and will be paid millions of dollars. Unfortunately, we know that one outcome of this heady combination of skills, brains, commercial instincts and money, is an environment that can be both aggressive and predatory. Be aware, this is the arena you enter when you invest in structured notes.

The derivative products business is one of the most complex and least transparent businesses on Wall Street. It is also one of the most profitable. Aside from listed futures and options, most derivatives trade *over the counter*, which means that transactions are singly negotiated between two parties. There are no quoted prices that define the market at a given point in time; you have to call other dealers and you will likely get a different price on each call. Professional dealers with their own sophisticated pricing models operate in this business, not the unwary retail investor. Here in the OTC derivatives business is where the knowledge gap between the professional trader and the average private investor is at its widest. This knowledge gap, combined with the lack of transparency, is very fertile ground for big profits.

The structured note is Wall Street's vehicle for getting complex derivatives into the portfolios of the much less knowledgeable retail investor. Few individual investors understand derivatives generally, much less the kinds of complex exotic derivatives that are often embedded in these notes, so the banks have created a framework of selling points supporting the use of these notes and describing the value they can bring to an individual's portfolio. With this positive spin, this rationale, individual investors feel a little more comfortable—seemingly a little smarter—and so are more willing to buy these complex securities. This leaves the banks in a position to exploit the knowledge advantage they enjoy, and it is this exploitation that produces significant revenues for all involved in the production and distribution chain. As we will see, the professional trading desks build considerable margins into these products at the retail investor's expense.

"Caveat emptor" if you are tempted into this market.


## STRUCTURED NOTE BASICS

Structured notes are a combination of a bond and a derivative, which is often some form of a complex exotic option. This derivative will essentially determine the return on your note. It might be linked to a single stock or a basket of stocks, an index or indices, interest rates, foreign exchange, or commodities. It can also reference any combination of these underlying assets.

Notes can offer high coupons or no coupons at all. Payments can be periodic or only occur at maturity. The coupon payments might be contingent on certain conditions being fulfilled, as is the case in accrual notes. In some notes principal is at risk and in others you are assured of getting your principal back at maturity. The variations and combinations are endless.

Many notes today promise the full return of principal, regardless of how the underlying derivative performs. Principal-protected notes are appealing for the simple reason that they will offer some participation in the upside of the market, or the potential for a coupon that is higher than prevailing market rates, but in the event that the derivative does not perform as planned, the investor will get his full investment back as long as the note is held to maturity.

Principal protection can come in two forms: the FDIC can insure it, or it will be subject to the credit quality of the issuing bank. There is a big difference between the two. FDIC insurance implies the full faith and credit of the US government. Notes issued with FDIC insurance are referred to as market-linked CDs, and are distinct from market-linked notes that are subject to the credit of the issuer. They will offer less compelling terms to the investor than similarly structured notes that have issuer credit risk.

Principal protection that relies on the credit quality of the issuing bank is an important consideration. Typically, the issuing banks are large, good-quality banks: JPMorgan, Goldman Sachs, Barclays, Morgan Stanley, and a number of the Canadian and European banks, for example. These banks are, generally, not high risk, and an investor can be comfortable with the credit quality of any of them, with one cautionary observation: structured notes are illiquid. They are not meant to be traded and are expected to be held until maturity. Some notes are also long dated. Some accrual notes that are linked to swap rates and play on the shape of the yield curve can be up to 15 years long. When long maturities are coupled with complete illiquidity, risk rises substantially. Fifteen years is a long time to sit with exposure to any borrower, but it borders on foolish when you cannot sell that exposure should the credit conditions of the borrower change during the life of the note.

This issue of credit quality was thrown into stark relief during the crisis of 2008 and the bankruptcy of Lehman Brothers. Lehman had issued billions of dollars worth of structured notes and many were marketed as "100% principal protected." These notes were subject to Lehman's credit quality and were not FDIC insured. When Lehman went bankrupt, these notes traded at pennies on the dollar and investors lost most of their money. Sadly, and unwisely in the context of structured notes, most retail investors did not read the prospectus and governing documents where it was clearly articulated that this protection was subject to the creditworthiness of the borrower. UBS, who sold many of the Lehman notes through its retail distribution network, subsequently put aside $120 million to settle claims that it improperly sold and marketed these notes. While the disposition of claims against UBS is pending, investors will still be left with far less than they invested. Principal protected notes without FDIC insurance should prudently be confined to shorter dated maturities.

In other structures, principal can be partially protected or not protected at all. These notes come with warnings throughout the term sheets that an investor can lose a large part, or all, of his investment. In any case, whenever the note is not a market linked CD, the investor is exposed to the issuing bank for all cash flows.

In addition to describing structured notes in relation to the treatment of principal, they can also be described by the underlying exposure. Notes might be equity-linked, interest rate linked, linked to commodities or foreign exchange. They might also be described as hybrids, which will provide exposure to a combination of asset types.

Comprehensive data for the structured note market is hard to come by, given its fragmented nature. This presents a challenge in any effort to describe it. Some individual issues run to more than $100 to $200 million in size, but many are below $5 million and even less than $1 million in issue size. For example, in the following table you will see that as of September 5, 2014, year to date issuance has been $28.9 billion. This has been achieved through 6,132 discreet issues representing an average deal size of just $4.7 million.

In addition to the fragmentation of the market by deal size, there is also a tremendous degree of variability in the types of structures being issued. This complicates the process of putting the data into neat buckets for analysis and discussion purposes. For the last several years, issuance of structured notes in the United States has held steady at a little more than $40 billion per year:

| | |
|---|---|
| 2010: | $49.4 billion |
| 2011: | 45.5 |
| 2012: | 39.0 |
| 2013: | 40.5 |
| 2014: | 43.3 annualized (year-to-date as of Sept. 5, 2014: $28.9 billion) |

(Note: these figures include only notes registered with the SEC. All data compiled by Bloomberg.)

While the overall volumes have remained steady, the types of notes have varied, along with the changing market view of interest rates and equities.

Equity-linked notes, broadly defined, accounted for 50% of all notes in 2011 and 75% in 2013. Year to date in 2014 (Sept. 5, 2014) equity-linked deals are up to 81% of all deals. This makes sense, given the bullish stock market in 2013.

Interest-rate linked notes were as much as 18% in 2011 and fell to 11.7% in 2013, and are down to 10% so far in 2014. Likewise, it makes sense that deals linked to interest rates have declined, given the end of quantitative easing and the general expectation of higher rates.

Commodity-linked notes have ranged from 6.7% of the market in 2012 to 3.3% of the market the last two years.

In addition to equity, interest rate, and commodity-linked notes, other categories include reverse convertibles, foreign exchange, hybrid, and "other" types of notes. Within each of these categories there is a broad diversity of underlying structures that present a challenge when trying to talk generally about this market.

So what of these notes? Do they deserve a place in the portfolios of individual investors?

## WHY BUY STRUCTURED NOTES?

A Google search regarding the pros and cons of structured notes will offer up a large number of articles and opinion pieces. Unsurprisingly, it is easy to find financial professionals, academics, and pundits on both sides of the debate. Given the variety of structured notes and the permutations on the types of notes that are being issued, it is easy to grasp that the debate is two-sided. Ostensibly, there is something for everyone in this market. Many structured notes do have merit, and yet, some have very little. Some notes are understandable to the nonexpert, but sadly many are not. The perspective of this chapter is that of the individual investor with limited *technical* financial knowledge. Sophisticated institutional investors might approach such a critique differently. They might focus more on the actual mechanics and pricing of the derivatives and, of course, many institutional investors would just enter the derivative contracts directly—no need for the note. Nevertheless, this chapter will alert nontechnical investors to some of the potholes surrounding these securities.

The conclusion is not definitively against these investments. It is, however, definitively against investing in these notes because your broker sells them to you and you trust him. If you are going to participate in these sorts of securities, do so from a thorough understanding of what you are locking your money into. Know the risks and limitations and engage in those risks with open eyes. The hope is that you will ask more questions, read more documents, and genuinely try to understand what you are being offered before committing your money. One useful principle to keep in mind as you think about structured notes: once these notes are in your portfolio it is very difficult, and very expensive, to get them out again.

Modify that Google search a little and it will turn up documents and brochures from the big banks and other financial commentators that provide selling points dressed up as arguments on why investors should include structured notes in their portfolios. These usually include several of the following purported benefits:

- Portfolio diversification
- Principal protection
- Reduced volatility
- Ability to customize a note to align with any view or forecast

There are others, but these are the most commonly recurring. Sadly, these arguments are, by and large, self-serving in favor of those who make a living selling these securities.

The diversification argument used to be a good one in favor of structured notes. Historically, asset classes like commodities, foreign exchange, and foreign stocks were more difficult for retail investors to access, but this is a much less relevant argument today. The explosive growth of exchange traded funds, for example, now offers the retail investor very specific exposures to a myriad of previously hard-to-trade assets. Foreign exchange and commodity ETFs are readily available, and using them, an investor can implement either a bullish view or a bearish view. ETFs can invest in a combination of global stock markets or single markets. They exist for subsectors of the equity market and for interest rate plays, too. Some ETFs provide leveraged exposure. In short, the individual investor today can gain access to almost any market, any market subset, and any commodity or foreign exchange rate. Unlike structured notes, ETFs have the added and significant advantage of being liquid.

Granted, ETFs do not offer principal protection and they are not embedded with triggers, barriers, cliquets, and other exotic options, so they do not provide an exact alternative to structured notes. However, when evaluated on the advantages of costs and liquidity, a strong case can be made that ETFs can be a better choice. In addition, there are a growing number of exchange-traded options on ETFs that, when combined with zero coupon bonds, can get closer to replicating the exposure of a structured note.

The idea that structured notes can reduce the volatility of a portfolio sounds technical, but it is not. The reduction in volatility is, generally, tied to principal protection. In the case of a standard equity linked participation note, for example, the investor will participate in some percentage of the upside of the underlying asset and yet will still be assured of getting his invested amount back in the event the asset declines in value. If a note promises to repay par at maturity, then this note will, of course, outperform in all instances of a declining market. Given that the note only pays a portion of the asset's upside, then by definition this note is less volatile than an outright investment in the market. Whether the market is down 20% or up 20%, the investor's return will range from 0% to something less than 20%, and that, by definition, is a less volatile investment.

This also applies in some cases where principal is not fully protected. Buffered Return Enhanced Notes, (BRENs), are a typical example. Instead of a full principal guarantee at maturity, an investment in these notes is subject to reduced downside market risk. A note with a 10% buffer will begin to lose principal if the asset has declined by more than 10% on the final determination date. If it declines 20%, the investor will lose 10%; if it declines 50%, the investor loses 40%. If the market, or asset, rises, the investor typically has leveraged exposure to that upside, but subject to a cap. If the market rises dramatically, the investor will only receive the benefit up to the cap rate. As in the case with equity participation notes, a BREN outperforms a declining market and underperforms a dramatically rising market. This also reduces portfolio volatility.

The argument that structured notes can be built to exploit any view or forecast is also a correct argument in and of itself, but it does not really tell us much. One would hope that *any* investment being sold to an individual investor provides exposure to a market move that the investor believes is likely or to which he would like to add exposure; structured notes have no special claim to this. On the contrary, it might be a better argument that structured notes can provide value when used as a hedge against the investor's core position or forecast and so offer an exposure that is opposite to the investor's forecast.

The remainder of this chapter concentrates on the negative aspects of structured notes; the most important of these are costs, illiquidity, and complexity.

## THE HEART OF THE MATTER: THE ARGUMENTS AGAINST

### Costs: These Notes Are Expensive

In 2012, the SEC began a dialogue with nine Wall Street banks with the intention of getting them to improve the disclosure around structured note issuance. Since then, banks have improved the information contained in their pricing supplements. It is now possible, for example, to find the estimated value of the notes on the date the issue was priced. Previously, this information was not disclosed and was closely guarded. The issuing banks had no interest in broadcasting the size of their margins on these deals. It is not a shock that these estimated values are less than the price investors paid on the same day; the magnitude of the difference, however, may be surprising. Usually, this number can be found within the final pricing supplement and often on the first page.

Broadly speaking, estimated values range from 90 cents to 96 cents on the dollar. As most investors pay par (100 cents on the dollar), they are buying notes that are immediately worth 4% to 10% less than the price they paid.

A random sample of 37 pricing supplements of notes issued in November 2014 produced consistent data. The issues included CDs, principal protected notes, partially protected notes, and others that had no principal protection. The assets they link to run the gamut from domestic and foreign stocks, to foreign exchange and commodities. A range of issuers was represented. The estimated worth of these notes on issue date were as follows:

| Values between | 90–91%: | 2 issues |
|---|---|---|
| | 91–92%: | 0 |
| | 92–93%: | 9 |
| | 93–94%: | 11 |
| | 94–95%: | 12 |
| | 95–96%: | 2 |
| | Above 96%: | 1 |

Additionally, supplements for eight reverse exchangeables showed estimated values ranging from 95.81% to 97.44%. These are steep fees for notes that are only 6 to 12 months long.

The difference between the price to investors, usually par, and the estimated value is a function of three types of costs: selling concessions, funding costs, and hedging costs. We will look at each separately.

The selling concessions paid are straightforward and are detailed in the final pricing supplement. These are fees that the issuing banks pay to induce brokers—either their own or third party—to sell the notes. Typically, fees range from 2% on six-month reverse exchangeable notes and up to 4% and 5% on longer and more complicated notes. These fees are deducted from the proceeds that go to the issuer. From the investor's perspective, these are direct charges taken from your investment. It is likely that your broker will be paid the bulk of these fees. In other words, if you invest $50,000 in a note that has 4% placement fees, there is a direct transfer from your wallet to your broker's of $2,000.

The funding spreads for the issuing bank are another cost borne by investors, but this is a cost that is harder to see. Term sheets refer to these funding spreads in various cautionary statements, but while no details are disclosed, we can approximate the point. A bank's credit default swap spreads (CDS) are a good guide to where a bank will issue plain-vanilla debt. For example, at the end of November 2014, five-year JPMorgan CDS were trading around 55 basis points. This roughly implies that Morgan could issue plain-vanilla debt at a spread of Libor +55 basis points. While not exact, it is close enough for this discussion. The relevant point here is that banks will target a much more advantageous cost of funds for structured debt issuance. Why? Because they can, essentially. Structured notes sold to the retail market are very difficult to reverse engineer even for other professional trading desks; the retail investor cannot possibly reverse engineer a complex note and so will be unable to calculate the cost of funds the bank will obtain through such a note.

An educated guess, however, will make the point. It is reasonable to assume that if JPMorgan were to issue a five-year structured note, instead of targeting a cost of funds around Libor +55, it might instead target Libor +25, thereby saving 30 basis points per annum. (This may well be a conservative number.) Why does this matter to the investor? It matters because that is 0.30%, every year, taken off the investor's return and left in the coffers of the issuing bank. Put into present value terms, on a five-year note, these 30 basis points equate to 1.45% that the investor forgoes.

There is an additional twist. In the event that the investor needs to sell the note before maturity, and in the event that the bank provides a bid price (banks are not obligated to do so), the funding cost implied will be substantially wider than Libor +25bps. They will price in a penalty rate that is in excess of its plain-vanilla cost of funds. Banks have no desire to buy these notes back given the advantageous cost of funds achieved when issuing them, and their bid price for the note will reflect that. Its bid for a structured note with five years remaining might be, conservatively, in the region of Libor +75bps. The 50-basis-point differential attributable to the bid–offer spread of funding costs is about 2.4%. This is an important cost that investors need to be aware of before entering the structured note market.

This is highlighted in the term sheets, albeit cryptically. Here is an excerpt from a recent JPMorgan pricing supplement (cusip: 48127DW46)

> The internal funding rate used in the determination of JPMS's estimated value generally represents a discount from the credit spreads for our conventional fixed-rate debt. The discount is based on, among other things, our view of the funding value of the notes as well as the higher issuance, operational and ongoing liability management costs of the notes in comparison to those costs for our conventional fixed-rate debt. If JPMS were to use the interest rate implied by our conventional fixed-rate credit spreads, we would expect the economic terms of the notes to be more favorable to you. Consequently, our use of an internal funding rate would have an adverse effect on the terms of the notes and any secondary market prices of the notes.

This sums it up succinctly.

It is prudent to have a discussion with your broker about the funding costs for the issuing bank when he is trying to sell you a structured note. It is probable he will not know the specific answer, but it is worth asking anyway.

The other category of cost is referred to as *hedging costs* in the pricing supplements. That sounds innocuous, but these costs are a direct reflection of the underlying profitability of the structuring process. A little explanation is in order. These notes are usually issued from either the bank or the holding company of the issuer, and they are issued on a fully hedged basis. In other words, they will not be taking the risk of the underlying derivative contracts—they will have swaps in place that guarantee to pay them whatever cash flows they are required to pay on the notes. Usually, these swaps and hedges are with the bank's own trading subsidiary. From the perspective of the issuer, then, these are indeed hedging costs, but the trading subsidiary that has structured the note is booking considerable profits at the time of deal pricing. The pricing supplement for a recent Credit

Suisse, a 15-Year Step Up Contingent Callable Yield Note (cusip: 22547QWJ1), sums it up clearly:

> The initial estimated value of your securities on the Trade Date (as determined by reference to our pricing models and our internal funding rate) may be significantly less than the original Price to Public. The Price to Public of the securities includes the agent's discounts or commissions as well as transaction costs such as expenses incurred to create, document and market the securities and the cost of hedging our risks as issuer of the securities through one or more of our affiliates (which includes a projected profit). These costs will be effectively borne by you as an investor in the securities.

Let's look at this particular security a little more closely. We notice that the estimated value on the trade date was 90.99%. The pricing supplement also tells us that the selling concession, or underwriting discount, is 4.566%. This is what your broker will get if you buy the notes from him. Subtracting this selling concession from par leaves 95.434%, but the value of the notes is only 90.99%. The difference of 4.44% is the profit retained by the structuring subsidiary of the bank. Some of that profit is accorded to the difference in credit spreads of the issuer, but the bulk of it is the margin—profit—built in to the underlying derivatives. Either way, it is money out of the investor's pocket.

Investors should ask themselves, in an environment of such low rates and low overall returns, whether they should be paying 5% to 10% upfront fees to their brokers. In exchange for these egregious fees, they get securities that are illiquid and overly complex. Investors should look for other ways of enhancing the yield on their portfolios.

## Liquidity (or Lack Thereof)

The liquidity of structured notes is another real concern. These notes should be held until maturity, plain and simple. Pricing supplements are littered with warnings that the banks are under no obligation to make a secondary market or to provide a price at which the investor can sell. If you need to sell, you will pay a steep price indeed.

As mentioned earlier, liquidity becomes more important when purchasing a note that is backed by the credit quality of the issuer, as opposed to one that is insured by the FDIC. Today, JPMorgan, Goldman Sachs, Barclays, and the other common issuers of structured notes have all rebounded nicely from the credit crisis of 2007 and 2008. Capital ratios are high, regulations are more strict, they have been forced to exit some volatile businesses, and they own less bad debt. The near-term probability of another Lehman Brothers type event amongst this group is low. Not all structured notes mature in the near term, however. Some are 7, 10, 15 years long. This is a long time to be exposed to a bank. Should the credit quality of an issuer deteriorate over the life of the note, investors will have virtually no chance of reducing their exposure to that borrower.

In the event you do need to sell your security prior to maturity, if you can get a bid at all, it will almost always be from the issuing bank. It is rare for any bank other than the issuing bank to step in and provide liquidity. If they do so, it will most likely be at the breakup value of the note. You should request that your broker provides details about its bank's trading activity in the secondary market for structured notes. The broker will likely reiterate the cautions in the pricing supplements that the brokerage firm or bank is under no obligation to provide a secondary market.

Occasionally, the investor can find nasty little potholes buried in the documentation of these notes. For example, JPMorgan recently issued "Digital Contingent Coupon Certificates of Deposit Linked to an Equally Weighted Basket of 10 Reference Stocks due November 30th, 2021" (cusip: 48125TF42). On the issue of liquidity and secondary market prices, JP Morgan informs us that should they offer to buy the CDs prior to maturity they will charge a "secondary market transaction fee." This fee is not small: 4% in year one, 3% in year two, 2% in year three, 1% in year four, and 1% in year 5.

Should the investor decide to sell before the CD matures, these fees will not determine the price he receives; they will be *subtracted from* the price JP Morgan is willing to pay. So in addition to the unwind prices of the embedded options and the spread at which the bank is prepared to buy back such advantageous funding, JP Morgan has added another cost the investor will bear. There is no explanation as to why this seemingly arbitrary fee exists; it is just another fee that works in the banks' interest and not the investors'. Whilst this twist is not common, it highlights the need for due diligence and a careful read of the documents.

As stated earlier, once one of these notes goes into your portfolio, it is very difficult—and painful—to remove prior to maturity. Evaluate your liquidity needs carefully before getting involved.

## Complexity, Suitability, and the Individual Investor

> Knowledge of the payoff structure is not equivalent to an understanding of the risks associated with a complex product.
>
> **FINRA Regulatory Notice 12-03**

One of the more relevant criticisms of these types of structures is their complexity and whether the average individual investor can really understand them. The answer is that it will depend on the specific structured note and on the sophistication of the investor. The broker must make a determination if such a product is suitable for an investor. We will discuss this shortly.

As the FINRA quote indicates, understanding these notes involves more than just being able to calculate what you will be paid under different scenarios. That is easy. It is not easy, however, to have a genuine understanding of things like volatility, all the "Greeks" associated with options (i.e., the delta, gamma, vega, and theta used to measure an option's price sensitivity), correlation risk when more than one asset is referenced, or the dynamics of interest rate swap spreads, credit spreads, and forward curves. These things are complex and deeply opaque to the average investor, and their prices and historical data are hard to find unless you are a derivatives market professional. And yet, these difficult concepts are the nuts and bolts of structured notes. This is the essence of the knowledge gap referred to earlier.

It seems that brokers make little effort to genuinely educate their clients about the inner workings of the underlying derivatives. A perusal of the marketing materials produced by the banks generally focus on how the notes work—that is, how they will pay out over time or at maturity. They contain little education on the workings of options, futures, swaps, forward rates, or the correlation of multiple assets.

Having said that, it is not the purpose of this chapter to provide derivatives education. It is rather to highlight aspects of these notes that may not be well understood. With that in mind, let's consider a few notes.

Simple equity participation notes are comparatively easy for most investors to understand. A zero coupon bond is combined with a call option on some stock or index. The zero coupon bond assures the investor will get par back at maturity (subject to the credit of the issuer and subject to the note being held to maturity). The call option offers some percentage of participation in the upside of the underlying asset. For those investors with a very basic understanding of bonds and options, this is not a complex security, and many investors would be able to replicate this type of note.

As notes progress in complexity, however, it becomes increasingly difficult to replicate the payout profile exactly. For example, notes involving buffers, triggers, knock-ins, knock-outs, and similar options are virtually impossible for a layman to price independently or to replicate easily. Each investor needs to decide if such investments are warranted, given the lack of knowledge and data around the embedded derivatives.

Of course, some notes just don't make much sense from a retail investor's perspective.

Goldman Sachs recently issued a CD that is linked to the performance of the S&P 500 index (cusip 38148D3F9). Placement fees were 3.5% and the estimated worth at the time of pricing was 92.70%. In addition to principal protection, the investor will receive a minimum payment of 6% at the final maturity. That is, for a $1,000 investment, the minimum the investor will receive at maturity is $1,060. Anything above that will be subject to the performance of the S&P index.

But it is not what you think. If the index rises 10% over the life of the note, it does not mean the note will pay 10%. If it rises 30%, 40%, or even 50%, it does not mean the note will return that. Nor does this note pay some participation rate of the upside. Why not?

This is called a *cliquet* structure, and it will not look at the overall index return, but rather, it will calculate the percentage gain of the index from quarter to quarter. In effect, every quarter is a new quarter when calculating the percentage return. Those 24 quarters worth of returns (6 years = 24 quarters) are then *added* together. The resulting sum of the quarterly returns is what is used to calculate the payout at maturity. If that sum is anything less than 6%, the investor gets the minimum return of 6%, or approximately 1% per annum. If the number is higher than the minimum, it will be paid to the investor at maturity.

With this specific structure, it is important to note that any negative quarters will subtract from the overall sum and there is no floor on those negative quarters. At the same time, quarters with strong positive performance are capped at 4.5%. In the event, for example, there is a significant correction in one quarter and the market is down 15% but rebounds sharply by, say, 17.65% the following quarter, theoretically the investor is back to break even but not with this structure. The investor gets all the downside of the bad quarter but will only get a 4.5% contribution (instead of 17.65%) from the rebound. Instead of emerging from this volatility with a 0% return, this note leaves the investor down by 10.5%. Another way of describing this point: If there is a decline of 13.5% in one quarter, it will require three quarters of maximum growth to make this up.

Some cliquet structures count only the positive returns while others have floors on the negative returns along with caps on the positive returns. This note, however, has a significant asymmetric return profile, and there are a limited number of scenarios where this will be an advantageous structure. It is unclear how many individual investors will actually understand this. Backtesting the data will prove the point, and it is an ugly one.

We have taken the payout formula for this note and applied it to the quarterly return data for the S&P index since the beginning of 1994. Since that time, there have been 58 complete rolling six-year cycles, with the last cycle beginning in Q3 2008 and ending Q3 2014. The results are startling.

Over these 58 six-year periods, this note would have paid 6%, the minimum, on 48 occasions.

The 6% minimum payout has occurred in 48 of the last 49 six-year cycles. In the 49 six-year cycles beginning in Q4 2001, the average payout has been 6.005%.

However, if quarterly returns were not capped at 4.5%, as they are in this note, then there would have been only nine times where the note would return 6%. The other 49 instances would have produced returns in excess of 6%. In fact, the average six-year payout would have been 32.77%.

This begs the question: How many of the brokers who sold this note did any homework on the bias that is inherent in the note (for which they earned the 3.5% placement fee)? How many understand this quirk of an asymmetric cliquet structure? How many of the investors who bought these notes understand this inherent bias? This is one note that should not have been sold.

JPMorgan recently issued a 5.5-year Certificate of Deposit Linked to the JPMorgan Optimax Market Neutral Index (cusip 48125TF34). This note will pay 140% of the upside of this index at maturity; there will be no interim payments. The selling concession for this note is 4.4% and its estimated value on the trade date was 92.46%. What is the Optimax Market Neutral Index?

It is a proprietary construction designed and managed by JP Morgan that is composed of 18 synthetic constituents that seek to represent specific underlying commodities. This is an index with a twist, however:

"The index employs a strategy that is based on modern portfolio theory and momentum theory."

Unlike most indices, the Optimax Market Neutral Index does not simply seek a weighted average portfolio of the underlying 18 commodities. Instead JP Morgan uses algorithms derived from portfolio theory and momentum theory to rebalance the index every month. This will result in long exposure to some constituents and short exposure to others. The algorithms will decide based on such variables as the last year's returns for each constituent, the relative return of the constituents versus each other (their covariance), their volatility, and various constraints relevant to each of the synthetic positions. The pricing supplement goes on to say that the resulting weights for each constituent will be such that the index will be long those with positive expected returns and short those with negative expected returns.

Despite the obvious idea that the index will be long where the formula expects upside and short where it expects downside, this is not an easy index for anyone to understand, especially the average retail investor. This index is not an index at all: indices do not employ strategies. The Optimax Market Neutral Index is an approach to trading, pure and simple. It is a model that allocates weightings to synthetic commodity positions and it makes those allocations based on mathematical algorithms that have been devised by the trading desk at JP Morgan. The investor who invests his money in this note is simply giving his money to Morgan's trading desk to trade according to their obtuse proprietary formulas.

Elsewhere in the pricing supplement we learn that when returns are calculated on this index, it will be after JPMorgan has deducted a "hypothetical" fee of 96 basis points per annum. There is nothing hypothetical about the reduction of almost 1% per annum from the investor's return. This looks very much like a fee that JPMorgan pays itself to run its trading algorithms.

This note is a pretty good deal for JPMorgan. The brokers and advisors in the Morgan network will get 4.4% of every note they sell; the trading desk that structured the note will get the bulk of the 3.14% left over (after selling fees and before the estimated worth); the bank's treasury will get the rest through their advantageous funding levels; and now we see that the guys who run the Optimax index will also be paid 96 basis points every year. An investor in this note would need to be very confident it was a winner before buying this.

How many retail investors truly understand the risks of this note and this index? For that matter, how many smart sophisticated derivative traders understand the risks inherent in this trading model, other than the Morgan team itself? How many of the brokers, who were paid 4.4% for selling it, truly understand this proprietary model?

This note may wind up doing very well and an investor may well decide to give his money to Morgan's synthetic commodity trading model, but it will be a rare investor indeed who can claim to understand it.

This next note looks attractive on the surface, and even after a deeper look, some investors may be willing to purchase such a note. That does not mean however, that they will really understand its inner workings.

Credit Suisse recently issued Step Up Contingent Callable Yield Notes due November 29, 2024 Linked to the Performance of the EURO STOXX 50 and the Russell 200 (cusip: 22547QWH5). Placement fees are 4.385% and the estimated worth when it was priced was 92.815%.

The note will pay a 9% per annum coupon during the first five years (quarterly in arrears); then 11% for the next three years and 13% for the last two years until it matures in November 2024. These are attractive rates in today's interest rate environment. What's the catch? There are a few, and they are complicated.

This note has both barrier options and knock-in options embedded within it. The barrier options are struck 25% below the initial level of each index; the knock-in options are at 50% below the initial level of each index. Prior to every quarterly coupon payment date, there is an observation date and if, on that observation date, either index closes below its barrier level, then no coupon will be paid for that period. If a barrier has not been breached, then the coupon is paid. This pattern of observations continues for the life of the note.

At maturity, there is an additional observation. If either index is below its knock-in level, the investor will get a lot less than par back. For example, if the index closes on the day of that final observation 50.01% below the initial level, thereby breaching the knock-in level, the investor will lose 50.01% of principal. If either index closes 60% below its initial level, then the investor loses 60%. And so on. If both indices close below their respective knock-in level, then the worst performer is used to calculate the redemption amount.

It might be reasonable to assume that both the barrier levels and the knock-in levels are a long way out of the money and therefore represent *de minimis* risk, and an investor with a sanguine view can look forward to 10 years worth of these high coupons. Not necessarily. The last quirk of this note is that the issuer has the right to call the notes at par on any coupon payment date. Evaluating call options embedded in traditional nonstructured bonds is a function of interest rates and credit spreads, and therefore refinancing costs. With this note, those factors are still at work but in addition, the costs of unwinding the barriers and the knock-ins need to be factored in. This makes it very difficult for a nontechnical investor to fairly assess the likelihood that these notes will be called and that future payments of the high coupons will or will not occur.

Do investors understand the correlations between both indices? How do these indices trade in relation to interest rate movements? Do lower rates/higher rates imply a greater or lesser probability that one of the index options comes into the money? Under what combination of market movements is this note likely to be called? Is it more likely the notes will be called when the equity options are far out of, or far in, the money? Given that this note is not principal protected, how might the investor protect himself if the knock-in option is coming into the money? The notes will have essentially no liquidity and if there is a bid at such time, it will be substantially below the investor's cost. How can he hedge this? What is his Plan B? Sadly, few individual investors will have confident answers to these questions. This is a reasonable discussion to have with the broker trying to sell these notes.

These are three notes pulled at random from recent offerings. The list could be extended at will. Structured notes are complicated and are, in the opinion of this author, generally beyond the technical capabilities of the average individual investor.

Notes like these raise questions about the extent to which brokers are adequately assessing the suitability of such notes for retail clients. The need to do so has been spelled out in FINRA's regulatory notice 12-03. (Note that the FINRA website has a wealth of warnings about structured notes that are worth reading.) Notice 12-03 discusses the general level of supervision that brokerage firms are expected to exert when selling complex products, and it also discusses the individual broker's responsibilities when selling notes like these. In relation to the latter, the notice states:

> Knowledge of the payoff structure is not equivalent to an understanding of the risks associated with a complex product. The registered representative also should understand such features as the characteristics of the reference asset, including its historic performance and volatility and its correlation with specific asset classes, any interrelationship between multiple reference assets, the likelihood that the

complex product may be called by the issuer, and the extent and limitations of any principal protection. The registered representative should be adequately trained to understand not only the manner in which a complex product is expected to perform in normal market conditions, but the risks associated with the product.

This is an interesting bar to set for any broker in relation to the notes above. It would be interesting to see how many genuinely pass muster. It is equally interesting to ask how many investors were deemed suitable enough to buy these securities.

FINRA standards apply to brokers, or financial advisors. These classifications are distinct from the designation of *investment advisor*. Investment advisors are not judged by FINRA's suitability standard; they are judged by a fiduciary standard and are essentially regulated by the SEC. The fiduciary standard is a tougher standard in that advisors are required to do what is in the client's best interest and to put the client's interest ahead of their own. It is reasonable to assume that what is in the client's best interest will sometimes produce different recommendations from those that are deemed merely suitable for that same client.

It would be interesting to see if those on the fiduciary standard treat structured notes differently from those brokers on the suitability standard. Does the fiduciary standard impose a hurdle that many structured notes cannot clear? Is it mostly brokers rather than investment advisors who are selling these notes? Sadly, little research exists on this question.

Structured notes are lucrative securities for the banks. Individual investors need to use caution when these notes are being marketed. Read the pricing supplements, note the fees and the complexity, and weigh the liquidity disadvantages of the particular note. Engage your broker in a vigorous conversation about these issues and see what kind of answers he offers. Pay particular attention to the answers he does not have.

Markets are tough enough these days. It is unlikely they will be made easier by investing in securities with no liquidity and that are too complex to understand—unlikely, that is, for all but the big banks. Caveat emptor.

# CHAPTER 4

---

# UPDATE TO *THE HEDGE FUND MIRAGE*

## HEDGE FUNDS REMAIN A GREAT BUSINESS

In January 2012, I published *The Hedge Fund Mirage; The Illusion of Big Money and Why It's Too Good to Be True*. Although hedge funds have long been associated with fabulous wealth, a little-appreciated fact was that substantially all the profits generated by hedge funds had been eaten up in fees paid to the hedge fund managers themselves. Funds of hedge funds and consultants had taken the rest, with the result that, while hedge funds had been fantastically profitable investments, those profits had not made their way through to the clients.

The book caused quite a stir within the hedge fund industry. All I had done was consider returns from the standpoint of ALL the investors. Conventionally, historic returns on most types of investment are calculated assuming a single commitment of cash by the client at the beginning of the period. By this measure, hedge funds indeed looked very good. Starting back in the 1990s depending on which hedge fund index you use, returns are quite decent, at 6% to 7%. And it's true, hedge funds used to be very attractive. In the late 1990s and through 2000 to 2002 when stocks were collapsing along with the bursting of the dot.com bubble, hedge funds did what they were supposed to do. They hedged, preserved investor capital, and earned a well-deserved reputation for delivering good, uncorrelated returns. The investors at that time did very well. There just weren't that many investors.

This success drew substantial amounts of new capital from institutions eager to find some way to diversify their traditional mix of equities and fixed income. It was a completely understandable decision, one that at JPMorgan at the time we supported. In fact, in 2001, anticipating just such a flood of institutional capital into hedge funds we set up a hedge fund seeding business, the JPMorgan Incubator Funds. Since many of the best hedge fund managers were already so highly sought after that they were turning away potential clients, we felt that the best new hedge funds would be highly sought after. The Incubator Funds' investment model was to try and identify tomorrow's top hedge fund managers today, before they were overwhelmed with capital. By using JPMorgan's vast network of financial market contacts, we were able to identify talented managers early and, at least as important, reject those whose background and pedigree were inadequate.

Perhaps most importantly, we were able to negotiate a share of the manager's business. Although we wanted hedge funds that would generate good returns, we were most interested in sharing in the lucrative fees that they charge, the now ubiquitous "2 & 20" (2% management fee and 20% of the profits, annually). We recognized that the *business* of hedge funds was likely to be a far better investment than simply being a hedge fund client. As subsequent developments showed, that turned out to be far truer than we could have imagined.

As money flowed into the hedge fund industry, generating attractive returns became more and more challenging. A swelling pool of assets gradually exhausted most of the arbitrage-like, uncorrelated return opportunities out there. Over time, hedge funds began taking more bets on the overall direction of the market, magnified by leverage. They became more reliant on their ability to quickly adjust their risk profile when markets moved against them. An industry that had earned its positive reputation by exploiting market inefficiencies with carefully designed, tightly controlled hedged strategies drifted toward more prosaic bets. As the years went by, more and more hedge fund portfolios were exposed to directional moves in equity and credit markets. This shift in investment styles, combined with the influx of money, led to the damning result that in the 2008 financial crisis the losses incurred by hedge funds wiped out all of the cumulative profits they had ever earned for their investors.

Although some tried to explain away this disastrous outcome as a completely unforeseeable consequence of market collapse that few expected, the fact is, hedge funds were found wanting at precisely the moment when their uncorrelated returns would have been most important to investors. During the 2000 to 2002 technology-driven bear market, hedge funds had delivered as promised. The contrast between that period and 2008 couldn't have been more stark. Clearly, something had changed.

In fact, the fundamental error that's still being made by today's hedge fund investors is that they never consider the natural limits to size facing the industry. It's quite an amazing oversight. There's lots of academic research to show that small hedge funds outperform big ones. Their small size allows them to get in and out of trades nimbly as well as to exploit minor inefficiencies that wouldn't be material for larger funds. Hedge fund investors generally agree that small hedge funds outperform big ones. Finding small hedge funds is expensive though, so it's not a practical approach for institutions with billions of dollars to allocate. It's also not an approach advocated by the consultants that advise these institutional clients. If your business is to recommend individual hedge fund investments to your pension fund clients, it's a far more efficient business model to research big hedge funds because they will accept larger investments, and as a consultant you can make the same recommendation to multiple clients, which cuts your own costs of research.

While investors recognize that small hedge funds are better than big ones, they also know that most big hedge funds they look at were themselves better when they were smaller. That's how they became big, by generating good returns while small. And yet, today's hedge fund investors and their advisors fail to make the third and obvious step, and realize that a small hedge fund *industry* was better than today's big one. The results speak for themselves, and in fact, if I was to write *The Hedge Fund Mirage* today, the results would be more negative. As I often say, I predicted in 2012 that future hedge fund investment results would be disappointing, and the industry has cooperated ever since in providing further empirical support!

## INDUSTRY REACTION TO THE DISMAL TRUTH

In early 2012 when *The Hedge Fund Mirage* was published, its controversial stance quickly caught the attention of the financial media. Everybody had become so used to seeing lists of unbelievably huge paydays for hedge fund managers that it seemed beyond question that the clients must be doing well, too. The revelation that this wasn't the case was itself newsworthy. The media interest didn't surprise me; I had thought it was a huge story myself as I was writing it. And as I point out in the book, I was by no means the first person to identify the gaping contrast between actual and perceived investment results. An academic paper by Ilya Dichev from Emory University and Gwen Yu of Yale had arrived at a similar conclusion. Not enough investors read their research (academic papers are not to everybody's taste). Their work inspired me to examine why this was the case and to present it in a form that could be more readily digested by the investors whom I was hoping to inform.

What did surprise me was the reaction of the hedge fund industry itself. Hedge fund managers are some of the smartest people you'll meet in the investing world. Big money attracts the most talent in any field. The vast majority of the people I've known since I first began investing in hedge funds in the early 1990s are reasonably intelligent. I publicly criticized an entire sector of finance, even an entire asset class (some people assert that hedge funds are not an asset class since they invest in other assets themselves; their precise definition is not important). Many people could have been understandably quite defensive as I bashed their means of earning a livelihood to the gleeful accompaniment of the mainstream financial press. *The Wall Street Journal,* the *Financial Times,* and *The Economist,* as well as many other print and cable TV outlets, interviewed me and provided balanced but favorable coverage.

To the eternal credit of many thoughtful hedge fund professionals, rather than reacting defensively or trying to ignore me, they engaged me. I was invited to speak at numerous hedge fund conferences. Some may have disagreed with me, or wished that what I was pointing out wasn't true, but they nonetheless invited me to present my ideas.

Even more surprising was the reaction of many hedge fund managers. I was frequently contacted by people running successful funds, and invariably the dialogue was along the lines that they loved my book, and that of course there was enormous mediocrity throughout the hedge fund world. Though not in their fund, of course!

This made perfect sense. Hedge fund managers are smart. They fully recognize the challenges of size in investing: "Size is the enemy of performance." Successful hedge fund managers often cap the size of their funds for this reason, because as they get richer their own investment in their fund grows and they become more concerned that excess capital will dilute the returns on their own money. You'll never hear a hedge fund manager recommend a diversified portfolio of hedge funds as a thoughtful approach. That's because they understand its limitations. They recommend their own hedge fund and maybe a handful of others where they know the manager personally. The smartest people in the industry already get it.

In fact, in the months following the book's release we struggled to find much of a negative response. I had simply shouted that the emperor had no clothes, and it turned out a great many people had quietly felt all along that something was very wrong. A group in London called the Alternative Investment Managers Association (AIMA), whose mission is to promote the use of hedge funds, did fortunately step up and gamely attempt a rebuttal. Since their job is to persuade investors of the value in hedge funds, they were only going to come out on one side of the debate. They put out a couple of write-ups that didn't directly address the issues and didn't convince many people. One academic referred to my book as, "... baby hedge fund analysis 101 at best," displaying arrogance from the safety of an ivory tower unburdened by the need to make actual investment decisions.

I watched in the blogosphere for reaction to the criticism. Felix Salmon is an erudite, well-informed financial writer for Reuters and others. Felix read my book and AIMA's response. In a truly memorable put-down of their PR effort, Felix wrote that AIMA had, "... convinced me of the deep truth of Lack's book in a way that the book itself never could" (Salmon 2012). The inadequacy of AIMA's response had provided further support.

More recently, AIMA partnered with the Chartered Alternative Investment Analyst (CAIA) Association and commissioned Hedge Fund Research (HFR) to figure out how hedge fund investors had done. All three groups, of course, make a living from a big hedge fund industry, so unsurprisingly, the HFR study commissioned by AIMA found hedge fund investors had made an implausible $1.5 trillion over the past 10 years (AIMA 2015). Their methodology wasn't disclosed, but somehow HFR was able to show that hedge fund investors had made, for example, $20.1 billion in 2011 even though HFR's preferred index, the HFRI Fund Weighted Composite Index, which represents the broadest measure of the industry, was down −5.25% that year. If you torture the data sufficiently, it will tell you whatever you want to hear. People have moved on, though. Few journalists picked up the story, most likely because they've already concluded AIMA is just a relentless sales organization with little objectivity.

## WHY HEDGE FUNDS ARE STILL GROWING

Over three years since the book's publication, subsequent hedge fund industry results continue to be inadequate at best if not downright disappointing. Yet investor capital has continued to flow into hedge funds, which have grown from around $2 trillion in assets under management to perhaps $2.5 trillion today. Apart from the fact that it shows not everybody who read the book was convinced, it also suggests that the returns I find so mediocre are in fact quite acceptable to at least those investors making the allocations. Perhaps the strongest riposte hedge fund apologists can mount is to point to the voting of clients with their money. They're all consenting adults, and capitalism's allocation of resources to products and services based on countless independent decisions is the best way we know of to let the best rise to the benefit of all.

The obvious response to this is that the history of investing is littered with episodes of capital flowing too readily to areas that ultimately prove poorly considered. It's not that every successful investment idea eventually blows itself up, but every one that does blow up was preceded by a thoughtless scamper to join the crowd. Early, smart money is followed by the less astute. So we'll put financial success for hedge fund promoters in the category of dubious support for the notion that a bigger hedge fund industry is better.

In the early days of hedge funds the investors were generally wealthy individuals, "high net worth" investors acting either through the private banks that covered them or on their own. Someone once asked me if I was saying that these generally self-made wealthy entrepreneurs were the dumb money. In fact, it's quite the contrary. Today's hedge fund investors are far more likely to be institutions especially US public pension funds investing the retirement savings of teachers, firefighters and other public sector workers. Wealthy individuals are far less significant investors today. In many cases, they represent the smart money, in that they enjoyed the successes of hedge funds 15 or so years ago.

This is good news. The point of this book is that too often, individual investors receive poor, expensively delivered advice. We hope that all investors big and small will find that this book helps them avoid some of the more egregious products we've written about. That individual investors are less committed to hedge funds reflects a more discerning approach.

So the case for hedge fund vindication relies on the investor acceptance represented by "sophisticated institutional investors" with all their research capabilities deploying some of their capital as they are into hedge funds. I often smile when I hear that phrase *sophisticated institutional investors*. It's usually used by service providers seeking to impose an imprimatur of quality on their own business by virtue of their clientele. Of course, many institutional investors *are* sophisticated. They have the resources to hire investment professionals to advise them on their portfolios, and many do. But just as not all hedge funds are bad, not all institutional investors are sophisticated. In fact, some of the least sophisticated are the public pension plans plowing their money into hedge funds.

The Trustee Leadership Forum is a group affiliated with Harvard University that brings together the trustees of public plans with the objective of sharing best practices and learning from one another.

I once had the opportunity to present the findings of *The Hedge Fund Mirage* to one of their events, so I traveled up to Cambridge, Massachusetts, to Harvard University.

The speaker before me was Diane Mulcahy from the Kauffman Foundation in Kansas City, Missouri. I knew Diane because she was co-author of a fascinating research paper titled "We Have Met the Enemy and It Is Us." It arrives at similar conclusions about venture capital (vc) investing to the ones that I reached on hedge funds, in that smaller vc funds are better than big, that the 1990s was a far better time to be invested than after 2002, and that fees had consumed far too much of the profits. I dubbed it "The Venture Capital Mirage."

When it was published I had chatted with Diane about their findings, which were largely drawn from the Kauffman Foundation's own investing experience. It remains an outstanding effort to inform vc investors, based on the experience of one very definitely sophisticated institutional investor.

Diane was giving her presentation and we were all watching with great interest as she went through the analysis they had performed on the Foundation's overall investment results. Examining private equity returns can be complicated, and Diane was doing a great job of walking her audience through the exercise with charts and figures. It wasn't a presentation you'd expect a high school student to readily grasp but was certainly appropriate for a roomful of public pension trustees, stewards of some of the largest pools of investment capital in the United States.

Midway through Diane's presentation, an audience member posed the most basic question. What did Diane mean by the use of the word *median*? For those of you for whom middle-school math is a distant memory, the median is the point at which exactly half the observations you're measuring are higher and half lower. It's not the mean but is often close to it. For someone in investing, you'd no sooner feel the need to explain what you mean by median than you would tell them who is the president of the United States.

Diane was only momentarily surprised by the question before she quickly regained her composure and politely explained the term. I was stunned. Not just that the questioner didn't know the answer, but also because he wasn't at all embarrassed to ask in front of his peers.

As the day wore on and I spoke to more people, it dawned on me why this was the case. His peers weren't investment professionals at all. At lunch I sat with a retired firefighter. At another table was a retired steelworker. These were some of the people who were pension fund trustees. They'd spent their careers working in fields as far from investing as it's possible to be, and were there to represent the interests of their former colleagues who no doubt trusted them to look after their interests. My overwhelming impression that day was of thoroughly conscientious people working very hard to improve their understanding so as to do a better job at managing retirement savings.

In fact, investing doesn't have to be that complicated. It's not a bad test to say that if it can't be explained to a retired firefighter (or teacher, nurse and so on) then maybe it shouldn't be recommended. Call it the Public Sector Worker Test.

## SOME ACCOUNTING RULES ARE DUMB

Now let's return to the growth in the hedge fund industry and examine why the increase in clients shouldn't be interpreted as a popular vindication of value to the typical investor. While the early investors in hedge funds in the 1990s were largely high net worth individuals, over the past decade or so institutions have become a far more significant source of hedge fund capital. Perhaps the most important among these have been the public pension plans, charged with managing the retirement of America's public sector workers such as teachers, firefighters, and so on.

Public pension plans use some pretty strange accounting. Since investing for retirement entails providing income for beneficiaries several decades into the future, pension funds have very long investment horizons. In calculating whether they have enough assets today to meet tomorrow's obligations, they estimate all of the cumulative payments they expect to make over the likely lifetimes of their beneficiaries. These future payments are then converted into today's money by discounting them using an appropriate discount rate. It's the *time value of money*. Commonly, corporate pension funds will use the rate on bonds of similar maturity to the timing of the pension's obligations.

The lower the discount rate, the higher the "present value" of those obligations and consequently the more assets are required in order to show that the pension obligations are fully funded. A low discount rate is more conservative than a high one, since the assets the pension fund holds need to be invested profitably so they grow sufficiently.

Many public pension funds in the United States are underfunded, which is to say the assets they own are unlikely to be sufficient to meet future retiree obligations. It's a steadily growing problem, and while it may never lead to a crisis, it will create a growing tax burden for the next generation of taxpayers as state governments are forced to close their pension deficits by raising taxes. It is an unfortunate legacy of the baby boomer generation that it has consistently voted for political choices that pushed such obligations into the future, something I wrote about in my book *Bonds Are Not Forever; The Crisis Facing Fixed Income Investors*.

Using bond yields as the discount rate to calculate the present value of future pension obligations is a sensible approach, and this is what most pension funds do. However, public pension funds follow a different set of accounting rules, and in an especially bizarre departure from private practice they use their expected return on assets to discount their liabilities.

To show how odd this is, you need only consider how shifting their asset mix can have a dramatic effect on their obligations. A pension fund expects to earn a long-term return on its assets based on the likely return for each asset class and the proportion of its assets in that asset. For example, suppose it invested half its money in stocks with an expected return of 7% and the other half in bonds with an expected return of 3%.

$$(50\% \times 7\%) + (50\% \times 3\%) = 5\%, \text{ their expected return on assets.}$$

Clearly shifting the mix of stocks and bonds will alter the expected return. Add more risky stocks and the expected return will rise, as will the risk of the resulting portfolio.

What's uniquely odd about public pension plans is that they also use this expected return as the discount rate for their liabilities. It's a perverse treatment, because it means that changing the mix of assets alters the present value of their obligations, although their actual obligations haven't changed. So a more risky mix of assets, through the higher discount rate it produces, lowers what they owe future retirees and therefore improves their funded position.

The *Economist* magazine, my personal favorite weekly publication, captured the problem with this approach quite elegantly in an article titled "Money to Burn" (*The Economist* 2013). The article noted that, just as increasing the share of your portfolio invested in higher return-ing, risky assets can translate into a lower obligation, so can removing low yielding assets. Cash, which earns close to 0%, is a drag on any portfolio's returns. The article colorfully notes that if a pension fund held cash and simply got rid of it (i.e., burned it as in the title of the article), this would drive up the expected return on assets of what remained and therefore drive down the present value of the liabilities.

In this way, the pension fund could appear to be better off through having a reduced obligation, even while the assets with which it planned to meet those obligations were now smaller because they'd burned the cash. It may sound like an absurd example, but it highlights that driving the expected investment return higher by increasing the allocation to higher returning assets does the same thing. So a more risky pension fund can appear to be in better shape than a less risky one.

Because an allocation to hedge funds carries with it that hoped-for 7% return (this seems to be what most hedge fund investors and their consultants expect of their hedge fund investments over the long run), public pension funds are incented to add hedge funds (burning cash might achieve the same result from an accounting standpoint but has unattractive optics).

This is what has happened. Hedge funds with their 7% return potential can appear very attractive to public pension funds grappling with insufficient assets to meet retiree obligations. They can serve to delay the inevitable day of reckoning with its politically unattractive tax hikes or spending cuts (or both) to make the numbers add up.

The problem is, no one is pointing this out. The consultants that advise public pension plans are conflicted because recommending hedge funds pays well, so there's little incentive to do anything else.

Moreover, the consultants themselves rarely demonstrate a track record of profitable recommendations. One study in 2013 found that investment consultants were "worthless" (Sorkin 2013).

Pension fund trustees are caught in a tough bind. They generally rely on consultants because the requirements of the Employee Retirement Income Security Act of 1974 (ERISA), which regulates pensions, places a heavy burden on trustees. ERISA includes civil and criminal provisions for those who fail to oversee pension fund assets in a way that's in the best interests of the beneficiaries, so it's little wonder that they use consultants.


## POLITICS DRIVES ASSET FLOWS

The other problem facing public pensions is that when they're underfunded, there's not much of a political consequence. A shortfall between the assets held by a pension fund and its obligations ultimately has to be made up by increased contributions. It's a brave politician who opts to raise taxes or cut services today so as to fully fund a pension, versus leaving the problem to grow for elected leaders to deal with 10 or 15 years later. Most voters will opt for policies that defer topping up pensions. It may be criticized as poor public policy, but it's the democratic process at work. New Jersey is just one example. In 2014, Governor Chris Christie slashed pension contributions (Magyar 2014) by $2.4 billion to meet a budget shortfall. Unions representing the beneficiaries challenged the move, but Christie evidently calculated that few voters would be that bothered. Short of ironclad legal requirements that such pension obligations be fully funded, political leaders responding to the desires of voters will kick the can down the road.

This was brought home to me quite memorably by a representative of the Los Angeles County Employees Retirement Association (LAC-ERA). During my presentation, she explained the actual dilemma they all faced. Noting my recommendation to drop hedge funds from their portfolio, she walked through the likely consequences. The expected return on their assets would fall, since hedge funds with a 7% return target was higher than their other holdings. No matter that 7% is an unrealistic figure to expect of hedge funds; it's provided by the consultants and therefore independent of the trustees even if based on dubious assumptions.

The lower expected return on the pension assets would then feed through to a lower discount rate on its liabilities as described above, which would then increase the underfunded position of the pension fund. "At which point, those Republicans will point to the gap and demand that we cut benefits," she continued. I never get into the politics of the issues, but I sympathized with her plight. Because of the political process that provides funding for public pension plans and their curious accounting, many people with responsibility for tomorrow's retirees unquestioningly cling to the fantasy of the kinds of hedge fund returns that we haven't seen for over 10 years. Those who believe that the growth in hedge fund assets represents vindication for the asset class are not thinking very deeply about the process through which such decisions are made.

Some public pension plans are responding to the continued disappointing returns. The California Public Sector Retirement System (CalPERS) is often regarded as a thought leader among other pension funds, and with over $300 billion in assets it is one of the largest institutional investors in the world. In September 2014 it announced (CalPERS 2014) the elimination of hedge funds from its portfolio, concluding that the cost of investing wasn't justified by the returns. One interesting disclosure was that in the most recent fiscal year through June 2014, CalPERS had paid $135 million in fees on a $4 billion portfolio that earned 7.1%. The approximately $280 million in investment returns ($4 billion × 7.1%) means that for every $2 in returns, it paid away a third dollar in fees. Of the gross returns (i.e., before fees), two-thirds went to CalPERS and one-third to the hedge fund managers. When you consider that it's possible to invest in equity index funds for less than 0.1%, this division of investment profits between the provider of capital and the managers must have appeared as absurd to CalPERS as it does to everyone else.

One seldom-acknowledged fact about hedge fund returns is that a simple 60/40 portfolio of stocks and bonds has beaten hedge funds since 2002. Prior to that, hedge funds had actually done a pretty good job, often justifying their hefty fees and the faith investors had in them. Few knew at the time that the best years of performance were already in the past. The plain-vanilla stocks and bonds portfolio hasn't just beaten hedge funds since 2002. It's done so every single year since then. Some years stocks have been strong and sometimes bonds, but the combination has relentlessly left behind the expensive and by now bloated asset class.

The response of some of the industry's proponents can make you smile. I'm often asked to give a presentation on my views on hedge funds. As I often note, although *The Hedge Fund Mirage* was published in 2012, hedge funds have co-operated by continuing to generate mediocre returns at great expense, which is causing more and more people to question the standard recommendation of a diversified portfolio of hedge funds.

Hedge funds used to be referred to as absolute return vehicles. It sounded very solid, portraying the talented navigation of a portfolio through the unpredictable waters of market volatility with the assurance that the eventual result would be a positive (i.e., absolute) return no matter what the prevailing conditions. Few use the term any more, since 2008 demonstrated so convincingly that almost nothing apart from developed market sovereign debt was immune to the hurricane unleashed by mass deleveraging. The Absolute Return moniker is long forgotten, although a monthly publication, *AR Magazine*, retains the title it drew from its coverage subject in a quaint reminder of what used to be.

Absolute returns were dropped in favor of generating attractive relative returns, which also seemed like a solid, reliable objective. However, the history since 2002 increasingly demonstrates that the relative returns being generated are relatively poor, at least compared with the stocks/bonds portfolio as described above. So the goalposts shifted again, to one of generating uncorrelated returns. This also appears like pretty safe ground. Although in 2008 hedge funds were unfortunately too highly correlated with everything else as they lost 23%, they do seem to be reliably uncorrelated and worse than other assets.

## TOO MUCH CAPITAL

The pressure on returns doesn't just come from the weight of assets under management, which has the effect of creating too much competition for the interesting opportunities that are out there. CalPERS found size to be a constraint in determining to end their hedge fund portfolio. An additional problem is the institutionalization of the business. As with other asset classes, big investors seek diversified portfolios following one of the core precepts of the capital asset pricing model (CAPM), which is that diversification is always a good thing.

However, for diversification to work, the risks of your individual holdings need to behave somewhat predictably. Since part of their original selection was based on their being uncorrelated with one another, it's important that they retain that feature going forward. Today's hedge fund investors are far more focused on the potential for a hedge fund to experience *style drift,* which simply means the manager begins to invest in a way that's different from the past.

It's easy to see why this might be a problem. If a portfolio of hedge funds that were previously uncorrelated with one another all begin to drift toward a new investment style or set of opportunities that they all deem attractive, they will no longer possess the diversification that led to their combination in the same portfolio. This is a potentially huge problem for the investor, and is one reason why the potential for style drift is carefully monitored.

However, an unintended consequence can be that by limiting a manager's freedom to roam where he sees the best opportunities, it also shields the investor from an important element of the manager's overall skill. Many of the best hedge fund managers back in the Golden Days of hedge funds (pre-2002) did just this, often to the benefit of their clients. The wealthy individuals who were the typical clients in those days held fewer hedge funds than today's institutions. They knew little and cared less about style drift. They just wanted their managers to make money. The constraints today's institutions seek to place on hedge fund managers reduce both the risk and the return potential.

I once wrote a post for my blog titled "The Dumbest Idea in Finance," which is how I described the conventional, broadly diversified portfolio of hedge funds that is so often the way institutions approach them. It was, of course, an incendiary title, but it was backed up with an interesting twist on conventional thinking.

Financial theory in the form of CAPM holds that a diversified portfolio is a good thing. In CAPM-speak, there is no excess return to idiosyncratic risk. What this means is that any time you spend selecting individual investments is not going to provide you any improved risk–adjusted return over and above what you could earn holding a highly diversified portfolio. It means that for investors in equities, for example, they should just hold an index fund rather than waste time on individual stocks. Put another way, you don't need any insight in security selection to be invested in equities.

Although the entire universe of active equity managers (which includes your author), by their very existence disagrees with this conclusion from CAPM, it's certainly also true that holding index funds is a perfectly legitimate way to be invested in stocks.

A crucial premise here is that over the long run, stocks have a *positive excess return,* which is to say they do better than the risk-free rate. Although equities can obviously have bad years and even a bad decade, the notion that they have a positive long-term return is not a contentious idea. Hedge funds are different. As I showed in *The Hedge Fund Mirage*, Treasury bills would have been a better bet for investors in aggregate. It's not at all clear that in the future hedge funds will outperform the risk-free rate. In such a case, the conventional thinking about diversification breaks down. In fact, if you're investing in an asset class with poor or negative future returns, you clearly need to be good at picking individual investments. For the hedge fund investor, this means you have to have skill at manager selection.

This is not just nice to have, it's so critical that if for some reason you're not good at selecting hedge fund managers, then you shouldn't bother investing at all. By contrast, equity investors who are no good at picking stocks can still invest in equities by using index funds. Hedge fund investors invariably believe they possess insight about picking hedge funds. Of course they can't all be good at it, but some are. For those that are good, diversification will only serve to hurt them, as the more diversified their portfolio of hedge funds, the more it will be drawn toward the mediocrity of the average return. Since the average has been poor and is likely to stay that way, investing broadly so as to dampen the impact of any one manager on performance is really counterintuitive. Therefore, diversification is really useful to hedge fund investors who are not good at manager selection. For them, the average return is better than they'll get relying on their insight. Conversely, good insight on manager selection argues that you shouldn't dilute it.

Therefore, a focus on fewer hedge fund investments where you have the highest conviction is more likely to be rewarding for the investor with manager selection skill. A highly diversified hedge fund portfolio is the sign of someone who knows he or she is not that good at picking them, and strives to achieve the mediocre average return because it'll likely be better than would be achieved with fewer managers.

Fewer hedge funds means a more concentrated portfolio, which naturally means you should allocate less to hedge funds. This isn't an attractive proposition to pension funds relying on hedge funds to help cover their underfunded retiree obligations, nor to the consultants who earn fees advising them on how to build their portfolio.

Nonetheless, this is what happens when you apply the world of CAPM to an asset class that wasn't contemplated in its design. Of course, few hedge fund investors would concede to the logic outlined above. They would claim that adding diversification simply provides greater exposure to the selection skill they already have. Nonetheless, hedge fund returns continue to be poor in aggregate.

Hedge fund managers are often held to be the smartest people in finance. Ted Seides, co-founder of Protégé Partners, a fund of hedge funds, once said, "The best and brightest spend their time where the compensation is best, and today in the public markets, that's clearly in the hedge fund universe" (Seides 2014). The irony is that I don't think a hedge fund manager has ever publicly recommended investing in hedge funds the way Seides and others do for their clients, through large, diversified portfolios. Just because the smartest people run hedge funds doesn't mean you should want to be their client.

An amusing exchange took place in late 2014 involving Seides and other commentators. Perhaps feeling that the recent decision by California's largest public pension plan to redeem its hedge fund investments demanded a public defense of hedge funds, Seides wrote a blog post suggesting the possibility of poor timing by the California fund's managers. The subsequent responses quickly poured cold water on Seides's position. Such is the contempt with which many nowa-days hold hedge funds, given their continued poor performance that humor at poor Seides's expense soon followed.

In 2008, Warren Buffett famously made a bet with Ted Seides that the S&P 500 would outperform any fund of hedge funds over the next 10 years. It is a bet that Protégé will probably wish had never been made. Certainly, by late 2014 Buffett was looking like a clear winner, and Seides's blog posting wound up drawing reminders of his rash decision to take on Omaha's Oracle. Even though the bet's time period included all of 2008 with a 37% loss in the S&P 500, hedge funds have still been a clear loser. Piling on the misery, one reader compared the performance of Protégé's own fund of funds with the S&P 500. Five years earlier, commentators may not have been so quick to knock hedge funds, but more recent history—perhaps aided in some modest way by *The Hedge Fund Mirage*—have provided the tools for more robust and pointed criticism.

## FOR ONCE, THE RETAIL INVESTOR WASN'T DUPED

Unusually, this is one of those rare cases where the unsophisticated retail investor has not been the victim of overpriced investments with high fees. Because hedge funds are generally offered via unregistered securities, in the United States and many other countries this has restricted their availability to high-net-worth investors and institu-tions, both of whom are regarded as smart enough to discern a good opportunity from a poor one. Somebody once asked me during one of my presentations if I was implying that high-net-worth investors were stupid to be invested in hedge funds. It raised an interesting point. To generalize, wealthy individuals were a far more important source of capital to hedge funds before 2002. Since then, they have shrunk as a percentage, and the unexpected imposition in 2008 of so many impediments to redemptions hastened their departure.

I'm always careful to point out that there are great hedge funds and happy clients. Some of the most talented investors around run hedge funds, because that's where the fees are highest and the most money can be made. That will always be the way. And there are happy hedge fund clients, too. Often, they only hold a handful of hedge funds, and rather than pursuing a diversified portfolio of managers, they've simply picked a small selection of talented people to manage their money. Those that are happiest with hedge funds aren't relying on them the way many institutions do to reshape their overall investment portfolios. A slim reliance on hedge funds with an opportunistic approach when circumstances permit is a more reliable way to achieve a successful outcome.

The high-net-worth individual investors of the past were the smart money. When private banks were the dominant allocators to hedge funds, they guided their rich clients to managers they liked, and returns were good. It was the arrival of institutions to hedge fund investing that coincided with the degradation of returns, which shouldn't have been a surprise because hedge funds have limited capacity to generate attractive results. It's fair to say that wealthy individual investors enjoyed the best years of hedge funds, and rather than being stupid were quite astute in their timing. I know quite a few individuals who were very successful with their hedge fund investments. Moreover, they often held only two or three such investments, illustrating the point above that sometimes less is more.

I don't believe any of the investors including today's can be characterized as stupid. Public pension plans are simply responding to the odd accounting described above and the politics of deferring financial pain as long as possible.

Today's hedge fund investors need to return to the approach that worked so well in the 1990s when the industry was less than a quarter of its present size. First of all, any analysis of future returns that fails to consider the size of the opportunity set is fundamentally flawed. This is the most obvious error being made by so many consultants and their clients today. They are extrapolating past returns into the future and creating an implausible vision of unlimited market inefficiency waiting to be exploited to their benefit. Diminishing returns to size are a common problem. Failure to contemplate the limits to size of an investing style or the industry overall has been a major mistake. It's really quite naïve. Recommending a substantial hedge fund allocation today either reflects a profound misunderstanding of how financial markets work, or a cynical appreciation of the quirky way public pension accounting renders hedge funds a plausible solution to a funding shortfall. Either way, we can look back on the consulting advice provided over the past several years to the trustees of billions of dollars of public sector retirees and question whose interests were really being served. Hedge fund research has paid well.

Since $2 trillion to $2.5 trillion has been shown to be an excessively large amount of capital for hedge funds in aggregate, the well-advised institutional investor should first rein in their expectations in terms of how much money they can profitably invest. Broad exposure (in some cases up to 20% of assets or more) to an overcapitalized industry is hardly likely to generate a satisfactory outcome. Instead, they should create a much smaller pool of 2% to 4% of their portfolio to be invested opportunistically in a few areas that are lightly trafficked and where additional capacity remains. This won't be easy—by definition, finding little-known investment areas requires some digging around. But this is where the investor is more likely to find market inefficiencies to exploit. They're also more likely to find managers with the time to sit down and really explain what they're doing.

Obscure investment opportunities are likely to be uncorrelated with the rest of one's portfolio, and may also provide interesting knowledge that can be applied in more size or elsewhere across certain core investments. It's quite likely the hedge fund exploiting a little-known area will identify related opportunities. It can be worth giving smart people a chance to do something a little different, so the investor ought to allow some flexibility of mandate here. Today's institutionally driven hedge funds with their carefully focused strategies that avoid style drift and multiple layers of risk are designed to be expensive but unexciting. The best hedge funds are risky, and risk mitigation comes through a thorough understanding of the risks being taken.

Small allocations to obscure strategies are likely to work best for hedge fund investors. Big allocations to well-known hedge funds work best for consultants. Consequently, the latter will continue to trump the former until continued mediocre results delivered at great expense provoke the ultimate clients into demanding a different approach.

Hedge funds continue to represent a disproportionate number of investment frauds. As I noted in *The Hedge Fund Mirage,* there is even a book devoted to them called *The Hedge Fund Fraud Casebook* (Wiley, 2010) by Bruce Johnson. It's not that hedge fund professionals are dishonest—even though I'm a critic of the broad industry, I don't believe the people in it are any less honest than other areas of finance. It's just that if you're looking to commit fraud, a hedge fund is the perfect vehicle. The securities are unregistered and the manager may also not be required to be registered with any state agency or the SEC. Creating a fictitious list of holdings in public companies is less likely to cause suspicion than, for example, claiming to own a building or private company that might not exist.

Madoff represents the biggest and most stunning fraud in history. Some quibble and say he wasn't running a hedge fund—it's a meaningless distinction because the clients believed they were investing in a hedge fund. Harry Markopoulos is known as the Madoff Whistleblower because of his gripping book, *No One Would Listen* (Wiley, 2011). When we were seeding hedge funds at JPMorgan, we met with Fairfield Greenwich Group (FGC), which was one of Madoff's feeder funds, channeling clients into the abyss. They described a structure that sounded very much as if the hedge fund was able to front-run orders received by Madoff's brokerage business. The salespeople at FGC didn't come right out and say this, but they described a "close working relationship" between Madoff's two operations that could be interpreted as such. We didn't have any subsequent meetings with FGC because the setup didn't sound right.

Later, I had the opportunity to meet Harry Markopoulos and we exchanged books, each signing a copy of what we'd authored for the other. In the copy of his book that Harry signed for me, his memorable inscription was, "Assume Fraud Until Genius is Proven." Harry had for years sought to warn the SEC of the fraud he believed was taking place in broad daylight at Madoff. His conclusion was based on careful analysis of public information, the crux of which was that Madoff's purported investment strategy would have required him to trade more than 100% of the available options in certain markets. I loved his book, and I can report that Harry is also an engaging public speaker. One of the items that resonated for me in his book and that Harry confirmed for me in person was that a great many investors in Madoff had concluded, like us, that front-running of brokerage clients was a significant source of their profits. Amazingly, therefore, these clients willingly invested with someone they already believed to be crooked based on the suspect logic that they understood the extent of his dishonesty and that it wasn't going to extend to them. There were some tragic stories of trust built over several decades crushed when everything was revealed. However, it's hard to have much sympathy for people who invest with the expectation that their return is based on exploiting other clients. These people assessed that they were simply passive beneficiaries of what they already believed was illegal activity, and doubtless assumed that when the gig was up they'd be allowed to keep their ill-gotten gains with no consequence. It was a Faustian bargain.

# CHAPTER 5

WHY IS WALL STREET
SO INEFFICIENT?

## WHY IS FINANCE SO EXPENSIVE?

Why do so many people pay so much for financial services? It's perhaps the most fundamental question policymakers could ask of today's banks and brokerage firms. Since Wall Street represents capitalism in its purest form probably more than anything else you could think of, why is the market for financial services so inefficient?

There's plenty of research that highlights the problem. For example, Wall Street's share of the economy, which is measured by looking at GDP value added of financial services, began growing in the 1980s and by 2007 had roughly doubled. I wrote about this in *Bonds Are Not Forever*. Finance hadn't just grown along with nominal GDP over that approximate quarter century, it had actually grown at twice the rate of GDP.

Banking jobs tend to be more highly paid than average, and this shift has in part driven the increasing income dispersion that's occurred in developed countries. Finance isn't to blame for this, but it's worth considering how we got here and if it's been the right direction.

One of the biggest innovations to impact banks was the development of the desktop computer. Banks spend enormous amounts on information technology (IT). In fact, much of today's trading in financial markets wouldn't exist in its present form without IT. My first job was in 1980 when I was a trainee broker on the floor of the London Stock Exchange (a "blue button" because of the color of the badges we wore with our firm's name on). Part of my job was to scribble down a "run" of prices on securities as they were rattled off by one of the market makers (called "jobbers" in those days; equivalent to specialists on the NYSE). I'd then read them off using a bulky "walkie-talkie" that was attached to a loudspeaker in the office where the brokers were waiting to call their clients.

A year later in another job at a different firm, I'd close trades by typing prices into a telex machine (a typewriter that can function like a telephone). Naturally, trades were recorded by being written down on tickets that would produce carbon copies when you wrote on them. In fact, so much of life was written down by hand back then.

That's now one if not two generations ago, and improved technology has changed so many businesses—perhaps none more so than finance. And yet, in another strange development the expenditure on IT hasn't impacted finance the way it has other industries.

If you're researching topics such as the cost of financial services, it doesn't take long before you come across Thomas Philippon. Philippon is a finance professor at New York University, and has written many academic papers on topics such as "Has the U.S. Finance Industry Become Less Efficient?" and "Wages and Human Capital in the U.S. Financial Industry: 1909–2006."

At a transaction level, there are countless examples of investors paying too much for poorly designed products. But at the 30,000 feet level, an increasing share of US economic output is devoted to financial services. After peaking around the time of the 1929 crash, finance shrank rapidly through the Depression and World War II. Following the end of hostilities, a steady uptrend began. In the 1980s it surpassed the previous prewar peak and accelerated upward. The faster growth coincided with the substantial impact IT was beginning to have on banking and financial markets.

There was never any public policy debate about whether more banking was better or not. As with other sectors of the economy, the government allows households and businesses to spend their after-tax money as they see fit. Finance is currently around 9% of GDP (Philippon 2012). At its most basic, finance is all about channeling savings to places where they can be used profitably as capital by businesses or governments. If it's done well, the result should be a more productive economy. All the banks and brokerage firms collectively exist to support the nonfinancial economy.

While finance has grown, it's hard to identify where the rest of the economy has benefited. Surprisingly, by some measures it's no more efficient than it was 100 years ago. Philippon adds up all the savings that flow through Wall Street into financial markets and back out to the issuers of debt and equity that use them, concluding that the cost of this intermediation is between 1.3% and 2.3% of the assets involved but has been heading higher since 1970. As Philippon says, "How is it possible for today's finance industry not to be significantly more efficient than the finance industry of John Pierpont Morgan?"

Financial services firms are some of the biggest buyers of IT services. There's little doubt that computers have revolutionized everything from retail banking to securities trading. Clearly, brokerage firms believe the money invested in new technology is good for business. But Philippon draws a fascinating contrast with the consumer retail sector. Wal-Mart perhaps most exemplifies the use of IT systems to closely track what it's selling so it can manage inventories and prices so as to maximize their profits. Selling products to the general public, whether online or in a physical store, nowadays relies heavily on IT. Interestingly though, the efficiency gains from better business management have translated into lower prices for consumers. When Philippon measures the share of GDP represented by retail trade since 1970, its downward path coincides with a big jump in IT spending. If the profits, wages, and bonuses of the retail sector are smaller, it's to the undoubted benefit of the consumer. The same analysis applied to banking shows no such equivalent drop in spite of a similar IT spending. If Wall Street operated more like Wal-Mart, the rest of the economy would be better off.

The argument in support of the status quo is that households and businesses buy the financial services they need, and if they're spending more on them it must be because value is delivered in excess of the money spent. It's a good place to start, because few would accept a public policy that sought to constrain the size of an industry without very strong justifications in the public interest.

But the facts revealed by Philippon do suggest that something is wrong. The growth in finance as a portion of the economy and the failure of intermediation costs to fall from their historic 1.3% to 2.3% range is in spite of decades of efficiency-enhancing IT investment. It's as if the improvements in productivity on Wall Street have remained with their companies and employees in the form of higher profits and compensation, rather than percolate down to the consumers. Although at ground level there seems to be plenty of competition to offer all of the services banks and brokerage firms provide, at the 30,000-foot level it doesn't seem to be that competitive.

## TRADING DOESN'T BUILD A SECURE RETIREMENT

Equity trading is one area where steadily declining transaction costs have led to enormous increases in volumes. Philippon shows that equity-trading volumes as a portion of GDP have increased by a factor of 10 to 20 times in a little over a generation. Numerous studies show that holding periods for stocks are becoming ever shorter. Commissions and other transaction costs such as bid/ask spread have certainly fallen, but not commensurate with the jump in volumes. Figuring out who's the winner or loser on an individual trade isn't nearly as objective as you might think. We all believe we get some positive utility, or value added, out of every trade. If an investor sells Apple stock only to see it continue to rise, the sell decision wasn't necessarily bad for that investor if he then reinvested the cash in something that went up even more. But at an aggregate level, returning again to 30,000 feet, since every trade incurs frictional costs from commissions and the bid/ask spread, trading volumes represent a wealth transfer into the pools of capital set up to provide market liquidity and to charge for that access. The transfer comes from everybody else.

It's easier to recognize that society is worse off from all the frantic activity than to identify the losers individually.

There can be little doubt that there's greater focus on the short term from the vast majority of market participants. The constant media attention paid to the market's near-term direction caters to the demands of everyone from professional money managers to individual retail investors for an insight that will gain them a short-term advantage. In the face of overwhelming evidence that short-term, market-timing activity is more often than not unprofitable, explanations for its continued growth must lie in areas such as behavioral finance. If we keep doing something that's financially not good for us, there must be a nonfinancial explanation. To my mind, it increasingly looks like a form of gambling, another activity in which the participants willingly engage in spite of their recognition that the aggregate winner is inevitably the facilitator (i.e., the casino), not the end user. For instance, Interactive Brokers, an online brokerage firm that offers very low-cost execution across stocks, bonds, and futures, discloses information on the profitability of its Foreign Exchange accounts as required by its regulator. It typically reports that about 43% to 44% of its accounts are profitable in any given quarter. Other firms' clients do worse; for example, FXCM, another active FX broker, reported that fewer than 33% of its clients were profitable in each quarter of 2014 (FXCM 2015). The firms don't report account turnover, but since FXCM's clients have a two in three chance of losing money in a quarter, assuming the results are random, around 20% of them would experience four straight losing quarters (that is, 0.67 to the 4th power). If the results aren't random, meaning there are some FX traders whose skill leads them to be profitable more often than randomness, that, in turn, implies that greater than 20% of accounts suffer four straight losing quarters.

It seems a safe bet that a year of losses would persuade most erstwhile FX traders to spend their time (and capital) elsewhere. The steady inflow of new, inexperienced traders flatters the statistics while increasing the numbers of people who lose.

And of course, nobody should be surprised. Short-term trading of most things is inherently unprofitable unless you have an informational advantage (such as being a market maker) or some other technological edge (such as those enjoyed by many high-frequency-trading firms). Notice how the ads for these firms all portray images of men in business suits thoughtfully turning some innate and hitherto untapped trading insight into unlimited wealth with no more effort than it takes to sit attentively at a computer terminal (as with FXCM's website). All that's missing is the adoring trophy girlfriend who will inevitably accompany such success.

The risks of amateurs trading FX were amply demonstrated in January 2015, when the Swiss National Bank shocked the market and abandoned its peg to the euro, allowing the Swiss franc to soar over 20% almost instantly. Many retail traders who had availed themselves of leverage at up to 100:1 to be short Swiss francs immediately lost their entire account, and because there had been no opportunity for their brokerage firms to cover losing positions, several retail FX firms suffered substantial losses and in some cases went bankrupt (Trevedi 2015).

The dawning horror of what has taken place is quaintly reflected in chatroom dialogue of some part-time currency traders as extreme Swiss Franc volatility spills into other currency pairs (Murphy 2015):

Amateur traders with names such as "Lord Flasheart" and "ChattiFX" note first with bemusement that their online broker has closed out positions and deducted value from their accounts. Shortly it dawns that this is not just a software error but an economic event. One trader notes that he had "… done quite well in the last 3 weeks. this (sic) has really upset me now!" It's comical to read.

These currency websites aimed at retail traders play directly to the behavioral finance issue of overconfidence. Men (and it is inevitably men, I'm afraid) are easily persuaded that they have more than the average ability to outsmart their fellow hunters in search of easy financial prey. Retail trading is often confused with investing when it's hardly different than betting on sports. Of course, in a free society people are allowed to engage in activities that are harmful; the best we can do is try to educate them so they don't risk their retirement savings on gambling.

The steady losses experienced by FX clients are not caused by rapacious brokers charging too much, either. In looking at the two-way markets quoted by Interactive Brokers, I have to say that they appear very competitive to me. No doubt the firm adds some mark-up onto the prices in lieu of a commission but the net result is still a market quote that looks very close to institutional standard. It doesn't need to charge a significant mark-up on each trade. The business model relies on a tiny sliver of each transaction combined with volume.

There's no easy way to calculate whether retail traders are losing more money than in the past. Equity volumes have grown enormously, and a substantial proportion of that is algorithmic trading by HFT firms. However, they obviously wouldn't be as active as they are if they were unprofitable. While investing isn't a zero-sum game, trading generally is. It's likely that part of the growth in financial services as a percentage of GDP over the past 20 to 30 years is the result of unprofitable short-term trading by retail investors. Self-directed IRAs and discount brokerages have certainly made it more possible, and the huge increase in equity volumes seems to support the notion. This is one case where the financial services industry has simply responded to demand and that much of the responsibility lies with the buyers themselves.

## INVEST TIME BEFORE MONEY

Investing is more expensive than needed because of the types of products offered and the way they're sold. But investors, especially retail investors, are their own worst enemy. It's been said that many people will dedicate more time to researching which refrigerator to buy than they will on investing many multiples of the cost of a fridge in a financial product. The problem starts with the most common question asked of financial advisors: What do you think of the market? It's not that there's anything wrong with discussing the news and how it's affecting the economy and securities prices. We do it all the time. To most people it's very interesting. Following events and developments is entirely appropriate, but too much of the focus is on trying to figure out the near-term direction so as to profit from it, either by investing now or waiting for a better entry point. The brokerage industry, whose very lifeblood is the commissions that come from trading, services this need for a short-term edge with its advertising, research on macro themes, and strategists talking on TV. They are meeting a very real need, but one that is fundamentally self-destructive to the financial well-being of the recipients. In financial services but unlike health care, individuals are deemed to know what's best for them. It is therefore incumbent on them to invest the time figuring out what really is best, recognizing that many firms exist whose objective is to generate profits from activities that may not always be in the individual's long-term interests.

In the United States and the United Kingdom, there has been a public policy response. While not directly targeting the size of the financial industry, it has focused on overall systemic risk and to a lesser degree compensation following the public outrage at the bailouts in 2008. Ironically, the biggest losses borne by the government from the crash in 2008 were sustained where they'd had the most influence, in the two government agencies that subsidize mortgages, FNMA and FHMC ("Fannie Mae" and "Freddie Mac"). Congress has a poor record of enlightened legislation regarding financial services, and after a few years of tighter lending standards the two government housing agencies are once again relaxing standards below those available from the private sector with the goal of seeking maximum home ownership.

The fault lies on both sides. Retail investors often have unrealistic expectations based on insufficient research. Often, what requires the least amount of careful thought is to buy what's been going up and dump what's been falling. Consumers are used to making purchase decisions based on reliable brands. It's an efficient way to spend your money. If everybody you know owns an iPhone, you're unlikely to be disappointed buying one. But while our phone needs are reasonably homogeneous, investment needs are clearly heterogeneous. A portfolio that is comfortable for one individual may be completely inappropriate for another, based on financial situation, age, or overall disposition. Because investing your savings is one of those issues that's always important but rarely urgent, it's easy to put off decisions or spend too little time on it.

## SEX AND INVESTING

One interesting area of behavioral finance relates to how men and women approach investing differently. Men are more prone to overconfidence in many things apart from investing. They tend toward risk-seeking behavior more readily than women. As a result, studies have revealed that brokerage accounts run by men tend to have a wider range of outcomes (i.e., more spectacularly good and bad results) than those run by women, but also a lower average return overall. That's right—women are on average better investors than men. I can tell you why that is from my own experience. Women tend to approach investing by acknowledging what they don't know and seeking to learn more before making a decision. Some men do that as well, but can also have a tendency to be overly confident about their knowledge and ability. There aren't just two types of investor of course, but I have found that many men could benefit from being more in touch with their feminine side. They'd then be less worried about the market's near-term direction and more focused on whether their portfolio was right for them and whether the costs of the products they're buying were appropriate.

Managing your investments requires a different mindset from almost anything else people buy. Most obviously, evaluating short-term results often represents a poor way to evaluate long-term results. On top of this, every document you ever look at warns that past performance is not an indicator of future results, as required by the SEC. So you're not supposed to consider the long prior history of an investment manager before becoming a client, and once invested you're to ignore near-term fluctuations in performance as being largely random. Every investor is trying to figure out the long-term prospects that a decision will be correct, and it seems as if the only thing you can consider is the long-term performance that you experience as a client.

This leads to a different decision making process than for anything else people buy. Suppose you were told to ignore the past reliability of an automobile, fridge, or TV before making your purchase? What if a lawyer's history of successful lawsuits was held not to be indicative of his ability? Or if a doctor's track record of botched operations didn't render her any less qualified than one whose patients leave hospital under their own steam?

Considering the past is so obviously important in making a selection that warning people not to do so becomes meaningless without providing them with an alternative framework. What it comes down to is a fundamental difference between the results you should expect from investments compared with all the other things you might buy, which is that results fluctuate. In most cases, you can expect that what you buy will perform as advertised 90% or more of the time. Investment results can't be held to the same standard because part of the result comes from fluctuations in the markets themselves, which are largely unpredictable over the short run.

However, it does seem reasonable to me for investors to consider long-term results for an asset class or an investment manager when making a decision. For example, public equities have shown themselves to be the most reliable way to grow your savings so that they at least keep up with inflation after taxes over periods of many years. The longer your holding period, the more likely you are to get the long-term return. So if you're thinking of investing in Vanguard's Extended Stock Market ETF, looking at the long-run return on stocks and Vanguard's low fees are two important items to consider.

Measuring the returns to active management is more tricky. The first thing is to choose the right benchmark. Too few investments are properly benchmarked at all. As soon as you move away from the cheapest way to gain exposure to an asset class, the correctness of your decision needs to be measured against the cheapest option that you passed up. Benchmarking their results is anathema to many investment managers. Since active management costs more, and on average does worse than passive, the average manager is quite rational in trying to avoid any comparison. Only the good ones want to have their results properly evaluated against the cheaper, passively managed alternative.

Probably the biggest step any investors can take to ensure the advice they get is worthwhile is to agree on a benchmark at the outset. Automobiles, lawyers, and doctors can be compared with their peers, increasingly so with Internet technology. Financial advice ought to receive the same treatment, but such is too rarely the case. There's an additional factor that I think must be unique to investment products, which is that an investment that has attractive returns but is uncorrelated with other things you own really can be more valuable to you, because of the diversification it adds. An investment with an uncorrelated, positive return is what everybody wants. So a manager who can persuade clients that there's no appropriate benchmark for his results not only avoids potentially unwelcome comparison with something better but also stands to argue that his uncorrelated returns are more valuable.

Hedge funds used to do this all the time. Back in the 1990s when I served on JPMorgan's investment committee that allocated to hedge funds, just about every hedge fund manager we met would, somewhere in their presentation, note that their particular type of investing couldn't be easily compared with any widely known style. The manager might be completely focused on technology stocks, but would nonetheless maintain that comparison with other technology-focused hedge funds wouldn't allow for a meaningful evaluation. This was self-serving but also spoke to precisely what hedge fund investors were seeking. I often point out to hedge fund proponents that their industry used to claim it was targeting *absolute returns*, with the promise that they'd make money over any reasonably long holding period and were uncorrelated with other major asset classes such as stocks or bonds. The 2008 crash showed how unattainable this was, and hedge fund proponents quietly adopted different descriptions of their objectives. These included generating attractive *Relative Returns*, and more recently when even this more modest objective proved to be beyond their collective ability the term *Uncorrelated Returns* gained favor. Since hedge funds have in recent years been worse than just about anything else it's been a good choice.

The lesson for investors is to identify a meaningful, objective way to evaluate your investment choices. I once sat on an investment committee that had chosen to hire a professional money manager to invest its endowment. That's not necessarily a poor decision, because investment committees meet infrequently and are generally not set up to make tactical, short-term decisions. A group that meets only quarterly or even monthly should focus on strategy and its implementation, which is to say they should choose the overall asset allocation they want (stocks versus bonds and perhaps other asset classes such as real estate). Having made the most important decision, which is asset allocation, it's OK to delegate its implementation to a full-time manager and then evaluate their performance against a passive alternative (such as Vanguard's ETF for equities for example).

The external manager we selected, who managed several billion dollars for individuals and institutions, claimed their expertise was in picking mutual funds that were better than average. However, unlike most of their clients, we compared the results as described and found they came up consistently short. During a strong market for equities, our endowment's value lagged where it should have been. It was up, but that was because our committee had made the right critical decision to be overweight stocks. But it had not done as well as the passive alternatives. When we pointed out this shortcoming, they responded that their investment choices had included mutual funds that tended to be more conservative, and that they believed this would provide better "risk-adjusted" returns going forward. They used that explanation on the wrong people. I pointed out that we expressed our risk appetite through our asset allocation, and that their job was to simply implement and not alter it. In effect, they were making it harder to benchmark performance, because in investing anything that takes the evaluation discussion away from the realm of numbers benefits the mediocre manager.

Although we were approaching the issues like the institutional client we were, there's no reason why an individual investor shouldn't ask how their advisor would like to be evaluated. Make sure the answer includes numbers and isn't full of holistic mumbo-jumbo. If it can't be measured, it doesn't really count. Investing, more than most activities, is something that lends itself to the objective measurement of results.

In *Backstage Wall Street*, Joshua Brown described his former life as a stock broker pushing poorly advised investments on uninformed buyers over the phone as he dialed for dollars. He includes a description of the various sales pitches that he refined over the years, which were designed to appeal to the male trait of seeking quick profits based on an overconfident forecast. In fact, Josh Brown notes that pitching ideas to women was usually a waste of time. They were far less willing to make a quick decision without more information.

Brown's book confirms the negative stereotype of brokers cynically trying to foist substandard, overpriced financial products on retail investors who ought to be more cynical. Although the vast majority of employees at brokerage firms are honest with the best of intentions toward their clients, brokers that earn fees on transactions have to balance the interests of their clients with their own natural desire to earn a living. Josh Brown was evidently ready to put his own interests ahead of everything else, but eventually grew disillusioned with the business model and now works for an investment advisory firm with a much clearer alignment of interests between him and his clients. Brown's book is an absorbing first-hand account of how someone who chooses to can abuse the system at the expense of clients with relative impunity.

## COMPLEXITY SELLS

Aggregation of products or services is a common technique with which businesses extract greater profitability. Technology companies routinely do this, meeting a desire for consumers to buy in a neat, self-contained package. It's how companies like Apple and Microsoft enjoy operating margins that can exceed 30% of revenues.

Financial services are no different, and the least complex products incur the smallest fees. Vanguard's Total Stock Market ETF provides investment exposure to approximately 100% of the publicly traded stocks in the United States for an annual fee of just 0.05% of assets. Vanguard has performed an enormous service to retail investors by offering simple products at rock-bottom prices. The company remains true to the values of its founder Jack Bogle as well. A couple of years ago I was invited to give a presentation at Vanguard's corporate campus in Malvern, Pennsylvania. Vanguard is in many ways not your typical investment firm. Because it is mutually owned by all the people who buy its investment products, it doesn't seek to make a profit like conventional firms. As I pointed out at the beginning of my presentation there, the first thing I noticed upon entering the parking lot was that I didn't see any German cars, demonstrating that their frugal DNA extended to buying cheaper domestically produced transportation (I confess that my car looked like the solitary German one in the parking lot).

A friend of mine once recounted an instructive story about Jack Bogle. The two of them had chatted during the conference and were both scheduled on the same train for the journey northeast from

Washington, DC, to their respective homes in Pennsylvania and New York. It was the Friday before Mother's Day, and with some time to spare at Union Station in Washington both men decided to pick up Mother's Day cards. It turned out they were to buy three: Bogle needed one for his wife, while my friend needed two cards, one for his wife and one for his Mother. Vanguard's founder quickly noticed a sign next to the cards promoting "Buy Two, Get One Free" and suggested they combine their purchase to save money.

Trivial anecdotes can be very revealing. The people at Vanguard with whom I later met and shared the story laughed but weren't a bit surprised. Their ethos is not to try and beat the market but, rather, to come close to equaling the market return at the lowest possible cost. Vanguard's more modest objective may not be for everybody, but because actively managed funds on average fail to beat the market and are more costly, Vanguard's approach allows it to do better than most. By focusing on a realistic goal and keeping costs as low as possible, Jack Bogle has offered millions of investors a fair deal.

Many of the investments that we're warning you about in this book are complex. They're often a combination of two or three simpler instruments; Wall Street has excelled at creating demand for complicated things, from mortgage-backed securities and other collateralized debt obligations to structured notes, non-traded REITs and funds of hedge funds. The insurance industry has also gotten in on the act with annuities. Although it's an overstatement to say that every complicated product should be avoided, a strong bias toward the financially simple is likely to get you into far less trouble than the opposite.

There's also no doubt that too many firms provide poor advice, expensively priced. I come across examples all the time. I recounted an example in Chapter 1 of the taxable trust invested in short-term bonds yielding around 1.5% and with an annual fee of 1.5%. Trust companies typically retain their clients more readily than most other firms, because trust agreements are time-consuming and expensive to change. In addition, my friend's late father had appointed the bank as trustee, something that's not easily undone after the fact. Common sense dictates that nobody wants to hold an investment that costs money after fees and taxes. Ultra-low interest rates have caused countless problems like this, but the trust company had a moral obligation if not a legal one to find a better solution. It could have waived its fee on the fixed-income portion of my friend's portfolio, or perhaps recommended an alternative trustee. It did neither of these things, thus contributing to the negative stereotype often applied to banks.

In another case, a friend showed me the portfolio allocation for his retirement savings that was recommended to him by a big European bank. Most research will show that asset allocation drives up to 90% of the returns on a portfolio (with security selection the other 10%). In other words, if you choose to put 60% of your funds in stocks, the return on the averages will likely be responsible for up to 90% of your return, with individual stock selection relatively unimportant. Of course, this varies widely and the fewer stocks you own the less diversified you'll be, making individual stock selection more important. But generally speaking, if you hold 20 or more names across several industries you'll have enough diversification that individual stock picks won't be that impactful.

Asset allocation decisions rely crucially on the expected return on the asset and its correlation with the other assets you may hold. Fixed income represents a particular problem, in that future returns are highly unlikely to look like the past. Of course every investment product carries this warning, as required by law, even though past performance is probably the most commonly used metric by investors. But for bond allocations it's especially problematic, because the most important predictor of your expected return on a bond is the yield at which you buy it. Historic bond returns may have been 6%, but if today's yields are 2.5%, that's your starting point as far as what you can expect to earn in the future.

The narrative included in the presentation acknowledged that bond returns might disappoint in the future but added that they were an important part of the portfolio because of their diversification. Somehow, including an asset with poor return prospects was going to be helpful.

Nonetheless, my friend was given a presentation that included a sizable bond allocation whose expected return was 6% *because that's what bonds had historically returned.* This is just intellectual laziness masquerading as analysis. It's hope rather than honesty. The result was an asset allocation whose forecast return looked attractive even though it had little chance of being achieved. It represents a disingenuous approach to advice, and is another example of what leads to individual investors drawing negative conclusions about big financial firms that they suppose hold their interests at heart even while they provide poor advice.

Complex products are attractive to financial salespeople because it's hard for the client to figure out how much profit is being made. Structured notes are a great example, in that they may combine two or three simple components (such as a long position in the equity market combined with a short call option and long put option), packaged up so as to be presented as a bond whose return is, within limits, linked to stocks. The investor is always getting a worse deal than buying the components himself, but it's often hard to figure out how much worse. Kevin Brolley's chapter on structured notes explains this very clearly and in more detail.

## THE HIDDEN COSTS OF MUNICIPAL BONDS

If complexity is good for firms selling products, so are opaque markets. Municipal bonds have long been one of the most expensive places for retail investors. As yields have fallen, transaction costs have become a bigger chunk of the overall total return. S&P Dow Jones (S&P Dow Jones 2014) found that the transaction costs for investment grade munis were 1.4% of the face amount, almost double that for similarly rated corporate bonds. Munis are widely owned, not least because of their tax-exempt status. This has made buyers more relaxed about the easy profits earned by salespeople, thereby dampening the competition that would otherwise drive spreads lower.

Of course, nobody in their right mind is going to trade bonds for short-term performance. In most cases, they're owned as investments—the transaction costs make any type of turnover prohibitive. Apologists note the one-time costs are justified by the benefits of stable, tax-exempt income. Although munis represent an attractive option for many investors, the problem is that the true costs of access aren't properly disclosed. There's plenty of research online with warnings like the report from S&P Dow Jones. In July 2012 the SEC published *A Report on the Municipal Securities Market* that was critical of the poor disclosures provided by issuers as well as the transaction costs faced by retail investors. More recently, SEC Commissioner Michael Piwowar has spoken publicly about the need for improved transparency to improve transaction costs. Interestingly, Piwowar noted that the relative complexity of many bonds increased costs for the municipality issuing them as well as contributing to the difficulty of comparing similar bonds. Although uniform standards would appear to benefit both buyers and sellers, it's likely that the firms that underwrite bonds have every incentive to promote complexity, since it allows for higher fees.

It's possible to do some simple math, pulling together data on the municipal market, to reveal just how much of the return on munis gets eaten up in transaction costs. Start with the size of the market, around $3.3 trillion, according to data from the Securities Industry and Financial Markets Association. Of that amount, households own around $1.6 trillion, or 43%. Let's further assume that the yield on the entire market weighted by volumes outstanding is around 4% (SIFMA calculates that the average maturity is 16 years).

So if households earn 4% annually on $1.6 trillion in bonds, that's $64 billion.

Now, SIFMA also tells us that daily volumes in munis average $11 billion. From S&P Dow Jones we know that transaction costs are 1.4%. That's for investment-grade munis—transaction costs for high-yield munis are around 2.4%, but for now let's just assume the lower transaction cost figure applies to all.

If households own 43% of outstanding municipal bonds, it's not unreasonable to assume they are also 43% of the daily volume. So now we calculate total annual transaction costs incurred by households in munis. For this we need to calculate annual volume in munis, which is daily volume multiplied by the number of trading days in a year (around 260), and multiply that by the 43% of volume we're assuming is households, and lastly take 1.4% of that for the transaction costs. The result is $16 billion. Therefore, it seems reasonable to assert that in aggregate, households incur $16 billion in costs on munis that in aggregate pay $64 billion in interest, annually. After transaction costs, that leaves households with $48 billion. They're spending $1 to earn $3.

Of course it's not evenly spread out—clearly some people pay more than others. And some investors may even feel that it's a fair price to pay. However, few probably look at it like this, and I suspect for many knowing that 25% of the total return is eaten up in the transaction may be sufficiently galling to induce them to invest elsewhere. Interest rates are so low nowadays that the costs imposed by Wall Street are a more meaningful portion of the whole. Somehow, muni brokers and their share of the profits on their investments now look a lot like hedge fund managers.

High mark-ups on municipal bonds sold to retail investors have been a thorny issue for years. It ought to be simple enough to provide information on trades so individuals can assess for themselves the costs they're incurring. But the industry has continued to oppose such measures. They argue, quite patronizingly, that the sort of useful information sought for investors by regulators would be misunderstood by technically unsophisticated clients. SIFMA and the Bond Dealers of America, who represent the securities dealers on the right side of these expensive transactions, have consistently opposed greater disclosure.

If the broker covering your account declined to provide you with information you'd requested by claiming you wouldn't understand it, you'd probably take your business elsewhere. And yet, that's exactly what the industry representatives of these firms are claiming.

Jeffrey Gottlieb, a lawyer from Michigan, spent $200,000 unsuccessfully suing Morgan Stanley for $1.4 million in undisclosed fees on municipal bonds (Burne 2015). Seeking redress in the courts is obviously a last resort. What buyers of munis should do is to recognize that if they're buying bonds from a broker, they're likely to be charged an undisclosed mark-up. The broker has to make a living. But you're entitled to know how much you're paying.

Many of the products and services that consumers buy don't fluctuate in price the way securities do. Comparing prices charged for a fridge or plumbing services is far simpler by comparison. The transaction fee charged by a bond broker is wrapped up in the overall price of the security, so if it costs more than you expected it's hard to discern the impact of market movements from the broker's fee.

Then again, the firm that delivers heating oil to our house provides us with an invoice showing the price we're being charged for the oil which I can compare with the heating oil futures market. There's a substantial mark-up there too, but that's intended to cover the cost of delivery of heating oil to our house and ongoing service to our furnace. At least I know what I'm paying above the wholesale price. Retail investors in munis deserve no less. If every reader of this book who invests in munis is provoked into a frank discussion of disclosure of transaction costs with their broker, we'll have achieved at least one worthwhile goal.

## SOME BANKERS JUST DON'T THINK

The reputation of finance professionals and bankers especially has never been that positive but took a bad knock during the 2008 crisis from which it's barely recovered. Inevitably, there's research that supports the view that bankers are somehow less trustworthy. A thought-provoking example was performed by scientists at the University of Zurich and reported in 2014 (Cookson 2014). They designed a game to measure honesty when no one is watching, using 200 volunteer bankers divided into two groups. The individuals in each group were asked to record how many times heads came up in a series of coin tosses. Each individual, without outside verification, was asked to report personal heads-or-tails results, and there was a small cash prize for flipping a certain number of heads.

Of course, across both groups you'd expect roughly 50% heads, which is pretty much what happened. However, one of the groups was asked questions about their jobs, which got them thinking about being bankers and all that entails. Following these questions and now presumably in "banker" mode, this group repeated the coin toss experiment. Individuals miraculously saw a statistically significant (and, to the scientists, implausible) number of heads. The conclusion of the experiment, which was hardly flattering to the participants or to the industry, was that otherwise honest people can become dishonest when their role as a banker is on their minds. The experiment was repeated with groups of volunteers from other industries, but only the version with bankers produced this curious result.

Of course, such a study is simply illustrative and other than being interesting doesn't represent conclusive evidence of weak ethics in finance. Incidentally, almost two thirds of the participants in the banker version of this experiment came from one bank—presumably Swiss, since the experimenters were based in Zurich. Therefore, it may say more about Swiss banking ethics than the industry overall.

But there remains this nagging suspicion that banks can't be trusted, and news stories often appear to support such feelings. To my mind one of the most egregious examples involves the "Libor scandal" of recent years. Libor (the "London Interbank Offered Rate") is a benchmark interest rate whose construction is a quaint holdover from an earlier era. When US regulations limiting interest rates led to the creation of the Eurodollar market in London in the 1970s where US$ denominated bank deposits could change hands at market rates beyond the reach of US regulations, Libor was devised as a single rate to reflect where transactions were taking place. Libor is set for bank deposits from overnight out to one year, and over many years it gradually gained importance as the basis for the cost of short-term credit for non-sovereign borrowers globally. Libor was set for all the major currencies, and the custom spread beyond London to the Eurozone (for euros), Tokyo (for yen) and so on.

One of my earliest jobs, in 1981, was as a money broker in London where it was possible to see all the different transactions taking place in the money markets. Although setting three-month Libor suggests that three-month deposit transactions take place at that rate, the truth is far less tidy. Banks borrow at varying rates, depending on the market's perception of the credit risk involved, and so a tiered market has always existed. The anachronistic custom around Libor was that it reflected the rate at which "prime borrowers" could borrow easily. In some ways it was a peculiarly British creation, borne of the same culture that operates without a written constitution but where the rules are understood. The banks that traded in the market for interbank deposits themselves set Libor; sometimes they'd post somewhat different rates but usually they weren't far apart.

The financial crisis brutally exposed the flaws in a process that was not robust enough for the rumor-charged environment about creditworthiness that prevailed. Subtle differences of interpretation were possible with Libor; did it reflect where the bank setting the rate could itself borrow as a prime name, since many more banks perceive themselves to be prime than are in fact regarded that way by the market? Or did it reflect where the bank in question would willingly lend to prime names? Since few banks will lend to a similar credit at a lower rate than where they themselves can borrow, the credit rating of the banks setting Libor started to matter and the system began to break down. At one point, Barclays received "a quiet word" from the Bank of England that its relatively high Libor settings were creating a poor impression about Barclays' own ability to access liquidity. It's quite likely that the providers of lower Libor rates at that time were unable to borrow themselves at the rates they posted, but maintained the charade when the interbank markets had pretty much shut down so as to avoid the unwelcome scrutiny drawn to Barclays.

The success of Libor as a benchmark over several decades had led to its use for a wide range of short-term contracts. The Eurodollar futures market remains the most important gauge of short-term credit market and settles against Libor. The interest rate swaps market has, since its inception relied on Libor to provide the floating rate reset on its transactions. Many forms of corporate credit as well as US residential mortgages had their cost tied to Libor. For these reasons, following the dysfunction of 2008, Libor and the process by which it's set came under increased scrutiny, which revealed some of the most shameful behavior by those in a position to influence the rate.

Since a 0.01% difference in the setting of Libor is one person's gain and someone else's loss, perhaps it was inevitable that ethically challenged traders close enough to the rate setting process would find a way to influence the process for financial gain. It is at its essence a judgment call; since Libor is not based on actual transactions but on the opinion of a seasoned market veteran about where a theoretical transaction could take place, that left plenty of room for manipulation once the money involved was big enough. The relentless growth of the swaps market had led to sometimes millions of dollars of potential P&L reliant on whether Libor was set at 2.01% versus 2.02%.

When you combine seemingly trivial differences with hundreds of billions of dollars of transactions whose value rested in part on that rate, ethically bereft traders grabbed the opportunity.

Nonetheless, the release of instant message dialogue between partners in crime not only exposes the moral failings of the protagonists but also exposes the tepid IQs of some former bank traders. For it takes an unflattering combination of extremely poor judgment and low intelligence to send an instant message saying, "… need 6m high as a drug addict" which in plain English is a request to set the 6-month Libor rate as high as possible so as to boost the trader's profits (Englesham 2013). A similar request drew the response, "Done … for you big boy …" and later in a reflection of the happiness increased trading profits can generate, "Come over one day after work and I'm opening a bottle of Bollinger" (Farrell 2012).

Royal Bank of Scotland and Barclays, whose traders' adolescent behavior was humiliatingly made public in court proceedings, understandably assessed a failure of culture and reacted accordingly. If their hiring process had simply screened out potential felons OR those with an IQ lower than room temperature (who else types such conversations on a keyboard nowadays?), the rest of us might not have learned with jaws agape just how devoid of scruples some supposedly trusted individuals are.

Was it always this way? Were bankers always at their worst prone to the type of rapacious, morally bereft behavior so shockingly on display in recent years? There's no quantitatively based answer. Personally, I think while the workforce is predominantly honest, the tendency toward this type of destructive behavior has increased over the 35 years that I've been in the industry (hopefully they're not connected!). When I began my career in the City, London's financial center, in 1980, "My word is my bond" was a phrase often heard and not taken lightly. Markets were far less integrated with one another; participants did frequent business with familiar people, many times face-to-face on physical exchanges. It's harder to rip somebody off when they're two feet away from you, and a transgressor would quickly develop a reputation that would lead to the trading community rejecting him for future business. When financial transactions were more often than not negotiated and closed through two people talking to one another, the system benefitted from the social pressures that promote good behavior. Since today so much trading is done electronically with the click of a mouse, there is never any visible injured party to dishonesty. The traders in the Libor scandal had no perception of any losses incurred by real people on the other side of their manipulative behavior. The homeowner paying a higher interest rate or the corporation experiencing a higher cost of funding were entirely abstract concepts. It was no more real than the carnage in a video game. We're unlikely to return to the past. The impersonality of financial markets is here to stay. Consequently, the regulatory framework will adapt for a world in which socially acceptable norms don't apply to one vast and impersonal community. Users of financial services will need to modify their expectations as well.

# CHAPTER 6

# THE UN-PORTFOLIO AND BETTER PORTFOLIO MANAGEMENT TECHNIQUES

## Bob Centrella, CFA

It was early in 2011 and I sat there opposite my new client thinking, 20 years of hard work to build a nice-sized retirement fund and THIS is what his broker bought for him since he turned the money over to him a few years ago. Fast forward a few years and I came to find that that thought was going to be a common one in my head as I met with clients.

Individual investors often find themselves at the mercy of the person they hire and trust to create and manage their portfolio of assets. Many don't have the time to review transactions and research securities and funds that they own. They don't have the luxury of institutional investors who often get to choose from seasoned professionals with research teams, long track records, and customized portfolios. More often than not, it can be a broker or advisor who was handed the account or a "friend" in the financial business who is really not a money manager and he turned the assets over to him as a favor. Or it can be a self-managed portfolio where the individual is not able to devote the necessary time. In the end, too many portfolios are often poorly constructed and don't meet the objectives of the investor. In this chapter I'd like to talk about some of the portfolios of assets I've seen that were poorly constructed and spend some time on various aspects of proper investment management.

As part of the service of my company, Forza Investment Advisory, I offer investors a free "second opinion" review of their existing portfolio and then talk to them about how it's structured and what I might recommend. Typically what I see are improperly constructed portfolios that really don't meet their needs, objectives, and risk tolerance. So, as I sat there on that Saturday morning in 2011 staring at that portfolio of assets that my friend (let's call him Fred) had brought to our meeting for me to analyze, I was actually annoyed at what his previous financial advisor (who, ironically, was a friend of his) had bought for him in his retirement account. I immediately thought of fiduciary duty** and the apparent lack of it. I'll have more on this often overlooked yet extremely important topic later. [NOTE: all terms indicated by ** can be found in a glossary at the end of the chapter.]

I also thought that this is the *exact* reason why I decided to go off on my own in 2010 and start my company after over 18 years managing money at other companies for institutions and individuals. Portfolio management is both an art and a science and there are too many brokers/advisors who *think* they are portfolio managers but haven't had the proper training on how to build a portfolio. As I go on, this chapter is not meant to be a rant against brokers as there are many out there who are honest, trustworthy, and smart. Also, I don't mean to imply that all registered investment advisors are great too, as many fall short (as I show in an example later). Finally, this is not meant to be an advertisement for my company and I'm not trying to imply that my company is the answer for everybody. My goal here is to try to educate the investor on what he/she should look for and consider when deciding what to do with their money and some of the pitfalls to try to avoid.

When I first started my business, Forza Investment Advisory, LLC (Registered Investment Advisor**) in 2010 it was not too long after the Madoff Ponzi scheme** had unraveled a year earlier. There was a growing distrust between individuals and their financial advisors and it was difficult to get people to "hand over" their hard-earned savings in many instances, to a stranger. As the Madoff scheme revealed, there was often a lack of transparency in strategy, holdings, and fee structure. It became clear that there was a void in the local wealth management industry for an independent, trustworthy, and highly transparent advisory firm that was focused on client service. In addition there was a need for an experienced money management professional to develop customized money management plans for individual clients not unlike what institutional investors can get. These are the founding core principles upon which I would start my firm.

During and after the time that the Madoff scandal came to light, many investors were shocked by the scope of it and held onto their money rather than look for investment advice. Also, investors were still in distress after the downturn in 2008 and early 2009, and many missed the rebound and thought it was too late to get into the market. Thankfully, a few good friends jumped onboard as my first clients and I was off. I decided that I wanted to try to "keep it in the family," and primarily offer my services to friends and their referrals. Some would say there is more pressure to manage money for friends and family, whereas I think a good manager should be confident enough in his process to offer his/her services to friends. Having been around the financial business for about 25 years, I was pretty certain that there weren't many ex-institutional money managers servicing smaller clients like I was doing.

There are many reasons why people may want help with their investments whether it be for retirement, a college fund, or maybe just getting their financial house in order. The investment industry and all its choices can be quite intimidating, and investing your hard-earned money really should be more than a part-time job. Unfortunately, finding the right person or company to manage your money can equally be as confusing and time-consuming. Often, I find that folks don't want to meet because they feel they will be pressured into doing something. They may also not want to pay a fee for a manager and decide to do it themselves or hire a broker because they think it is cheaper. However, when dealing with your money, leaving even a percentage point of performance on the table can be quite costly in the long run. Hiring a professional to manage your hard-earned money is a very personal decision and shouldn't be taken lightly. But I get the feeling that investors put more time and research into buying a car, a TV, computer, or taking a trip than in managing their own money.

## BACKGROUND

Before I go on, I'd like to back up a bit and start with a little business background and my "street cred" before proceeding. I might give a little more detail than necessary but want to establish the amount of financial and management experience I have so you know where I'm coming from when I pick apart the portfolios I see. I've been working in the field of Finance since 1985 when I took my second-ever job as an internal auditor for a small investment shop in Rosslyn, Virginia. You see, I had an Accounting degree and was sure I wanted to be an auditor or accountant for the rest of my life—a very good job, stable income, and lots of work to be had. It took me about a month of talking to the money managers and performing internal audits to realize I loved finance and particularly the investment field. I laid out a long-term plan on how I was going to get to the point of becoming a money manager. I even considered becoming a broker for a short while but then realized that being a broker really meant being a salesman, not a money manager. This is something I'd say that the most successful brokers realize even today—hire professionals to run the money and concentrate on service. It took me 7 years and few financial job stops on the way that included me getting my MBA in finance and becoming a CFA®** charterholder (Chartered Financial Analyst®) before I was hired by my first mentor at Foxhall Investment Management in DC in 1992. Foxhall was a great place to work and learn the trade. I quickly began providing equity and fixed income research, as well as shadowing my boss (the president of the firm) and learning how to talk to clients, trade securities, and construct and manage balanced portfolios. It couldn't have been a better place for me to start. I slowly took on my own portfolios and spent time talking to clients. It was here I also had my first exposure to working with brokers. Our investment firm had a relationship with one of the broker houses at the time, and the broker house used us to manage the portfolios for them while their brokers concentrated on marketing and raising assets. I could write a whole chapter on those early days of "wrap accounts" where brokers charged their clients up to 3% to have their money managed by someone else. What a scheme that was. But I digress …

One of the sadder days of my young career was when Foxhall was acquired by Prudential around 1994. By 1995, I moved to New York to work for Pru, but within a year landed a new job in the Institutional world of investing at MacKay Shields (ironically in the same building as Prudential), where I joined the Growth Equity team. Working in New York fast-forwarded my career and investment acumen exponentially. At Mackay, I was allowed to be both an equity analyst and a portfolio manager. The institutional world opened up a smorgasbord of learning opportunities. There were brokerage industry and investment conferences, face-to-face analyst meetings, one-on-one meetings with company presidents and CFOs, lunches, dinners, more research material than I could ever read, along with daily phone calls from equity sales people and analysts.

At Mackay, we not only managed mutual funds but also dealt with large institutional clients. I met with institutional investment boards regularly and presented to the brokers who sold our mutual funds. I was also able to talk daily with our other managers of various asset classes of small cap, value equity, fixed income, convertible securities, high yield, and international equities, both informally and as a member of the investment committee for our total return funds. I became managing director and co-manager of the equity group in 2006 but then in 2008 the financial crisis hit and in a mind-boggling move the whole equity department was dismissed in June 2009, just about at the market bottom, as the executives at our parent (another big insurance company) decided to close down the domestic equity operations of the value, growth, mid-cap and small-cap teams. Of course, the equity market hasn't looked back since, but fate allowed me to come full circle in 2010 when I opened the doors of Forza Investment Advisory, LLC. Thank goodness I decided against opening a hedge fund (the author of this book wrote his own book on hedge funds) and decided to go back to my roots and try to bring institutional quality investment management to individuals, families, and small institutions. So in summary, I've seen a lot of portfolios, big and small, managed a lot of portfolios of all sizes including mutual funds, and provided both equity and fixed income research in my career.

## UN-PORTFOLIOS AND DIVERSIFICATION

Over the years, I've come to refer to what I often review for potential clients as *un-portfolios*. I call them un-portfolios because usually they appear to have little rhyme or reason as to why the assets have been grouped together, offer minimal diversification benefits, are costly, and actually tend to have assets that are highly correlated**. I found that Fred's "un-portfolio" was what I was going to see many more times in the years to come. First, the broker had put him in a managed account and was charging him a fee of about 1.5%. Fred didn't know what the fee was that he was paying because it wasn't discussed and he didn't have an Investment Advisory Agreement (IAA**). An Investment Advisory Agreement is the very first thing any client should get from his advisor/manager before parting with a penny. An IAA is a formal arrangement between a registered investment advisor and an investor stipulating the terms under which the advisor is authorized to act on behalf of the investor to manage the assets listed in the agreement. Since Fred was working with a broker, there was no IAA.

Upon reviewing the assets, Fred's un-portfolio consisted of a smorgasbord of high-fee mutual funds. I counted *32 different mutual funds* for a portfolio of about $400K! I asked Fred what his manager's portfolio strategy was and how it related to his goals and objectives. He replied that he really wasn't sure. That's because he didn't have an Investment Policy Statement (IPS)**. AN IPS is the next most important agreement any investor should get from his advisor. Every institution having money professionally managed has an IPS. The IPS is a document drafted between a portfolio manager and a client that outlines the rules for the manager as related to the client's objectives. Most investors do not have an IPS or IAA unless they are working with a registered investment advisor, who is required to provide them to clients.

You must think that with 32 mutual funds there had to be a ton of diversification in that un-portfolio. In its simplest terms, diversification is a risk-management technique whereby the manager mixes a variety of investments within a portfolio to minimize the impact any one security will have on the overall performance of the portfolio. Especially over a longer time horizon, downside risk can be limited through diversification. This is important because there is a risk-reward inverse relationship in any security or portfolio. In theory, the more risk you take, the greater the return potential. Individual stocks have several kinds of risk, including firm risk, industry risk, and market risk. Firm risk and industry risk are diversifiable risks; that is, you can theoretically lessen the risk by adding other securities. In a portfolio, these risks can be reduced by diversifying among different stocks and different industries. Market risk is nondiversifiable because all stock portfolios contain market risk. That is, being in the market itself and subject to those risks of the overall market. There are many studies available that have been done over the years and I suggest that all investors should research this topic to understand just what diversification is and how it works before they invest.

For instance within equities you can diversify the portfolio in many ways, including by the following:

- Individual stocks—If building your own portfolio, there are numerous studies that show the more stocks the greater the diversification benefits. At a minimum, to receive diversification benefits I believe a portfolio generally needs at least 25+ different stocks. The S&P 500, aptly named, has 500 stocks. Mutual funds and exchange-traded funds vary widely and can hold hundreds or thousands of companies. There are also funds that hold less than 50.
- Sectors—There are 10 major sectors that professionals use to divide the market. These are healthcare, financial, industrials, consumer staples, consumer discretionary, energy, technology, utilities, materials, and telecommunications. The sectors are then subdivided into hundreds of different industries. Having exposure across sectors can help reduce risk of overconcentration to one sector.

- Market capitalization—The three most common sizes used are large, mid and small cap. Large-cap companies are above $10 billion, mid-cap from $2 billion to $10 billion, and small-cap $200 million to $2 billion. (Below that are micro-caps.)
- Weighting—Each stock, sector, or cap size should be allocated a target weight. Weights can vary by capitalization (S&P 500) or can be equal-weighted, or can be arbitrary as chosen by the manager.
- International stocks—International stocks generally can offer lower correlations to domestic stocks, which provide risk mitigation benefits. Holding individual positions can be costly, but there are securities called American depository receipts (ADRs)** that can be bought on exchanges (which I won't get into).

You can also diversify a portfolio by allocating different weights to varying asset classes, with stocks, bonds, and cash being the primary allocation strategy and then real estate and commodities being secondary. (For higher-net-worth individuals there are alternative asset classes like private equity, venture capital and hedge funds that also offer diversification benefits but these classes have their pros and cons and are not part of this discussion.)

Remember that diversification does not necessarily mean you are increasing your expected return. You are lowering your return in exchange for a lower level of risk. Thus, the risk–return trade-off. For example, below are the calculated returns and standard deviation (risk) for the period of 1991–2013 for stocks and bonds:

|  | S&P 500 | Barclays Bond Agg | 50% Stocks/50% Bonds |
| --- | --- | --- | --- |
| Annual Return | 10.04% | 6.41% | 8.22% |
| Std Deviation | 18.95% | 5.08% | 9.98% |
| Range | −37% to 38% | −2.9% to 18.5% | −16% to 28% |

Without getting too technical for this discussion, standard deviation is a common measure of risk in finance used by investors as a gauge of the amount of expected volatility of returns. The higher the standard deviation, the riskier the investment. The range shows how wide the returns ranged on an individual year basis.

Stocks have had higher returns than bonds but your annual volatility as measured by standard deviation was 3.7x higher during the period than for bonds while average annual return was 1.6x higher. In this simple example, I show the effect of a portfolio of 50% stocks and 50% bonds on risk and return. This allocation would have lowered the volatility from an all-stock portfolio to about 2x an all-bond portfolio while increasing return by 1.25x. In summary, bonds have had lower returns than stocks but also are less volatile. Combining stocks and bonds will lower both return and risk. This is the effect of diversification. As an investor, you must determine the appropriate trade-off for you going forward. This also requires an estimated expected return over your investment horizon of the different asset classes.

## FEES AND THE BLACK-BOX MODELS

Many advisors or brokers use a standard model that spits out a recommended allocation and places you in different mutual funds across various asset classes almost regardless of your personal objectives or the economic environment. This is what I refer to as the *Black-Box Model*. You put some parameters into the magical black box (computer program) and you get a one-size-fits-all diversified portfolio, in my experience usually for a management fee of 1.25% to 1.5%. Only, one-size definitely doesn't fit all when it comes to money management. You need to factor in each person's individual set of circumstances as well as the environment in which we currently reside. That's called the human element!

Now, back to Fred's portfolio. So yes, many of the boxes were checked—domestic equity, international equity, fixed income, real estate, private equity mutual fund, absolute return. You name it, it was in there. You can have as many funds as you want, but if they own similar securities, then you are not getting diversification. I'm not saying they all did, but the overlap was very big in each asset class. Rather than owning 32 funds, the manager could have achieved similar diversification benefits by owning one or two funds in each asset class. And given the economic environment and his objectives, there wasn't a need for every asset class to be represented. Upon closer inspection, I also estimated that the mutual fund fees probably averaged around another 1.5%. (A more detailed review I did later confirmed this.) So just to break even, the funds had to deliver 3% return. On top of that, the advisor put him in load funds (which charge a one-time transaction fee) for about half the holdings with a front-load fee of 5% to 6%! So he was collecting a load and charging a management fee. I call that *double-dipping,* and it is a clear potential conflict of interest and example of not having a fiduciary standard. So now, you have to earn 8% to 9% return on those load funds just to break even. I will speak more about load funds a little later. Finally, many of the funds were within the same fund family, which most likely meant that his firm had a deal with this fund family—another potential conflict of interest. You see, often times a brokerage firm or other broker/dealer firm will have either their own proprietary funds or fund families with whom they are connected in a tighter relationship. Usually, the advisor can get a higher payout or some benefit if he steers his clients into those funds.

When I asked him about performance, Fred said that his portfolio did not seem to be doing too well. So at that point, I decided to break it down for him and show him all the hidden fees he was paying, as well as talk to him about proper diversification.

Perhaps you are thinking that there has to be a fee and it is the price of doing business. I agree, since I charge a fee for my services. But it's all in the magnitude. Consider the following table where you can see how even a 1% difference in fees and returns can have a significant impact on your returns and nest egg over the long run.

| | | CAGR Gain % | | | | |
| | | 1.0% | 2.0% | 3.0% | 4.0% | 5.0% |
|---|---|---|---|---|---|---|
| 5 | Years | $525,505 | $552,040 | $579,637 | $608,326 | $638,141 |
| 10 | Years | $552,311 | $609,497 | $671,958 | $740,122 | $814,447 |
| 15 | Years | $580,484 | $672,934 | $778,984 | $900,472 | $1,039,464 |
| 20 | Years | $610,095 | $742,974 | $903,056 | $1,095,562 | $1,326,649 |

The table shows the value of an initial investment of $500,000 over various time periods at different rates of return (CAGR—constant average growth rate). That seemingly small 1% difference in return can be quite material over even 5 years. For example, the difference between a 3% and 4% return after 5 years in the simulation above is $29,000. After 20 years, this 1% difference is $192,000. That's a lot of money that could have gone a long way in someone's retirement. Too many investors don't realize this, and too many times the fees are hidden. Anybody having their money managed for them has the right to be shown in full transparency the fees they will be paying. Whether you hire an attorney, CPA, or money manager, the professionals will charge a fee for their expertise. But those fees should be discussed and transparent. Add in the fact that many portfolios are being managed improperly and the investors' loss of a few percent return can be quite significant.

## OTHER EXAMPLES OF UN-PORTFOLIOS

Fred's situation is just one example of an un-portfolio. Another example is an equity-only portfolio I saw from a very reputable investment professional's firm, a name many people hear every day in the investment world with several billion dollars under management. Another acquaintance of mine was unhappy with his 10-year relationship and asked me to take a look at his history. I was shocked to see the level of underperformance over 10 years from 2001 that he had endured when he gave me the portfolio to analyze, lagging the benchmark by about 15%—which in his case may have cost him $300,000 in underperformance! I saw poor asset allocation to domestic versus international markets, questionable security selection, and at one point a wholesale selling and purchasing of securities into a whole new allocation. That smacked of desperation and was a major red flag. Aside from the weak performance over 10 years, the investor paid management fees equal to half of what the performance was in that time frame (plus trading commissions). Finally, the portfolio contained about 9% allocation to banks, a sector in which the investor had specifically noted to the firm *not* to invest as he was employed in that industry and owned a good portion of his company stock. My guess is that the portfolio (over 7 figures) was still not big enough for a large firm to give it the proper attention it deserved. So yes, even reputable professionals can do a bad job if the allocation is structured improperly.

One final example of a portfolio of assets I was asked to analyze and later unwind is another common occurrence. In this instance, an individual had done well to save a nice amount and was trying to generate income from it for retirement. Unfortunately, that individual passed away and left the money to his wife, who had never dealt with any of this before. Spread across seven different accounts was a large array of holdings ranging from cash, individual securities, higher-fee mutual funds, a couple of non-traded REITs, a non-tradable CD, and a very large position (30%) invested in two telecom stocks. I usually see this in older individuals who have compiled assets themselves using a broker that they've dealt with a long time. Typically, the individual properly saves money during their life but improper portfolio construction and the lack of a disciplined investing strategy may have cost countless thousands of dollars left on the table.

Over the years, I've seen numerous types of "un-portfolios," so let me try to summarize what I see when I review the holdings. It tends to fall into the following list of mostly "don'ts" in terms of building a proper portfolio:

- There is usually at least one non-publicly traded REIT. (This book deals with that security in another chapter.)
- Almost always, there are annuities that have been purchased for them and 99% of the time the investor doesn't know what type of annuity it is. There may be a place in a person's overall allocation for an annuity but it should be bought for a specific purpose. (This book also deals with that security in chapter 7.)
- Load mutual funds. In my opinion, there is NO place in a portfolio for load funds with high fees. Load mutual funds will have an entry and/or exit fee that may range from 0% to a substantial maximum fee. See discussion following.
- Various types of mutual funds, but often several funds that cover the same asset type.
- Mutual funds with very high embedded management fees.

- Too much allocated to international funds, not enough in fixed income. This varies by individual, but my opinion is that advisors or brokers are not allocating enough to the good old USA.
- A managed account that is often invested in a generic model portfolio that usually is not a customized portfolio constructed to meet the person's objectives. Often their fee is at least 1.25% to 1.5% and then they are using funds that also charge a fee.
- The "Black-Box" model portfolio that has too many funds and asset classes.
- Random individual stock positions. These positions are often at sizes that are too big and subject the owner to large amounts of individual stock risk. They often are concentrated in one or two sectors that don't offer proper diversification. And there are always some small-cap speculative issues that generally have lost money.
- Closed-end mutual funds (CEFs) bought at their IPO price. Clearly, these are bought by the broker for a significant commission and maybe represent a deal that the firm is sponsoring. *Never* buy a closed-end-fund on the IPO. CEFs are traded like stocks and typically trade at a discount to the true NAV (net asset value). At the IPO, the CEF is priced equal to NAV. Inevitably the traded price drops to below NAV over a short period. Wait and buy CEFs at a discount to NAV.
- Exchange-traded Funds (ETFs). Although not necessarily a "don't," I'd like to say a few words about ETFs that you should keep in mind.

## EXCHANGE-TRADED FUNDS

An ETF is an investment fund that trades on a stock exchange at its underlying net asset value (NAV). Prices are updated through the day and ETFs can be bought and sold at any time during trading hours, unlike a mutual fund, which is priced once a day at the end of trading. However, that also means you pay a commission (although several discount brokerages offer no fee ETFs). ETFs have blossomed over the years and have drawn a lot of interest from investors both on a retail and institutional level. It is estimated that there are now over 1,600 ETFs with over $2 trillion in assets compared to $13 trillion in mutual funds. Most ETFs are passively managed, meaning that they are based on a particular index and are structured to be a liquid substitute for that index. Low-fee ETFs can be a good way to gain exposure to a particular asset class in a passive management way. But there are tons of ETFs out there, and the fees can vary significantly. There are also actively managed ETFs now proliferating, and then there is the cousin of the ETF called an ETN (exchange-traded note) that is often confused with the ETF. I won't get into defining an ETN, other to say that an ETN is really a debt instrument underneath with credit risk and a maturity date, and investors should know the differences. Always verify that the ETF is liquid and the embedded fees are not too high. I like ETFs and think they are good for individual investors as well as institutional investors for exposure to certain areas especially international stocks and small- or micro-caps. However, be careful of leveraged ETFs that give you two to three times the exposure to a particular asset class by using derivatives.

I would like to wrap up this discussion of portfolios and un-portfolios with a definition—maybe a definition with which I should have started this chapter. What is a portfolio? Investopedia says that a portfolio is a grouping of financial assets such as stocks, bonds, and cash equivalents, as well as their mutual, exchange-traded and closed-fund counterparts. Portfolios are held directly by investors and/or managed by financial professionals. Portfolios come in many shapes and sizes, and there are many portfolio strategies. But remember, there should only be one overall portfolio strategy for each of us, and that strategy is the one that will help you reach your own unique set of goals and circumstances.

## MUTUAL FUNDS AND FEES

I mentioned mutual funds in my prior example, and I'd like to spend a little time covering the topic. Don't get me wrong, mutual funds can have a place in many portfolios. For instance, investing in small, regular amounts a low-fee mutual fund that doesn't charge commissions is a good way to start building an investment egg. There are many good fund managers out there with solid track records in whose fund you can invest. I myself was a mutual fund manager for over 13 years. They come in all shapes and sizes and cover just about any major asset class you can think, of as well as some alternative classes. There are many ways to research funds to find out what they own, see the fees involved, check their historical performance, and other fund facts. Funds can be actively managed where the portfolio manager selects a particular strategy and tries to beat his benchmark—or funds can be passively managed where they are tied to a particular index and try to mimic that index. This chapter will not delve into the pros and cons of active vs. passive, as it is beyond the scope. As an active manager myself, I also can find a place in my portfolios for some passive investments so I guess I am a believer in both. My problem is not with mutual funds, but more the lack of fee transparency and misuse of mutual funds by brokers/advisors in structuring a portfolio. Too many times I see a portfolio with five or more funds allocated to an asset class that all do the same thing and are highly correlated. What this means is that if one fund goes up or down a particular day, they all follow. So there is little benefit to diversification. That is because they all probably own the same group of stocks making up the top holdings.

What many investors I talk to don't realize is that each mutual fund has a fee embedded in it that is charged by the fund manager. Fees can range all over the place with passively managed funds (those tied to an index) usually having the lowest fees and actively managed funds the highest. Morningstar (http://corporate.morningstar.com/US/documents/researchpapers/Fee_Trend.pdf) estimates that the average mutual fund fee on the universe of mutual funds was 1.25% in 2013. There is also another fee buried in the fund that is called the 12-B1 fee. This is a separate fee charged by the fund administrator for marketing the fund. This usually runs around .15% to .25%. So if you have a managed account and your advisor or broker is buying mutual funds, you are usually paying three fees—the managed account fee, the embedded mutual fund fee, and 12-B1 fees. High fee funds aren't necessarily a bad thing, but it does raise the bar for performance to recoup the fee and return a profit. Often this is done by taking on more risk.

Many investment companies have both proprietary and third-party funds. Proprietary funds are those managed in-house by the firm's investment group or investment subsidiary, while third-party funds are available on the platform and are managed by an outside advisor. This is important to you as an investor if you are represented by an agent, advisor, or broker of a particular firm. There is an inherent conflict of interest for the advisor to utilize the firm's in-house funds, as it is more lucrative for the firm as well as the advisor. Back to fiduciary duty, if the advisor is not acting as fiduciary, there is no requirement to disclose this potential conflict, so there may be a bias to push the in-house fund even though another fund might be less costly and more appropriate.

## LOAD FUNDS

Now what about load versus no-load mutual funds? A load fee is a sales commission charged to an investor when they purchase or redeem shares in a mutual fund. It drives me crazy when I see a portfolio that I might be reviewing with a handful of high fee load funds in it. A load fund is a mutual fund sold to you by a broker, advisor, or insurance agent that charges a *load*, or fee, for putting you in the fund. According to Investment Company Institute (ICI), the average maximum sales load on equity funds in 2013 was 5.3%, but the average load paid on load funds was just 1.0% due to discounts on larger purchases and fee waivers. Therefore, you are at risk of paying more if you are investing smaller amounts in load mutual funds. This may be one reason Fred had so many smaller allocations to similar mutual funds. This load can either be front-end, where you get charged when you first buy the fund, or back-end, where you get hit when you sell the fund. So just to break even you have to gain a potentially substantial load fee, plus the embedded mutual fund fee, plus the management fee you are being charged by the broker/advisor. That could be a substantial hurdle just to get your money back! Some no-load funds can also charge an early redemption fee where you are charged upon selling if not held for a minimum specific time frame. However these go back to into the mutual fund for the benefit of other investors and are usually limited to months. So be aware of what you are buying or own. In my mind, there is no reason for a broker or agent to buy a load fund other than to generate a commission for themselves so they can get paid. I understand that commissions are part of the business. But there are thousands of mutual funds they can choose from that don't charge loads. This gets to the concept of fiduciary duty.

## FIDUCIARY DUTY

Earlier in the chapter I mentioned fiduciary duty. Anyone evaluating hiring an advisor should always first ask, "Will you be acting as my fiduciary?" I think this is one of the most important yet most over-looked topics that any investor should be aware of when choosing someone to manage their money and become their advisor, and is also one of the biggest differences between an investment advisor** and a financial advisor** or broker**. Although the terms sound similar, investment advisors are not the same as financial advisors and should not be confused. Investment advisors are registered and governed by the Investment Advisors Act of 1940**. The term financial advisor is a generic term that usually refers to a broker (or, to use the technical term, a registered representative). By contrast, the term investment advisor is a legal term that refers to an individual or company that is registered as such with either the Securities and Exchange Commission or a state securities regulator. An investment advisor is governed by and held to the fiduciary standard** while the broker is held to the lesser suitability standard**. Fiduciary duty is a higher legal standard that legally requires an investment advisor to put their client's best interest ahead of their own. The Suitability doctrine requires a broker to know a customer's financial situation well enough to recommend investments that are considered suitable for that particular client. You may be asking, "Why does this matter? It sounds the same to me." It is most definitely not the same and the brokerage industry is fighting an ongoing battle to require brokers to adhere to the fiduciary standard. In laymen's terms, a broker may in fact sell you the investment that pays him/her the most commission, so long as the investment is deemed suitable. Brokers are also able to sell you proprietary products if their firm offers them. A firm's proprietary product usually brings more revenue to the firm, and they may have a higher payout to the broker who places their clients in the product. Finally, they may be subject to conflicts of interest that could influence their investment recommendations while at the same time not being required to disclose those conflicts of interest to the client.

Below is a summary of the differences between an RIA and a broker.

### Independent Registered Investment Advisor (RIA):

- RIA is in the business of giving advice
- *Independent* RIA firms are typically not owned by another and not beholden to any platform of products or services
- *Fiduciary*: legally required to put clients' interests first (a higher standard than suitability)
- Typically fee-based or fee-only compensation for advice
- Regulated by the SEC or states (as applicable) primarily under the Investment Advisors Act of 1940 and the rules adopted under that statute

### Registered Representative (Stockbroker):

- Brokerage firm primarily in the business of buying and selling securities for a commission or fee
- Registered representative is an employee/contractor of brokerage firm
- Typically compensated by commissions on product transactions
- Often experience greater profit from selling company's own proprietary product
- Held to suitability standard, not the higher fiduciary standards
- Often "look like" an advisor in marketing and websites (read the fine print)
- Regulated primarily by NASD (but also by SEC and states)

There are many articles that talk about the difference between suitability and fiduciary standard and I suggest that you take to the Internet and read several of them and make your own decision whether this is important or not. Personally, this is one of the top things I would require before I moved forward with any investment relationship.

## PORTFOLIO MANAGEMENT BASICS

I thought that now might be a good time to talk about the basics of portfolio management. Whether building a portfolio yourself or hiring someone to do it for you, you can follow these concepts to help you build a diversified portfolio or see if your manager has diversified your holdings:

1. **Investment Philosophy**
   Establishing an investment philosophy is the starting point for building your portfolio. You can accomplish this either by yourself or with a professional by doing the following.
   - Review your overall financial situation, past and present, to identify your financial objectives.
   - Set your financial priorities for the future. Determine your monthly and annual cash flows based on expenses and revenue sources.
   - Determine the tolerance for risk you are willing to undertake to capture the potential return.
   - Identify the resources you will need to meet your goals and outline a systematic plan to meet your objectives.
   - Determine solutions for reaching your goals by developing a customized investment portfolio and asset allocation based on your unique situation.
   - Monitor and update the plan on an ongoing basis, making adjustments when there is a change in your priorities or long-term objectives.

   The most basic of goals is to achieve consistent and competitive returns while managing risks and lowering investment costs. How do you do that? First, you have to have a plan.

   The trait most common among successful investors is discipline. Disciplined investors use a set of proven rules that protect them and guide them through the ups and downs of the market. A common disciplined investment approach (and the one that I use) combines elements of *top-down macroeconomic analysis* and fundamental *bottom-up company and security analysis.* The macroeconomic analysis—which includes an assessment of factors such as GDP growth, interest rates, inflation, monetary policy and demographic trends, world economics—serves to create a strategic backdrop for portfolio construction. The bottom-up analysis is done more on the individual security level where you determine the investment merits of a particular investment. Whether you use a top-down or bottom-up approach, you must have discipline in executing and following your strategy. My old boss in my early years in the business used to like to say, "You gotta have a plan. It doesn't necessarily have to be a great one, but you gotta have a plan!"

2. **Asset Allocation**

   Proper asset allocation is crucial to balancing risk and return. With proper asset allocation, it may be possible to lower the amount of risk in your portfolio while still producing a decent return. What does *asset allocation* mean, and why is it important? Asset allocation is an investment strategy that aims to balance risk and return by allocating a portfolio's assets among different asset classes according to one's individual financial goals, risk tolerance, and investment time horizon. Each asset class (stocks, bonds, cash, commodities, international, etc.) has a different level of risk and return, so each will behave differently over time depending on the macro environment. This level of behavior can be measured by a statistical figure called correlation. In general, assets that are highly correlated will act the same and don't offer much diversification benefit. Since we cannot predict the future, we will always face risks in making investment decisions. One asset class may be down while another may be up in the same timeframe. Although there is no simple formula to find the right asset allocation for every individual, it has been well documented through various industry studies that asset allocation policy is the single most important factor in determining portfolio performance. In other words, your selection of individual securities is secondary to the way you allocate your investments across asset categories. Asset allocation allows more control over how much return you can possibly get in exchange for assuming a certain level of risk.

Let's step back for a second and look at the big picture. Following are three common ways to manage money:

1. *Market timing*—making an investment decision and moving money among investments by attempting to predict future price movements based on a forecast over a specific time frame.
2. *Security selection*—deciding which security to buy or sell compared to others in the same asset class.
3. *Asset allocation*—the process of deciding how money gets divided up between different asset classes. Asset allocation can be dynamic (market timing) or static and long-term in nature.

Each investment decision utilizes at least one method and more than one method may be used. For instance, you can combine asset allocation with security selection to build your portfolio.

To understand the benefits of asset allocation, you must also understand correlations and returns. *Correlation* is simply defined as the degree to which one asset class moves in tandem with another. Correlations among classes can vary significantly over the long term. *Returns* may also vary from year to year and asset class to asset class. In general, you build a diversified portfolio by combining asset classes with low or negative correlations. One caveat to keep in mind, correlations are backward looking, and there may be periods (such as 2008) where correlations may be high among asset classes, thereby reducing the benefits of asset allocation in the short term.

To summarize, one's investment strategy can be based on the following building blocks:

- *The future can't be predicted therefore we all face risks.* These risks include economic risk, geopolitical risk, interest rate risk, inflation risk, market risk, business risk, credit risk, currency risk, and reinvestment risk among others. We attempt to manage these risks through investment diversification.

- *Diversification is achieved by asset allocation.* Asset allocation is the most important factor in the investment process and is a long-range planning decision that has little to do with market timing—it should not be tinkered with solely because of short-term market fluctuations and is achieved by allocation among assets with low or negative correlation. Asset allocation requires diversification among different asset classes as well as within an asset class.
- *A disciplined investment process for choosing securities is the only way to provide replicable results over the long run.* I believe in investing for the long-term with a disciplined strategy and low turnover that reduces transaction costs and tends to provide tax-efficient results. The investment process should focus on long-term results of the entirety of one's assets over a market cycle.
- *Remember that risk and returns will vary among asset classes over the long term.* Asset allocation should be made based on a belief in long-term results that can produce a satisfactory reward while reducing overall risk.

So remember, asset allocation is a planning tool that allows you or the investment manager to structure the investment portfolio in a manner most likely to accomplish the goals of each specific individual. An *asset allocation plan* is a long-range, semi-permanent planning decision that has little to do with market timing or hedging—it should not be tinkered with solely because of short-term fluctuations. Properly diversified and allocated portfolios can help protect you from severe market fluctuations.

3. **Benchmarking**

One of the key attributes of determining if your portfolio is performing at a high level and according to your specific set of goals and objectives is for the manager to utilize benchmarks. In the institutional world all portfolios are measured against benchmarks. So why shouldn't an individual's portfolio be measured against them? A benchmark is an index or combination of indexes that varies for each individual based on their goals and objectives. The two most basic benchmarks are the S&P 500 for

US equities and the Barclays Bond Aggregate for Fixed Income. When working with my clients, I construct a custom index for each client and report performance along with the indexes each quarter so they can see how their portfolio is performing relative to our agreed-upon objective and the financial markets. I see no reason why individuals shouldn't have the benefit of utilizing benchmarks just like institutions. Even if you manage your own money, you should utilize a benchmark to monitor your relative performance rather than just looking at your total return as an absolute number.

## SUMMARY AND CONCLUSION

I touched on a lot of topics in this short chapter but barely touched the surface. There's so much more and every day can be a learning experience, which is why I love this profession. But I hope I was able to educate you on some of the things to look for in deciding on how to manage your own hard-earned money, whether by hiring someone or doing it yourself. Rule #1 is, do your homework. Managing money is a full-time job, and since you worked hard to build your nest egg you should have proper time devoted to managing it. The loss of even a percentage point of performance can be costly in the long run. Determine your objectives, know your risk tolerance, and develop a disciplined investment plan and strategy. Have a properly constructed portfolio that meets your objectives. Stay away from high fees and assets that don't offer any benefit to your particular situation. If hiring a professional, ask questions. After all, this is your money. Ask about fiduciary duty and conflict of interests. Most importantly, don't take everything you are told at face value. Demand transparency and if you can't get it, move on and find someone that will give it to you. Above all, remember that investing comes with risk. Even diversified portfolios with asset allocation can and likely will go down in a particular year based on a host of factors. So there is some luck involved, too. But if you know your tolerance for the risk you are taking and stick to your plan over the long term, then in baseball parlance you are ahead in the count and your odds of success are better.

BONUS SECTION

## The 20 Biggest Money Mistakes

I'd like to end this chapter with a list that is not all encompassing but I think covers a lot of bases. We all make investment and money mistakes. Years ago, I came across an article that talked about some of the biggest investment mistakes people often make. I updated it over time and added my own. I'd like to give credit to the original author but honestly don't know who it was or when I found the original. So here is a list of what I think are the *20 biggest money mistakes* (not in any order). By cutting down on the number of mistakes made we can improve our chances of increasing our return. Let's face it, that's the name of the game!

1. Procrastinating about financial decisions. Start early and be disciplined.
2. Having goals that are too general, undefined, or unrealistic.
3. Not having a plan, or having one that won't work.
4. Ignoring the effect of taxes in your plan.
5. Going uninsured against death, disability, and liability.
6. Ignoring the cost of inflation in your plan. It is real and costly over time.
7. Being overweight in your portfolio in the current fad. Diversify.
8. Making decisions based on emotion (fear and greed).
9. Wanting to do it yourself to save a few bucks when you are really not qualified.
10. Being too conservative or aggressive. Know your tolerance and couple it with your time frame.
11. Not understanding the concept of asset allocation.
12. Concentration rather than diversification. Concentration may be higher reward but is also higher risk. Understand risk versus reward.
13. Placing bets on hot companies (Don't operate on tips and speculation versus investing).
14. Being overly influenced by others (friends and family).

15. Placing market-timing bets (speculating versus investing).
16. Failure to take profits or losses.
17. Idle assets (having too much cash).
18. Assuming things will just work themselves out (not selling a loser).
19. Demanding immediate results and satisfaction. Market cycles do exist.
20. Lack of spending/savings/investment discipline.

## Glossary of Terms

**ADRs (American depository receipts)** A negotiable certificate issued by a US bank representing a specified number of shares (or one share) in a foreign stock that is traded on a US exchange. ADRs are *denominated in US dollars*, with the underlying security held by a US financial institution overseas.

**Correlation** In the world of finance, a statistical measure of how two securities move in relation to each other. Perfect positive correlation implies that as one security moves, either up or down, the other security will move in lockstep, in the same direction. Alternatively, perfect negative correlation means that if one security moves in either direction, the security that is perfectly negatively correlated will move in the opposite direction. If the correlation is 0, the movements of the securities are said to have no correlation; they are completely random.

**Broker (financial advisor)** According to FINRA, a broker-dealer is a person or company that is in the business of buying and selling securities for a fee or commission—stocks, bonds, mutual funds, and certain other investment products—on behalf of its customers (as broker), for its own account (as dealer), or both. Individuals who work for broker-dealers—the sales personnel whom most people call brokers—are technically known as registered representatives. Broker-dealers must register with the Securities and Exchange Commission (SEC) and be members of FINRA. Individual registered representatives must register with FINRA, pass a qualifying examination (Series 7, Series 63, or others), and be licensed by your state securities regulator before they can do business with you. Registered representatives are primarily securities salespeople and may also go by such generic titles as financial consultant, financial advisor, or investment consultant.

**Chartered Financial Analyst (CFA®)** Some professional investment managers and analysts study to become CFA® charterholders. CFA® is a professional designation given by the CFA Institute (formerly AIMR) that measures the competence and integrity of financial analysts. Candidates are required to pass three levels of exams covering areas such as accounting, economics, ethics, money management, and security analysis. Before you can become a CFA® charterholder, you must have four years of investment/financial career experience. To enroll in the program, you must hold a bachelor's degree. The CFA® charter is one of the most respected designations in finance, considered by many to be the gold standard in the field of investment analysis.

**Investment advisor** (See Registered Investment Advisor)

**Fiduciary Duty** - A legal duty to act solely in another party's interests. Parties owing this duty are called fiduciaries. The individuals to whom they owe a duty are called principals.

**FINRA (Financial Industry Regulatory Authority)** A self-regulatory organization (SRO) that assists the SEC in regulating financial markets, notably exchanges and companies that deal with securities. FINRA has jurisdiction over all broker-dealers and registered representatives, and has authority to discipline firms and individuals who violate the rules. It regulates trading in stocks, mutual funds, variable annuities, corporate bonds, and futures and options contracts on securities. It also acts as the SRO for a number of securities exchanges. FINRA reviews materials that investment companies provide to their clients and prospective clients to ensure those materials comply with the relevant guidelines. The FINRA website also provides investor education and alerts on current issues of importance to investors. Through its BrokerCheck database, FINRA provides a resource for investors to check the credentials of people and firms. In addition, FINRA resolves disputes between broker-dealers and their clients, through either mediation or arbitration. It was created in 2007 with the merger of the National Association of Securities Dealers and the NYSE regulatory board.

**Financial Planner** Unlike the terms *investment advisor* and *broker*, *financial planner* is not a legally defined term. However, it generally refers to providers who develop and may also implement comprehensive financial plans for customers based on their long-term goals. A comprehensive financial plan typically covers such topics as estate planning, tax planning, insurance needs, and debt management, in addition to more investment-oriented areas, such as retirement and college planning. Some planners own the CFP (Certified Financial Planner) designation after passing an exam.

**Investment Advisors Act of 1940** The Investment Advisors Act is a US law that was created to regulate the actions of investment advisors (also spelled "advisers") as defined by the law. It is the primary source of regulation of investment advisors and is administered by the US Securities and Exchange Commission.

**Investment Advisory Agreement (IAA)** An IAA sets the terms of the relationship between the client and the advisor and the fee being charged to manage the listed assets. The agreement establishes the extent to which the advisor may act in a discretionary capacity to make investment decisions based on a prescribed strategy.

**Investment Policy Statement (IPS)** The IPS provides the general investment goals and objectives of a client and describes the strategies that the manager should employ to meet these objectives. Specific information on matters such as asset allocation, risk tolerance, and liquidity requirements are part of the document and should be unique to each individual.

**Madoff Ponzi scheme** Bernie Madoff is the former chairman of the Nasdaq and founder of the market-making firm Bernard L. Madoff Investment Securities. Madoff, who also ran a hedge fund, was arrested on December 11, 2008, for running an alleged Ponzi scheme; his hedge fund lost about $50 billion, but kept it hidden by paying out earlier investors with money from later investors.

**Registered Investment Advisor (RIA)** Refers to an investment advisor (legal term) that is registered with the SEC or a State Securities Agency and typically provides investment advice to a Retail investor or registered Investment company such as a Mutual Fund, or Exchange-Traded Fund (ETF). Registration does not signify that the SEC has passed on the merit of a particular investment advisor. A registered investment advisor (RIA) is an entity who, for compensation, engages in the business of advising others, either directly or indirectly, of the value of securities or of the advisability of investing in securities. They receive a management fee and do not receive commissions ("RIAs receive fees, stockbrokers receive commissions"). RIA's act as fiduciary in representing their clients and must put their client's interests ahead of their own. Common names for investment advisors include asset managers, investment counselors, investment managers, portfolio managers, and wealth managers. RIAs are governed by the Investment Advisors Act of 1940.

**Fiduciary standard** The anti-fraud provisions of the Investment Advisors Act of 1940 and most state laws impose a duty on RIAs to act as fiduciaries in dealings with their clients. (Brokers are only held to the lesser suitability standard.) This means the advisor must hold the client's interest above its own in all matters. The Securities and Exchange Commission (SEC) has said that an advisor has a duty to:

- Make reasonable investment recommendations independent of outside influences.
- Select broker-dealers based on their ability to provide the best execution of trades for accounts where the advisor has authority to select the broker-dealer.
- Make recommendations based on a reasonable inquiry into a client's investment objectives, financial situation, and other factors.
- Always place client interests ahead of its own.

**Suitability standard** Broker-dealers only have to fulfill a suitability obligation, which is defined as making recommendations that are consistent with the best interests of the underlying customer. Broker-dealers are regulated by the Financial Industry Regulatory Authority (FINRA) under standards that require them to make suitable recommendations to their clients. Instead of having to place his or her interests below that of the client, the suitability standard only details that the broker–dealer has to reasonably believe that any recommendations made are suitable for clients, in terms of the client's financial needs, objectives and unique circumstances. A key distinction in terms of loyalty is also important, in that a broker's duty is to the broker–dealer he or she works for, not necessarily the client served.

# CHAPTER 7

# ANNUITIES

## Dave Pasi

This section begins with a history of my personal experience with investments in annuities. I will then describe the basics of what annuities are, who sells them, potential tax implications, and why buy them. I will review basic types and cost structures. Next, a brief tutorial on some current issues and applications relevant to the insurance industry, government regulations, and recent policy changes, with specific examples of typical annuity scenarios, trade-offs, benefits, and costs. Most importantly, I'll give you questions to ask an annuity salesperson next time you meet one. This will leave you knowing much more and will show that you probably don't need what he's selling.

## INTRODUCTION

This is NO time to purchase annuities.

Annuities are high-fee, illiquid investments that make insurance companies a boatload of money. Does this sound too critical? Not really; don't get me wrong, there are investing situations that call for an annuity, but they are just few and far between.

Since the depths of the "Great Recession," the insurance industry has capitalized on the fear most investors felt when the stock market swooned from September 2008 to March lows in 2009. You might recall that the market was down over 50% from its high. Fear can be a great motivator, but not when it comes to annuities. When fear grips investors, insurance sellers soothe them with words like "safe," "guaranteed," and "never worth less than your initial investment." Insurance agents, brokers, and some financial advisors use a lot of hype to sell the products to unsuspecting, unsophisticated investors. Advertising for annuities bulked up every financial and nonfinancial publication. These musings came from the insurance industry touting annuities as the alternative to the risky stock market. Then, as now, annuities seem like the safety net investors are looking for; forget it!

Before you decide to invest your hard-earned dollars in an annuity, an investor should read the fine print. There are different types of annuities, with the majority being very complicated insurance policies that are difficult to decipher and may result in unintended outcomes. Any investor should understand what they are purchasing and should not buy these products with expectations of a great return. You may even find that you will not receive any return over time.

The following chapter could help you save hundreds of thousands of dollars, avoid making a lousy investment, and prevent the difficulty of reversing a very inappropriate and costly investment decision. Let's take a look at this arcane investment that uses slick ads to entice you and then issues you a 200-page tome to explain what you purchased.

If you have trouble falling asleep, begin reading an annuity contract and you will certainly pass out.

My experience with insurance products—and specifically, annuities—dates back to late 1988 as a result of my father's sudden death. As one of five children and the only one having experience in the financial markets, I was the logical choice to assist my mother in addressing the settlement of my dad's life insurance and guiding her financial future (she was 54 at the time). Shortly after my dad's death, my mother and I met with two very well presented insurance agents to review my dad's life insurance settlement and discuss the potential investment options and opportunities that the insurance company offered. The agents immediately tried to persuade my mother to purchase an annuity product. I asked them to leave their presentation and their shiny brochure and escorted them out. As a novice in their field, but having enough experience in the financial markets, I knew it was going to take some research (there wasn't any Google or Internet) and examination to evaluate their presentation. As I read through the reams of documentation that no layperson could comprehend, I noticed many embedded fees throughout the structures and realized that the sale of the product heavily benefited the agent and not my mother. However, we decided that it would be prudent to allocate a small portion of the life insurance proceeds into a *fixed annuity* and reluctantly purchased the product. As it turns out, the timing couldn't have been better. The fixed annuity at the time yielded close to 10% and was fixed for 20 years, outperforming the 20-year treasury during that time period. We benefited from purchasing an annuity at the beginning of a three-decade decline in interest rates and rode the bull market; even though we weren't making a market call or an interest rate prediction, we ended up being on the right side of the market for that portion of her assets.

Fast-forward 27 years, and the insurance industry has not changed much, but as most of the current and soon-to-be retirees know, interest rates certainly have dropped and the US equity markets are trading near their all-time highs. The insurance companies still market annuity products using shiny brochures and complicated documentation and claim to provide excessive above market guaranteed returns.

## WHAT IS AN ANNUITY?

Annuities were originally developed in Roman times; A.D. 225—A Roman judge produced the first known mortality table for "annua," which were lifetime stipends made once per year in exchange for a lump-sum payment (Marvin Feldman 2012).

An annuity is a contract between you and an insurance company that is designed to meet retirement and other long-range goals, under which you make a lump-sum payment or series of payments to an insurance company. In return, the insurer agrees to make periodic payments to you beginning immediately or at some future date (SEC.GOV n.d.).

Annuities typically offer tax-deferred growth of earnings and may include a death benefit that will pay your beneficiary a specified minimum amount, such as your total purchase payments. While tax is deferred on earnings growth, when withdrawals are taken from the annuity, gains are taxed at ordinary income rates and not capital gains rates. If you withdraw your money early from an annuity, you may pay substantial surrender charges to the insurance company, as well as tax penalties.

Here's how an annuity works: You make an investment in the annuity (give the insurance company an upfront lump sum), and it then makes payments to you on a future date or series of dates. The income you receive from an annuity can be paid out monthly, quarterly, annually, or even in a lump-sum payment. The sizes of your payments are determined by a variety of factors, including the length of your payment period. You can opt to receive payments for the rest of your life, or for a set number of years.

Annuities aren't one-size-fits-all panacea investments, and they are not too good to be true, even though too many are sold that way. Sometimes they work well when placed properly in a diversified portfolio, and fully understood for the contractual realities of the policy. So let's take a closer look at the different types and the reasons you might want to stay away from the annuity sellers.

## WHAT ARE THE DIFFERENT TYPES OF ANNUITIES?

Annuities can come in many different shapes and forms, but generally are either fixed or variable. The payments can start immediately (an immediate annuity) or after some accrual period (a deferred annuity).

Many investors may choose to purchase an immediate annuity by making an upfront payment, which will then be paid out over your life. If you chose an *immediate annuity,* you begin to receive payments soon after you make your initial investment. For example, an investor might consider purchasing an immediate annuity when approaching retirement age. In the current interest rate environment, it does not make any financial sense to purchase an immediate annuity. An investor can get a similar return investing in AAA-rated US government securities and avoid the salespeople and the annual fees.

*The deferred annuity* can have both an upfront payment or be paid over time. With a deferred annuity, your money is invested for a period of time until you are ready to begin taking withdrawals, typically starting in retirement. The deferred annuity accumulates money over time while the immediate annuity pays income streams immediately. Deferred annuities can also be converted into immediate annuities when the owners decide that they want to start collecting payments.

The most effective way to use a deferred income annuity is to buy one with a small portion of your portfolio and then delay the income distribution to the distant future to ensure a stream of income. You may pay much less for the product and peace of mind.

## Characteristics of Annuities

Can annuities be the right choice for perpetual income or an investment layered with expenses?

Annuities may be a popular choice for investors who want to receive a steady income stream in retirement (CNN Money n.d.). While annuities can sometimes be useful retirement planning tools, they can also be a lousy investment choice for certain people because of their notoriously high expenses. Financial planners and insurance sellers will frequently try to steer seniors or other people in various stages of retirement into annuities. An investor can be very vulnerable at this stage of life and may look toward the insurance salesman for those comforting words such as "guaranteed and secure" to assist them in making the investment decision. Many of the fees are upfront and payment of sales commissions and fees are imbedded in the contract. In some instances, fees can be as high as 8% of principal invested. Anyone who considers an annuity should research it thoroughly first, before deciding whether it's an appropriate investment for someone in his or her situation.

There are two basic stages, accumulation and annuitization. Very simply put, the accumulation stage is where an investor deposits funds into the account and at the end of the accumulation the investor can convert the deposit of funds into periodic payments or annuitize the account. All annuities grow tax deferred during the accumulation period, but the growth is taxed as ordinary income when withdrawn.

This description seems simple and is described in the most basic form; however, if you dig into the weeds, the product is extremely complex and requires significant analysis and evaluation. Language, terms, and conditions vary from insurer to insurer. These products carry high entry fees and annual fees; investors should read the details in the fine print, should understand what they are purchasing, and should not buy with expectations of a high-yielding return. A retiree just can't get low-risk, high-yielding returns given today's rate structure.

## Types of Annuities

Let's dig in further and take a look at the basics types.

*Fixed annuities* aim to provide a guaranteed income rate of return over a specified period of time and may provide additional death benefits. In today's market, the current income guarantee is less than 2%. I am extremely biased, but who in their right mind would lock an investment at 2% for 10 years? The most simplistic comparison would be to compare a fixed annuity to a certificate of deposit. Many annuity contracts entered today give the insurer the option to reset the fixed rate of return at the end of each time period or term; this, of course, would be to the benefit of the insurer not the owner. As noted above, each company has its own terms, which vary greatly.

If you choose a *fixed-rate annuity,* you are not responsible for choosing the investments—the insurance company handles that job and agrees to pay you a pre-determined fixed return. (CNN Money n.d.)

Fixed annuities may not protect an investor from inflation. Inflation erodes purchasing power over time. An investor can purchase an inflation protection rider for a *fee.* Additionally, if you decide to make any inflation adjustments to your monthly payment later in the contract, you will certainly pay penalties and/or additional fees. For an investment alternative that will protect you from inflation increases please refer to section on Series I Bonds on page 166.

When you invest in a fixed annuity, you also choose how you want your eventual payouts to be calculated. You have four options:

1. *Income for guaranteed period (also called period certain annuity).* You are guaranteed a specific payment amount for a set period of time (say, 5 years or 30 years). If you die before the end of the period your beneficiary will receive the remainder of the payments for the guaranteed period.
2. *Lifetime payments provide a guaranteed income payout during your lifetime only; there is no survivor benefit.* The payouts are fixed. The amount of the payout is determined by how much you invest and your life expectancy. At the time of death all payments stop—your heirs don't get anything.
3. *Income for life with a guaranteed period certain benefit (also called life with period certain).* A combination of a life annuity and a period-certain annuity. You receive a guaranteed payout for life that includes a period-certain phase. If you die during the period-certain phase of the account, your beneficiary will continue to receive the payment for the remainder of the period. For example, life with a 10-year period-certain is a common arrangement. If you die five years after you begin collecting, the payments continue to your survivor for five more years.
4. *Joint and survivor annuity.* Your beneficiary will continue to receive payouts for the rest of his or her life after you die. This is a popular option for married couples.

## VARIABLE ANNUITIES

The insurance industry defines *variable annuities* as offering flexibility, investment choices, and legacy protection to allow premiums to be invested in a limited number of subaccounts, similar to mutual funds. Typically, the investment choices are heavily fee-laden. The subaccounts may be invested in a broad investment class of stock funds, bond funds, or cash. The variable annuity may offer a guaranteed minimum return even if your investment choices underperform (additional fees apply to purchase that rider) (Money.cnn, 2013).

Variable annuities involve greater investment risks and can lose value. The typical investment is in the equity market. When choosing a variable annuity you as the investor make the decision on how to allocate your money. You have a choice of subaccounts offered within the annuity. The value of your account depends on the performance of the funds you choose. While a variable annuity has the benefit of tax-deferred growth, its annual expenses are likely to be much higher than the expenses on regular mutual funds—I would recommend investment in ordinary mutual funds, which would certainly be a better option.

## ASSOCIATED RISKS

Variable annuities can and do lose money. There is no FDIC or bank guarantee on variable annuities. If you are looking for a place to save money with no risk of loss, consider fixed-return vehicles such as US Treasury notes and bonds, bank certificates of deposit, or money markets.

The insurance company's financial strength will affect its ability to pay added benefits such as a death benefit, guaranteed minimum income benefit, and long-term care benefits. If the insurance company fails, annuity owners may not receive all the benefits they were expecting. Since 2009, there have been many legislative reforms enacted to better protect investors from failing financial services companies, and financial firms' balance sheets have been strengthened significantly. However, it is still important to evaluate the providers' financial strength and remain wary of the possibility of a financial services firm to not meet its financial obligations.

As with all purchased insurance products, investors should question the reliability and financial strength of the insurance company and its ability to consistently make payments in the future—that is, the creditworthiness of the insurer should be evaluated.

Check the insurer's credit rating, a grade given by credit bureaus such as A.M. Best, Standard & Poor's, and Moody's that expresses the company's financial health. Each rating firm has its own grading scale. As a general rule, limit your options to insurers that receive either an A+ from A.M. Best or AA- or better from Moody's and S&P. You can find the ratings online or get them from your insurance agent. It is possible an investor could lose money if the insurance company you invested with goes bankrupt. So it is critical to purchase annuities only from insurance companies that you're confident will be in business when you retire. There are, however, state guaranty funds that protect annuity owners if an insurance company fails, but the coverage is limited and varies from state to state.

## OTHER RISKS ARE LACK OF FLEXIBILITY

An annuity is a long-term investment that requires a multiyear commitment. But an investor can never be certain about the future. Keeping financial flexibility and liquidity can be worth real money to an investor. Annuities lock you into a limited pool of investments. If your situation or plans change, or the investment climate changes, or annuity returns are mediocre, it is extremely difficult and costly to cash out and switch to a better or more appropriate investment.

*Equity index annuities* can provide guaranteed minimum interest and beneficiary protection. Equity indexed annuities contain features of both fixed and variable annuities. Potential for additional growth is linked to the return of an index like the S&P 500. Most of the insurance companies will typically cap your return, so in an extreme up market year, the investors' upside returns are limited.

Following is a brief example of our new client Fred's (76 years old) previous purchase of equity indexed annuity and fee structure associated with the unwind.

In the fall of 2009, Fred purchased a product called Group Flexible Premium Deferred Annuity. When I questioned as to why he purchased the equity linked annuity, he told me it offered full S&P equity exposure and that the salesman gave him a 10% premium bonus when signing the contract. The product carried a 3.5% annualized cap rate with a 120% participation rate, which meant that he was taking outsized risk with limited upside reward. Additionally, the product carried surrender charges of 18% in year 1, reducing 2% per year through year 9! This investment offered very little liquidity, and in order to get his money out without penalties he would have needed to wait 10 years! Although the product with the bonus looked attractive on the surface, it offered Fred no ability to either capture gains or provide liquidity.

## VARIABLE ANNUITY RIDERS

Investor fear and greed drive insurance sellers. A few short years ago, several major insurance companies promoted getting a minimum guaranteed income for life, catapulting investors into pouring over $1.5 trillion into variable annuities (Money.cnn 2013). Driving the sales were buyers attracted by the living benefit rider, an optional feature ensuring that you can draw a base income from your investments regardless of how the markets perform or whether you drain your account.

Before the 2008–2009 financial crisis, annuity riders sometimes guaranteed returns over 8% (much of this actually is a return of your own dollars) with annual withdrawals of 7% and investors rushed into these insurance products seeing them as a guarantee with limited investment risk. However, over the past few years, most of the insurance companies selling these products had to scale back the guarantees while raising fees on new products and reducing investment choices and allocations.

A few companies even offered to buy out current customers' contracts and cancel their riders because the riders were too expensive to the insurance companies (great deals for the policy holder and bad deal for the insurers). Why would they do this? Well as interest rates collapsed and people were living longer the ability for insurers to guarantee their contractual commitments fell and left them with a questionable ability to meet future payment streams.

A lot of insurance companies got hurt and needed to restructure the terms of their contracts. If you already have a variable annuity you should review your contract, your current account value and the potential changes in terms. Many of the insurance terms are changing or have already changed to protect the insurance companies, limiting investment choices, lowering minimum returns and income guarantees and of course raising fees. Sometimes insurance companies screw up and misprice their products; savvy investors from time to time may have an opportunity to get a good deal.

There are now instances where the insurance companies need to restructure clients' long-term care policies due to inappropriate introductory pricing. The big insurance companies have the ability to petition their state insurance boards and ask for rate adjustments and subsequently apply policy payment increases. The odds are in the insurance companies' favor if they screw up a product as their lobby is very powerful and has the ability to force and make change to insurance contracts. This is not a fair and level playing field for the novice investor.

Here is an example of more structural changes to annuities as insurance companies continue to revamp their products:

Jackson National unveils tiered pricing for variable annuities (Mercado 2014).

A new pricing plan for Jackson National Life Insurance Co.'s popular variable annuity living benefit riders is scheduled to take effect starting Monday, September 15, 2014. Jackson will apply a five-tiered pricing scheme for single life versions of its LifeGuard Freedom Flex and LifeGuard Freedom 6 Net guaranteed minimum withdrawal benefit contracts.

"It's a continuation of our philosophy of building variable annuity products," said Greg Cicotte, president of Jackson National Life Distributors. "We try to give advisors options to be able to customize the product for each individual." The five tiers are meant to enable clients to choose a variable annuity based on what means most to them: *higher withdrawals or lower cost.*

Two components to understanding the tiers are income the client will get versus the cost, according to a June 11, 2014 filing Jackson made with the Securities and Exchange Commission.

First there's a level of income. *Lower tiers offer less guaranteed income at a lower cost.*

Jackson's move is one that permits the wildly popular variable annuity seller to mitigate flows into its contracts without calling for an outright ban on 1035 exchanges into Jackson contracts (more on 1035 exchanges on page 162).

Advisors might remember that last October the company decided to temporarily block transfers into its variable annuities, a repeat of a move it announced in late 2012. Effectively, such moves halt transfers for the remainder of the year.

With the new structure, however, Jackson can slow transfers and sales without rattling the reps who sell its contracts.

Is there any benefit to the investor? Not really, given level 5 sales being temporarily halted clients can still choose to purchase the slightly-cheaper and slightly less rich level 4 version of the riders. This type of variable annuity continues to raise concerns with the regulators.

So why have five tiers? In my view, it provides more room for confusion, hidden fees, and sales commission.

Investors need to know what to expect when purchasing an annuity.

Many unsuspecting clients purchased annuities from unscrupulous insurance sellers during the 2008–2009 downturn, preying on the investor fear and offering guaranteed returns. Let's take a real-life example; one of our 2011 clients, Maria, was sold not one but three annuities by a financial advisor/salesperson who regards the sales of multiple annuities and placing them in an IRA as suitable for this 46-year-old. Not that all advisors/salespersons fall into the same category but when we researched this one on the FINRA site we found details of improprieties (see the following recap). The reason for selling various annuities is all about sales credits and the payout associated with the sale of another annuity; having three annuities staggered enables the salesperson to benefit greatly while making it more difficult for an investor to unwind their investment in a liquidity event.

It is pretty easy nowadays to research just about anyone. Thoroughly check out your broker using FINRA Broker Check to learn whether your broker is licensed and has a history of complaints. When I searched their site I found compromising details about the salesman who sold the above annuities to Maria. This information is entered by the reporting source (broker, firm, or regulator). If Maria was an educated investor she certainly would not have purchased the annuity knowing the agent had numerous complaints. Simply having this many blemishes on your record is a red flag and cause for concern.

As a financial advisor we come in contact with many retirees who have been misguided and some by their local trusted Bank. Last year I met with a retired couple who went to their local US Bank branch where they knew the tellers by their first names and were very comfortable with them.

As often the case a teller suggested that they meet with the bank's investment brokers. Discussions and an evaluation ensued, and the bank investment specialist sold them a variable annuity. They invested more than $625,000. The annuity promised to generate lifetime income payments.

Of course the retirees wanted to make the most amount of interest they could.

What they didn't fully understand was that the variable annuities came with a steep annual charge: about 4% of the amount invested. That came to more than $25,000, annually—enough to buy a new car every year. What's more, if they needed to tap the money right away, there would be a 7% surrender charge, or $43,750 taken from their principal.

Many local banks claim that these investments are appropriate and that fees were disclosed, and that the sales are completed after months of consultations. But the retirees now question whether they were given financial advice that was truly in their best interests.

Like many consumers, they say they didn't realize that their broker wasn't required to follow the most stringent requirement for financial professionals, known as the fiduciary standard. It amounts to this: Providing advice that is always 100% in the consumer's interest.

## ILLIQUIDITY, OR THE LACK OF BEING ABLE TO GET TO YOUR MONEY

Annuities offer unique features and benefits not found in traditional or classic investments like stocks, mutual funds, and bonds. In addition, the annuity contract is more restrictive.

However, one of my biggest peeves across the product is the lack of liquidity. Annuities require a specific investment period. Many minimums are 7 years and some are blindingly longer before investors can start receiving income from the account. During the accumulation phase, the annuity contract may allow for an annual 10% withdrawal of original principal, however if the investor really needs to tap into the funds and withdraw more than 10% the penalties are severe.

Additionally, many annuities offer other insurance type products including death benefits; some of the variable annuities noted earlier offer built-in riders for insurance. The contract may include a death benefit ("basic life insurance") with a guarantee to pass money to a beneficiary in a lump sum or overtime. However, like all riders in annuities, the investor must pay for the additional insurance. The alternative would be to buy a much cheaper life insurance policy outside of the annuity.

## EVALUATION OF RETURNS: INVESTMENT OPTIONS INSIDE OF VARIABLE ANNUITIES

Though "guaranteed," a variable annuities return may be much less than traditional investments like stocks and bonds over time. Prior to entering a multiyear contract, investors should compare other investment alternatives. For example, fixed annuities provide guaranteed interest, but the insurance company may reset the rate annually, perhaps below what investors can get from investing on their own in government, municipal, or corporate bonds or other plain-vanilla fixed rate investments.

The account values of variable annuities generally follow the performance of the subaccounts' underlying investments—bonds, mutual funds, stocks, or money markets. However management fees, operating expenses and other charges that are associated with variable annuities can reduce returns relative to directly investing over time. In addition each subaccount manager should be evaluated on performance fees similar to an evaluation of any other pooled investment of mutual fund.

Let's take a look at the returns of traditional indexed annuities; in many cases the return is calculated from a benchmark rate of return minus a fee that can include a margin, a spread or an administrative fee. For example, if the benchmark index rose 8% and the fee was 3%, you would receive a 5% rate of return. A few percentage points over time can make a significant difference in an investor's overall return. Let's compare $100,000 invested in the S&P 500 Index versus buying a hypothetical annuity for 30 years ended December 31, 2013. The annuity offers 100% participation to the S&P 500 Index with an annual 3% minimum guaranteed rate of return and cap of 10%:

Investment of $100k: S&P 500 versus Annuity

| | Amount Invested 12/31/1982 | Time Horizon | Annualized Return | Ending Value 12/31/13 |
|---|---|---|---|---|
| S&P 500 Index | $100,000 | 30 Years | 10.79% | $2,164,428 |
| Index Annuity | $100,000 | 30 Years | 7.40% | $851,409 |

Additionally, some of the annuities tie their performance to an index that does not include dividends or their reinvestment; therefore, although very obvious, the annuities return will be significantly lower than an index with dividends reinvested over time. A number of companies promote "S&P-like" returns without including dividend. This type of marketing is deceiving the investor who thinks he is purchasing an investment that is matching the benchmark return, and they will most likely not ask if dividends will be included as part of their investment. Note this occurred in the previous Jackson National product sold to our client Fred.

## FEE AND CHARGES

Annuities generally come with more protections and guarantees than other investment vehicles, such as mutual funds, but at a cost. Annual expenses for variable annuities can be much higher than the expenses for a similar portfolio of mutual funds. Annuities often carry high, ongoing fees when compared to traditional investments such as mutual funds.

## Commissions

For starters, most annuities are sold by insurance brokers or other salespeople who collect a steep commission—as much as 10% or so.

Beware of the surrender charge: Some annuities have ridiculously high initial surrender charges that can be as high as 20% if withdrawn in early contract years, but check your contract's rules and federal law before you surrender, because some annuities will allow you to withdraw up to 10% of your initial investment annually without having to pay the surrender charge.

If you decide to withdraw from the contract within the first five to seven years that you own the annuity, you probably will owe the insurance company a charge of between 7% and 10% of your withdrawal amount. That is a pretty stiff penalty to get your own money back. Typically, that penalty fee declines by one percentage point a year until it gets to zero after year seven or eight. The surrender charges are to pay the insurance company back because, upon execution of the contract, the insurance company pays the agent for the sale of the annuity. The agent does not follow up on the investment strategy deployed—he simply moves on to the next sales victim. Additionally, if you make withdrawals before you reach age 59½, you will be required to pay Uncle Sam a 10% early withdrawal penalty as well as regular income tax on your investment earnings. (The amount you contributed to the annuity will not be taxed.)

## High Annual Fees

If you invest in a variable annuity you'll also encounter high annual expenses. You will have an annual insurance charge that can run 1.25% or more; annual investment management fees, which range anywhere from 0.5% to more than 2%; and fees for various insurance riders, which can add another 0.6% or more. The only ones that benefit from the fees are the annuity salesman and the annuity providers.

Add them up, and you could be paying 3.5% to 4% a year, if not more. That could take a huge bite out of your retirement nest egg, and in some cases even cancel out some of the benefits of an annuity. Compare that to a regular mutual fund that charges an average of 1.00% a year, or index funds that charge less than 0.50% a year.

The following chart highlights some common separately charged fees and their impact on a $100,000 investment in a variable annuity.

| Variable Annuity Expense Description | Annual Expense | Annual Expense in Dollars |
|---|---|---|
| Mortality and expense risk | 1.25% | $ 1,250.00 |
| Administrative fees | 0.15% | $ 150.00 |
| Optional guaranteed minimum death benefit rider | 0.61% | $ 610.00 |
| Optional guaranteed lifetime withdrawal benefit rider | 1.03% | $ 1,030.00 |
| Fund expense for underlying mutual funds | 0.94% | $ 940.00 |
| Total Cost | 3.98% | $ 3,980.00 |

The mortality and risk expense pays for the guarantee, sales commissions, and administrative expenses associated with the contract.

The optional minimum death benefit rider is for purchasing life insurance. An investor can purchase term life outside of the annuity for much less than 0.61% annually.

The optional lifetime withdrawal rider provides guaranteed income in retirement through a "withdrawal benefit" that is protected regardless of how the market performs.

Eliminating the three fees above leaves an investor with an approximate appropriate cost of 1.09%; there are a number of companies that will provide annuity products for approximately 1.25% total fees today.

The withdrawal charge is a schedule lasting seven completed years following each premium as shown below, and there are two optional withdrawal charge schedules (that are shorter) available (state variations may apply), also shown in the graphic:

Withdrawal charge (as a percentage of premium payments)

| | Completed Years Since Receipt of Premium | | | | | | | |
|---|---|---|---|---|---|---|---|---|
| | 1 | 2 | 3 | 4 | 5 | 6 | 7 | 7+ |
| Base Schedule | 8.5% | 7.5% | 6.5% | 5.5% | 5.0% | 4.0% | 2.0% | 0% |
| Five-year Schedule | 8.0% | 7.0% | 6.0% | 4.0% | 2.0% | 0% | 0% | 0% |
| Three-year Schedule | 7.5% | 6.5% | 5.0% | 0% | 0% | 0% | 0% | 0% |

Not all annuities have high fees; some investment companies sell annuities without M&E fees and riders and without charging a sales commission or a surrender charge. These are called direct-sold annuities, because unlike an annuity sold by a traditional insurance company, there is no insurance agent involved. With the agent out of the picture, there is no need to charge a commission. Firms that sell low-cost annuities include Fidelity, Vanguard, Schwab, T. Rowe Price, Ameritas Life, and TIAA-CREF.

## Fiduciary Standard of Care

In a fiduciary relationship, one person vests confidence, good faith, reliance, and trust in another whose aid, advice, or protection is sought in some matter. In such a relationship, good conscience requires the fiduciary to act at all times for the sole benefit and interest of the one who trusts. The fiduciary standard versus suitability debate will continue in regards to appropriateness of an annuity contract as part of a balanced investment portfolio.

Most investors do not understand what a fiduciary relationship means, and the process to educate them will take years. Most investors don't know the difference between a broker dealer, an insurance salesman, and an independent financial advisor. In order to make the difference clearly understood, the investor must carry out significant research.

## OPTIONS IF YOU ALREADY OWN AN ANNUITY

Should I exchange my current annuity for a new one, known as the 1035 exchange?

Be especially cautious if an annuity salesperson suggests you should exchange your existing annuity for a new annuity. This may be the only way the salesperson can generate additional fees. Read all the sales documents yourself and make sure you are aware of every potential fee. Never rely on the salesperson's explanation alone. You should ask for an annuity cost comparison report where your agent should be able to clearly document the current contract's expenses and surrender charges versus the new contract costs. You should exchange your annuity only when it is better for you and not better for the person selling the new annuity contract. Exchanges are known as 1035 swaps, after the section of the IRS code that regulates them. An insurance salesperson may tell you a 1035 swap is a great deal, because it allows you to get the features of a new annuity without incurring any taxes. What you might not be told is that the exchange earns a fat sales commission for the insurance agent.

What's more, by moving into a new annuity, you will start a new surrender period. For example, say you have owned an annuity for 10 years. You probably could close out your account without paying a surrender charge. But if you swap that annuity for a new one, you may be hit with a surrender charge.

The 1035 swap is not all negative; one appealing aspect is the tax-deferred growth of the funds in accumulation. Money that you invest in an annuity grows tax-deferred. When you eventually make withdrawals, the amount you contributed to the annuity is not taxed, but your earnings are taxed at your regular income tax rate.

But again depending on your tax status, an additional negative is that the gains in an annuity portfolio are taxed as ordinary income, for most investors the long-term capital gains tax rate is lower. Also, unlike traditional life insurance payouts the gains on the death benefit payouts may be fully taxable. Of course, with any structured investment you should consult with your financial and tax advisor before making any long-term decision—particularly with the purchase of an annuity, which imposes harsh penalties for any contract changes or withdrawals.

## WHEN SHOULD YOU CONSIDER USING AN ANNUITY?

Typically, you should consider an annuity only after you have maxed out other tax-advantaged retirement investment vehicles, such as 401(k) plans and IRAs. One of the biggest advantages as a result of the very dated 1986 tax laws, an investment in an annuity allows you to put away a large amount of cash and defer paying taxes. Unlike other tax-deferred retirement accounts such as 401(k)s and IRAs, there is no annual contribution limit for an annuity, which allows you to put away more money for retirement, and is particularly useful for those that are closest to retirement age and need to catch up their savings.

If you have additional money to set aside for retirement, an annuity's tax-free growth may make sense—especially if you are in a high-income tax bracket today. All the money you invest compounds year after year without any tax bill from Uncle Sam. That ability to keep every dollar invested and working for you can be a big advantage over taxable investments. When you cash out, you can choose to take a lump-sum payment from your annuity, but many retirees prefer to set up guaranteed payments for a specific length of time or the rest of your life, providing a steady stream of income. Additionally, the annuity can serve as a complement to other retirement income sources, such as Social Security and pension plans.

Sometimes annuities are sold to unsuspecting investors inside of IRA or other retirement vehicle. It is probably not a good idea to hold an annuity inside of an IRA. Since one of the main advantages of an annuity is that your money grows tax-deferred, it makes little sense to hold one in an account like an IRA, which is already tax-deferred. It's a little like wearing a raincoat indoors or a belt and suspenders. There are a few exceptions. If you're retired or very close to retiring and you feel you need more guaranteed income than Social Security will provide, it can make sense to use a portion of your 401(k) or IRA money to buy an immediate annuity that will pay income for life.

## RECENT DEVELOPMENTS WITH ANNUITIES

The following excerpt from *Investment News* says that now the Treasury and the IRS are onboard saying it is OK to put annuities in your 401(k)! This is absurd! Read on:

**Investment News** (Schoeff 2014)
The Treasury Department and IRS approval of the use of annuities in target date funds in 401(k) plans, including as a default investment, will make lifetime-income features more popular and help

ensure that droves of baby boomers don't outlive their nest egg, industry officials and experts say.

The Department of Treasury released guidance for plan sponsors on how they can expand the use of deferred-income annuities, providing a special rule that allows defined-contribution plans to offer target date funds that include annuities among their assets.

Treasury will permit deferred annuities to be offered at prices that vary with a participant's age. That means discrimination rules would no longer apply if the plan includes both people who are younger than the age limit for the annuity and those who qualify for the annuity.

The department also will allow retirement plan participants to mix annuities with other savings vehicles.

"Instead of having to devote all of their account balance to annuities, employees use a portion of their savings to purchase guaranteed income for life while retaining other savings in other investments," Treasury said in a statement.

The agencies' moves will make plan sponsors more comfortable adding retirement-income guarantees, said Jason Roberts, chief executive of the Pension Resource Institute. This does not seem logical.

"It's making it like target date on steroids," she said. "The idea of guaranteed income for life is very powerful. Something needed to be done to enable 401(k)s to do their jobs. I've seen a lot of mediocre retirement plans out there." This is scary, potentially packing junk into 401k plans. Ms. Prince supports Treasury's effort to boost retirement security, but said that while the new TDF rules "sound good on paper," it remains to be seen whether they will be effective. "There are a lot of unanswered questions," she said. "It depends on how [a plan] is constructed, how well it's explained to participants and the fees."

Is this really a good thing, having fee-laden annuity products inside of a 401(k) and available in other company retirement plans? Most investors don't have a clue as to what basic mutual funds to choose in their plans, let alone a complicated insurance product. Again, given today's rate structure, it would be difficult for someone to get any return buying a fixed annuity.

A few years back, I identified a relatively sound solution that provides inflation protection and is safer than an annuity. Buy US Series

I Bonds annually. Series I bonds can be purchased free using US Treasury Direct.

The current rate set as of May 1 is zero, as of November 1, 2014 it was 1.48%. The next rate will be reset on November 1, 2015.

## SAVINGS BONDS: LITTLE-KNOWN GOOD DEAL

Tired of low interest rates? Money market funds and one-year bank certificates of deposit pay less than 1%. Pretty lame.

But the much-ignored US savings bond Series I (meaning it tracks inflation) is a pretty good antidote to the low-rate blues. Because the bond is backed by Washington, it is very safe.

The current 30-year savings bond pays 3.06% over six months. That's comparable to the annual yield on a 30-year Treasury, which doesn't have the virtue of adjusting its rate to follow the Consumer Price Index, as the savings bond does. The government issues an inflation-tracking bond, called a Treasury Inflation-Protected Security, or TIPS. But due to strong demand, the 30-year TIPS yields less than the comparable savings bond.

Savings bonds are far less popular than they used to be. People bought $1.5 billion in savings bonds during 2011, about a fourth of the amount sold 10 years before. Part of the reason may be that you can trade a standard Treasury bond on the open market, any time you like. Savings bonds can only be redeemed from the US Treasury after 12 months, and if you do so early (within five years), you pay a penalty by forfeiting the most recent three months' interest.

Another factor is that, four years ago, the government reduced the maximum yearly purchase to $10,000 from $30,000. The $10k annual restriction makes it difficult for the high-net-worth investors to make a difference in their portfolio; however, duplicating an investment annually for a husband and wife can build a portfolio to over $250,000 over a 10-year period. One bond costs a mere $25, and is sold at face value. Maybe savings bonds' withered appeal also stems from their stodgy image: First issued during the Great Depression, they for decades were a favorite gift to grandchildren, about as welcome as a new pair of socks.

But so what? Many investors are missing out on a great opportunity. There are other types of savings bonds that pay far less than the inflation-linked kind, such as the Series EE (0.6%). The Series I variety is a no-brainer purchase.

Rates for I bonds change each six months, reset on May 1 and Nov. 1. So the 3.06% earnings rate for I bonds bought from November 2011 through April 2012 also will apply for the succeeding six months after the issue date.

Series I bonds were introduced in 1998. Interest accrues monthly and compounds semiannually for 30 years, and the interest is tax-deferred until the bond is redeemed

You can buy, manage, and redeem I Bonds online by setting up an account with the government's Web purchasing service, called TreasuryDirect. Starting this year, the bonds are no longer issued in paper form, a move to save printing costs. TreasuryDirect account owners may convert their Series E, EE, and I paper savings bonds to electronic securities. (*Exception:* You can still get paper bonds if they are purchased using part or all of one's tax refund.) For more information on this feature, visit www.irs.gov.

The bonds are exempt from state and local income tax. Plus, there are additional tax benefits when the interest is used for education expenses. Qualified taxpayers can exclude earned interest from their gross income. Eligible education expenses include tuition and fees.

In closing this chapter, I will conclude with why you don't need an annuity, how to protect yourself, and a few questions to ask yourself and the annuity salesperson. In summary, you don't need an annuity:

1. *If you can manage the money yourself or have hired a suitable professional.* Annuities should only be owned for their contractual guarantees, so if you are adept at managing your own money and feel comfortable performing that task, then you should not deviate from that plan. If you have an adviser who has proven themselves to be really good at managing your money, then consider yourself fortunate and stay the course with that professional.

2. *If you don't need additional lifetime income.* As noted earlier, annuities were created in Roman times for pension-type lifetime income guarantee. Even though variable and indexed annuities can be unbelievable complex and unfortunately represent the

vast majority of annuities sold each year, the primary reason that most people should own an annuity is to solve for longevity risk (i.e., outliving your money). If you don't see yourself needing additional income guarantees for the rest of your life and you are pretty good at managing your own money, then you probably have no need for an annuity.

3. *If you want equity market growth.* Annuities aren't growth products, regardless of the brokers' hypothetical growth dreams that are overly promoted. Even the best no-load variable annuities have limited investment choices and restrictions on moving the money between separate accounts (i.e., mutual funds). Indexed annuities were designed to compete with CDs, and their historical returns noted earlier reflect the realistic return percentages, and also noted today's interest rates are ridiculously low to purchase fixed annuities. Load variable annuities have limitations and restrictions from an investment standpoint, and their typical high fees severely eat into any annual returns.

4. *If you want everything packed into one product.* Riders are attached benefits that you can add (with an annual fee for the life of the contract) to some annuity policies to try to solve for solutions like lifetime income, legacy, or long-term care. Insurance carriers and their agents love to promote these one-size-fits-all product scenarios, but you are best served by solving for one solution at a time with any annuity strategy. In most cases, the contractual guarantees are higher when you implement a single focus solution. The more isn't the merrier with annuities.

5. *If you are only being shown one product from one insurance carrier.* Because annuities should be owned for their contractual guarantees, you should always shop numerous carriers for the solution you are looking to solve for. It is a good practice to shop around just like you would for any product. It is also important to remember that annuity guarantees are only as good as the company backing them up, so do your homework on the safety of the carrier.

Annuities have some significant drawbacks, and brokers recommending variable annuities must explain to you the important facts—including liquidity issues where you must be willing to sock away the money for years, potential surrender charges and other fees, as well tax penalties for withdrawal, mortality and expense charges, administrative charges, investment advisory fees, and, of course, market risk. As already noted, if you purchase a variable annuity, ongoing investment management and other fees often amount to close to 4% a year. These fee structures can be complex and unclear. Insurance agents and others who sell them may tout the positive features and downplay the drawbacks, so make sure that you ask a lot of questions and carefully review the annuity plan first. Before you invest, you should compare their fee structure with regular no-load mutual funds, which levy no sales commission or surrender charge and impose average annual expenses of less than 0.5% (for index funds) or about 1.0% (actively managed funds), and determine whether you might be better off going that route on your own.

If the sales pitch sounds too good to be true, then write down in detail exactly how you think the annuity being proposed is going to work according to what the agent said. Then sign and date that list, and have the agent sign and date it as well so you can have the agent fully endorse the recommendation. This is just an effective and simple idea to fully flush out the contractual realities of the policy. If you are getting pressured into buying or a red flag is raised for any reason, then it's probably best to move on. Ask the salesperson: How long will my money be tied up? Will you be paid a commission or receive other compensation for selling the annuity? How much? What are the risks my investment could decrease in value?

And finally, ask yourself, am I already contributing the maximum to my 401(k) plan and other tax-deferred retirement plans? Do I have a long-term investment objective? Am I going to need the money before the surrender period ends? Will I need the money before 59 1/2? Do I fully understand how the variable annuity works, the benefits it provides, and the charges I have to pay? Have I read and understood the prospectus? Are there special features provided such as added long-term care insurance that I don't need? Have I shopped around and compared the features of variable annuities, such as sales load and other fees and expenses? Do I understand the effect annuity payments could have on my tax status? If I am purchasing a variable annuity within an IRA, do I understand that IRAs already provide tax-deferred savings? Am I being pressured into making a quick purchase?

Hopefully, the chapter was able to point out the strengths and many weaknesses of annuities. On the surface, annuities seem like a safe asset allocation and, as noted, prey on investors' fears during market volatility. However, as mentioned throughout this chapter, there are many drawbacks that aren't obvious to the average investor. Be sure to thoroughly research and ask many questions before purchasing an annuity.

**CHAPTER 8**

# IS THE MOST IMPORTANT PROFESSIONAL IN YOUR LIFE EVEN A PROFESSIONAL?*

## John Burke[‡]

## MY START AS A BROKER

"Welcome to Prudential Securities; here is your desk, good luck."
That was my abrupt introduction to the second brokerage firm
I worked for. I was not yet 30 years old. I had trained elsewhere, so
I wasn't coming in completely inexperienced, but I soon found out
that the brand-new reps got only a little more training than I did—
basically, just enough to help them study for and pass the Series 7
exam, something most of them did in three months.

I joined Prudential Securities in 1988 as a vice president. Functionally, my position was financial advisor, responsible for financial
planning and all investment advice for my 200 clients.

It was a lot of responsibility. If you, the client, are healthy, your
financial advisor is more important than any other professional in your
life. Even if you're not, he or she is more important than your accountant, architect, attorney, dentist, mortgage banker, or insurance rep.

Your financial advisor's advice will determine what kind of college
your children attend. Your financial advisor's advice will determine
not only when you will retire, but also your standard of living in
retirement. Will you eat at home every night, or can you afford to eat
out? Will you be able to travel? Will you get the best medical care?

Despite the importance of the position, financial advisors are more
often than not uneducated in their field. Typically, even today, it takes
just a few months to get a license. Given how important a financial advisor is, the position should require more than a few months
of training.

Financial advising is the youngest of professions—if we can call it
a profession at all. Until May 1, 1975, commissions were the standard
form of payment. That date is called May Day in the brokerage world
because that is when fixed commissions were relaxed, and an advisor's
performance actually started to influence his or her earnings. Until
May Day, if you wanted to buy 100 shares of IBM, you were charged
the same commission wherever you went. Stock brokers sold shares
and executed trades; there was no incentive to add value by including
financial advice.

Philip Loomis, Commissioner of the Securities Exchange
Commission, commented in a June 1975 speech that prior to May

Day, "the New York Stock Exchange established the rate ... some years ago, the studies on which these rates were based included a fairly generous allowance for the compensation of salesmen who were expected to generate such orders" (Loomis 1975). Rates were deregulated, he said, because a separate market had developed, away from the New York Stock Exchange, which the Exchange, "in its more uncharitable moments, referred to (this market) as a 'parasite.'" In other words, market forces finally forced the SEC to deregulate.

These market forces moved at a glacial pace. When I got my license in 1984, commissions were generally 2% or more for stocks and up to 3% for bonds.

Investors did not even have the choice of paying advisors a fee (as a percentage of assets or hourly). I could even earn a commission of as much as 8.5% on certain products. It was a salesman's world.

As part of my initial training, I spent two months in Manhattan with new brokers from all over the country. I use the term "training" loosely. We were told to cold call and were given help finding lists of prospective customers. We sat in a very large "bullpen," one cubicle after the next lined up in a room with close to 100 advisors. Like the brokerage firm in the movie *Wall Street*, the atmosphere was far from professional.

When I sold my first big investment ($50,000, earning a $2,500 commission), the training manager came over and stood on my desk, wing-tipped shoes and all, announcing the sale to a loud ovation. He later brought me a chocolate cake.

Meanwhile, the financial planning profession had gotten off to a slow start. Even in 1984, nine years after May Day, we were nearly all brokers or salesmen, functionally, and few of us were giving consideration to planning or something approaching a professional relationship with our clients. The newly formed International Association of Financial Planners graduated its first class of 42 students in 1973 (Brandon 2009), but the certification did not gain momentum until much later. As told in *The History of Financial Planning*, "before financial planners could help the public, they had to help themselves create a credible profession. They faced substantial hurdles."

Among those hurdles were a lack of university studies and classes in the field, a lack of funding, and, until May Day 1975, a total lack of interest from stock brokers due to a lack of incentives. May Day would unleash competitive forces upon Wall Street, slowly forcing brokers to become something other than stock salesmen.

My career began nine years after May Day in 1984 and the office I started in resembled a scene right out of the 1987 movie *Wall Street*. Merrill's Staten Island office had four veteran producers and about a dozen of us new guys and one woman. We spent the day cold-calling, selling product. Selling anything with a commission of less than 4% simply didn't interest us; we had to make quotas. The quotas were not based on the number of clients or even assets that were brought in—they were based on commissions.

Because the odds were not with us when it came to making our quotas, most of us would be let go within five years. Though I had a degree in finance, that was unusual, and in the end, irrelevant. I was hired because of my success as a door-to-door salesman the summer before, between my junior and senior years at college. A successful sales record in another industry was the typical entree.

We received little support. I shared a sales assistant with six or seven other advisors. I shared a Quotron machine with another advisor. From this device, I could get quotes and client positions but little else. Posting of cost basis was done daily, into a written record, which was called our "book" of business. I can remember my manager inspecting our books, and if we did not post in a timely fashion, he would dump the loose-leaf pages all over the floor.

## PRESSURE TO GENERATE BUSINESS

We were under tremendous pressure. Once a week, the manager would send out a list with each of our names and our total commissions for the week. Most of us were young and worked long hours. Our motivation was simple: commissions, so we could keep our jobs. There was certainly nothing resembling professionalism. And none of us were doing any financial planning.

Even my stock picks came from analysts' recommendations. I was 22 years old. I did not know how to construct a stock portfolio and no training into how was offered. I had to pick from a large list of "favorites" from the analysts. As time went by, I started to track the analysts' picks. Returns were not good, and worse, it seemed like there was too much activity. Sell recommendations were too frequent, which was good for commissions but not for client returns. Eventually, training programs were offered, but they were certainly not required and most did not take them.

Still, outside forces were gradually forcing change upon us. May Day was having an effect—all of us were losing clients to discount brokers, something that did not exist until 1975. In 1975, the so-called wirehouses, such as Prudential, had a 100% market share of investments.[1] The wirehouses resisted change—but to a certain extent, we, the brokers, did not. Slowly but surely, we started taking courses to become a Certified Financial Planner™ (CFP©) or Chartered Financial Consultant (ChFC), despite the wirehouses' absence of leadership, and despite any direct financial incentives.

Donald Priti, president of financial publisher Arthur Weisenberger and advisor to IAFP (the International Association of Financial Planners), recalled that the early years were "difficult ... The existing financial companies wouldn't return our phone calls, much less see us" (Brandon 2009).

But if the companies could not see a need to change, advisors could. We were losing business to discounters. To earn a living, we needed to be more than salespeople, because the products we were selling were becoming easier and easier for customers to invest in without paying us commissions. We did not want to call ourselves brokers; we wanted to be known as financial advisors.

Further, those of us who wanted to be part of the newest profession wanted to distance ourselves from salespeople, especially the worst of them. At Prudential, the welcome was short and training even shorter. The manager's office had a revolving door. In my seven years there, I had seven different managers. And with such turnover, scrutiny of the sales force was lacking.

This is where I learned firsthand how bad things could be for clients when they hired the wrong advisor. Though it is hard for

---

[1]Wirehouses got their name from the way trades were made—over a wire to the stock exchange.

one advisor to judge another's stewardship of client money, there is an opportunity to see another advisor's work when they leave. The accounts from departing advisors are reassigned to the remaining advisors. Often, I was startled to find out how clients had been treated.

My first experience getting someone else's reassigned accounts were those from Jeff, an advisor I knew from playing softball. Jeff had a gambling problem. While he had forsaken the casinos, he made his accounts his own little gamble. He would drop a bunch of trades in client accounts, without authorization. He was gambling that they would be profitable and would use this line: "The trade was a mistake but since it worked out, do you want me to leave it in the account?" Jeff's incentive for this scheme was financial—the commissions.

It was the 1990s, and stocks were going up, so Jeff lasted a while, but when Reebok cratered after he had gambled with a bunch of Reebok buys (unsolicited and unauthorized as was his scheme), he was out. When the accounts were assigned to me, I was told to not get involved with the unsolicited trades. The firm did not want to automatically make the client whole—they would do so only if forced and they did not want me forcing the issue (taking the clients' side).

This was not the first nor last time I was advised against helping clients.

The most shocking experience I had with reassigned accounts was with those from Mike, who had done more damage than to just place a few unauthorized trades. Mike was not a friend to any of us. He was so absolute in not making eye contact that it was difficult to have even the shortest conversation with him. And he spoke very softly.

But Mike messed up some lives in a very loud way. He concocted a means to make huge commissions without bringing in any new clients or even churning accounts, the most common type of client abuse. Mike was more inventive than other rogue brokers that I had met.

## WHY YOU DON'T INVEST WITH BORROWED MONEY

Mike had his clients margin (borrow) against current positions to buy more commissionable product. While it is possible that margin can increase returns if the assets make more than the interest charged, it magnifies the risk as well as the commissions. Worse, he convinced clients that their investments were worth the gross value, not the net value after deducting the amount borrowed and interest paid. That is, clients consented to borrow against their investments to buy more funds. But that created a gross value (one that did not net out the debt) and a net value (a value with the debt netted out). Mike convinced clients that they could effectively ignore the debt.

After he was fired, some of his clients were reassigned to me. One of them was a retired priest who had invested his life savings. Mike had mismanaged the investments because he was in it for the commissions. The priest's investments had declined and he didn't even know it; he thought that his investments were worth the gross value.

I explained to the priest that there was one number, the larger number that was the gross value, and another number, which was less, because the debt was subtracted out. When he realized his investments were only worth the smaller number, he was devastated. After our meeting was over, I saw him walking in circles outside the building. Watching the priest helped me realize that I wanted to be entirely different than Mike.

I learned that Mike found another brokerage firm to hire him because of his ability to generate commissions, which are shared by the brokerage firm.

Over time, I have realized that lonely, elderly people were the most vulnerable to the likes of Mike. Mike would visit and spend time, and this encouraged the clients to look the other way on questionable trades. Or perhaps they liked Mike so much for spending time with them that they were blind to his transgressions.

Many of us took steps to differentiate ourselves from advisors like Mike. But there was certainly no wirehouse requirement to move in this direction. I spent another 10 years at wirehouses, admittedly unable to say no to the "prestige" they offered in the industry. I believed the scorn they heaped on advisors who didn't work for wirehouses. And I should have been more suspicious after each of the two wirehouses I worked at after Prudential greeted me the same way on my first day: "Here is your desk. Good luck."

Face it; neither brokers nor financial advisors are saints. We go to work to get paid like everyone else. But over time, I came to realize that if I worried about more about my clients' welfare than I worried about making money, the money would take care of itself.

But that was not the culture at the wirehouses. In fact, there was no culture at all. Shouldn't there have been some effort to create a culture? There may have been a fancy advertising slogan like "we make money the old fashioned way—we earn it" but it was an empty slogan. If there was to be a culture of "earning" it, there should have been policy or training that made it true. There wasn't. There was nothing that these firms did, policy wise or through training that was taught to new hires, regardless of their prior experience.

For my own part, I accepted large bonus checks with each of my moves, before leaving the wirehouse environment almost 10 years ago. (The practice of paying these bonuses is still common. The wirehouses pay up large bonuses to attract veterans with a large list of clients.)

It took me 21 years to leave the wirehouse environment and in the early years after I left, I frequently questioned myself—why did it take so long? The principle reason is that the alternatives were not very attractive. It took a long time for companies like Charles Schwab, Fidelity, Raymond James, and LPL Financial to offer financial advisors a viable alternative to wirehouses.

## HAS THE INDUSTRY MADE ANY PROGRESS?

Is the commissioned broker still the norm? I go back to *The History of Financial Planning* for the answer. They asked the question in 2009: "Forty years after financial planning's inception, had the dream of a dream of a profession been realized? Was financial planning on par with the traditional professions of law, medicine, and theology? Was it in fact 'the first new profession in four hundred years'"? (Brandon 2009)

Before I get to their answer, consider again that the financial-planning profession can both help people more and hurt them more than other professions, save your doctor. The financial advisor's recommendations will determine how early you can retire, the quality of life that you have in retirement—and even whether you'll outlive your money.

When I discuss this at conferences with my peers, especially when I point out how important it is to give good investment advice, I am often asked, somewhat defensively, isn't it the responsibility of the brokerage firm to invest well, and not the advisor?

To some extent, yes, the financial advisor normally passes on the responsibility of security selection (choosing which specific bond or stock to buy) to a portfolio manager. Security selection, however, is the least important aspect of investing. Much more significant is asset allocation—deciding how much to put into stocks and how to put into bonds, whether a mutual fund is recommended or portfolio of stocks—and that's a financial advisor's job. It's the financial advisor who interviews the client to determine how much risk is appropriate, not the fund manager. The financial advisor plays that most important role in guiding the client to the appropriate amount of risk.

In 1986, an award-winning article by Gary P. Brinson, L. Randolph Hood, and Gilbert L. Beebower determined that asset allocation was responsible for 93% of a portfolio's return (Brinson 1995). The article received much attention and even debate, but the basic concept is really not debatable. How much an investor puts in stocks rather than bonds is far more important than which stocks or which bonds. How much money goes into junk bonds instead of safer bonds is more important than which highly leveraged or AAA-rated ones are chosen.

The financial advisor and the client jointly, or in many cases, the financial advisor alone, determines how much money to put in bonds, how much to put in junk bonds, how much to put in stocks or how much to put in foreign stocks.

The asset allocator answers all of the important questions: Should the client buy small-company stocks or large-company stocks? Should the client use index funds? Which investments should go into an Individual Retirement Account and which should go into the taxable account? If a client needs money, where should it be taken from? Where should new deposits go? These are asset allocation decisions, and they are made between the client and the advisor, not by the fund manager or someone in the home office of a brokerage firm. The advisor can and usually does hire someone else to pick the stocks or bonds, but the crucial asset allocation decisions are made by the advisor and the client.

The advisor therefore needs to be very qualified and should put forth every effort to make sure the asset allocation decisions are well thought out and researched. Have financial advisors realized this, accepted the increased and large responsibility, and advanced past their commission-based roots? Are financial advisors becoming professional in their approach to investing?

The evidence is mixed. A *Journal of Financial Planning* article, "Reducing Wealth Volatility: The Value of Financial Advice as Measured by Zeta," studied results from a US Bureau of Labor Statistics survey (Grable 2014). Respondents were repeatedly interviewed over many years, but in 2006, a retirement module was added to the survey in which questions were asked about their wealth.

In the retirement module, respondents were asked whether or not they had asked a financial advisor for help. Wealth was measured again in 2007 and 2009, providing an opportunity to compare the change in wealth of those who had gotten help from a financial advisor and those who had not. And the period covered the Great Recession.

The conclusion? Those who had met with a financial advisor increased their wealth by a cumulative 3.31% over a four-year period as compared to those who had not met with an advisor. Helpful, but not significantly so.

Dalbar, a research firm, releases a study each year showing investor results as compared to various indices. In one of those studies (Dalbar 2006), Dalbar compared the results of those who had an advisor to the results of those who did not. Similar to the survey by the Department of Labor, results were better for those who had an advisor, but not by much.

Neither the *Journal* article nor the Dalbar study tries to differentiate between the results of advisors who were commissioned-based or sales-oriented and those who might be considered professionals. It would be interesting to see investment results comparing those two sets of advisors.

## IS FINANCIAL ADVISORY A PROFESSION?

*The History of Financial Planning* is asking whether financial advisors attained the status of professionals.

The authors conclude that, well, there's really no conclusion, at least not yet. Even within the ranks of financial advisors, opinion remains divided. But they make an interesting point that it will not be the financial advisors who will ultimately answer this question, or even the government. "Bill Carter, who served on national boards of several financial-planning organizations in the 1980s and 1990s, spoke for many when he observed in 2008, 'We are in the baby stages of being a profession. But we don't determine if we are a profession. The public determines it'" (Brandon 2009).

That sounds good, but I'm just not sure it's right. So let me try to answer the question throughout the rest of this chapter.

My experience is that the public struggles with the question. I have worked with thousands of families as a financial advisor, for more than 30 years. In conducting initial interviews, I have found that people who ask the right questions are rare. People can judge the service level that they are getting, and that often becomes the only basis for whether they choose and stay with an advisor. Let me give you an example to illustrate my point.

Pat was a broker from the second wirehouse I worked at, what I call the rogue broker office. Pat was one of the most enjoyable people I have ever had the chance to be around. He laughed often, complemented people at every chance, remembered names, and liked to have fun. And his clients also liked him because he returned phone calls and called them frequently.

But for all his great qualities, Pat was not a hard worker, and he did not have enough clients because he did not put in much effort to recruit more. Like most brokers at that time, his income was based on commissions. He could increase his income if he did more trades.

Making a trade for a client strictly for the purpose of generating a commission is called *churning*. Clients may struggle deciding the difference between churning and making a legitimate trade. Where is the line drawn between the two?

In Pat's case, he ventured well into the realm of illegality because many of his trades were put through without the knowledge of his clients. It is clearly illegal to put in a commissioned trade without client authorization. That he was doing this was not obvious to me until after Pat left and some of his accounts were assigned to me. (Pat left before being fired and ended up doing time after he promoted a Ponzi scheme in his next job.)

In looking at Pat's account records, I could see frequent trading. The clients told me that they had not authorized the trades. Since I knew that confirmations would have been mailed, I asked them why they did not complain once they saw the confirmations. They said that because they trusted Pat, they felt he was doing this to help them.

Most statements do not show returns. They usually show the results of specific holdings, and how much the investments are up or down since the client bought them, but the statements usually do not show the returns. Worse, many statements show how an account is growing but include deposits as part of the "growth."

In Pat's case, it would have made it easier for clients to see if in fact Pat was working on their behalf if they could have seen the investment returns for the account. Showing returns on the statement make it harder for the advisor to twist the truth. If there are deposits and withdrawals, most clients cannot calculate the returns. If the returns aren't known, the advisor can dance around the facts by pointing to the winners and not the losers, for example.

More surprising to me, when I interviewed Pat's clients that were reassigned to me, none of them had an interest in pursuing any resolution of the losses from Pat's bad trades because, they told me, Pat was such a nice guy.

To the extent that clients hire us because we are nice guys or women, we are not professionals. Even if we are good at returning phone calls, making clients laugh, or are nice enough to send birthday cards, we are only professionals if we have pursued the knowledge we need to help clients with asset allocation and other important investment decisions. Being nice to the clients and being likeable are certainly desirable traits, and probably good for business, but those are not the traits that make us professionals.

What about the government? Does the government have an opinion as to whether we are professionals? Again, quoting from *The History of Financial Planning*, "Law professor Jonathan Macey told the *Journal of Financial Planning* in 2001, 'They don't. They're very compartmentalized—securities regulators worry about securities and insurance regulators worry about insurance. They don't really know what financial planning is and they certainly don't view it as this holistic profession like those practicing do'" (Brandon 2009).

The good news here is that since Macey made that quote, there has been change from the government, along the lines of helping investors. While the government has not demanded that financial advisors become professionals by requiring more education, they have moved to differentiate between those advisors who are salespeople and those who meet a fiduciary standard.

## WHY YOU WANT A FIDUCIARY

The fiduciary standard is a higher standard than that which is applied to commissioned salesmen. Commissioned salesmen merely must be truthful. The fiduciary standard requires that the advisor do what is in the best interests of the client, even if it means the advisor doesn't maximize his or her own earnings.

While commissioned salesmen do not have to meet the fiduciary standard, many of us do. For example, those who use the CFP® certification and charge a fee instead of a commission, must meet the fiduciary standard. This is how the CFP® Board puts it: "All CFP® professionals who provide financial planning services will be held to the duty of care of a fiduciary." (CFP Board) For the discerning public, a CFP® certification is helpful in discriminating between a salesman and a professional, but it is not the only professional designation for financial advisors—those are covered later at the end of this chapter.

Clearly one would rather work in a relationship defined by the fiduciary standard than one with only a standard of truthfulness. If Carter's observation that only the public can decide whether financial advisors have created a new profession is true, then certainly the advisor meeting the fiduciary standard is closer to that ideal.

The fiduciary standard is causing quite a stir within the profession. The Securities and Exchange Commission and the US Department of Labor are currently pushing for the fiduciary standard to be applied more frequently. Mary Jo White, the current head of the SEC, speaking at an industry conference, said it was her "personal view" the SEC should act to implement "uniform fiduciary" standards among the brokers and other financial professionals overseen by the agency (Baer 2015).

The Department of Labor is pushing to have the fiduciary standard applied to all qualified pension plans, which it regulates. To which the CFP® Board responded: "As a fervent advocate for strong fiduciary standards in the provision of investment advice, the CFP® Board is pleased to see the White House and Department of Labor take a critical step toward protecting American investors and their retirement savings through a fiduciary rule."

There are those within the industry fighting the standard, however. Many of us feel that there are situations where the fiduciary rule should not apply. Clients may insist on a commission-based structure, where they pay a commission and not a fee, because trades are infrequent. In those relationships, there may be years where there are no commissions. It would not seem fair to require a higher standard to that type of relationship because it is not a relationship between a professional and a client; rather, it is a relationship between a salesman and a customer.

For anyone who wants to have an ongoing relationship with a financial advisor, it seems to be common sense that they would like that financial advisor to act in accordance with the higher standard, the fiduciary standard.

For that part of my career that I was a wirehouse employee, I was encouraged to be a salesman and not a planner. Not only were there the lists ranking advisors' revenues, but we were encouraged to sell investment products that were more lucrative to the firm. In one instance, I was scolded by the firm's wholesaler (salesperson selling mutual funds) for not selling more profitable (to the brokerage firm) mutual funds.

I ignored the wholesaler, but shortly after that I was called into New York headquarters. The regional manager asked me why I wasn't selling the more profitable funds. I answered that I thought there was a conflict of interest because my compensation was higher for those funds. He got very angry and told me that I was not a team player.

Being a team player is a conflicting idea. All compensation should be aligned so that it is in the interests of the client. The team concept should not apply to loyalty between firm and employee; it should support a structure where the team's interests are in making happy clients.

Most of my clients have told us that they would like us to meet the fiduciary standard. The fiduciary standard is a desirable trait in the relationship between client and financial advisor. A financial advisor who accepts the fiduciary standard is closer to the "professional" ideal. Are there other traits that the public can look for to help distinguish between a professional financial advisor and a nonprofessional financial advisor?

Or put another way, how can you make sure the financial advisor is qualified, especially given the importance of their role in your life?

Good service and having a nice person as a financial advisor are good traits but those are traits most people can discern for themselves. What are the traits that are not so obvious?

This is a list of questions that I would recommend in conducting interviews with financial advisors, and in order of importance:

1. How many years of experience do you have?
2. What is the fee structure?
3. What designations do you have and what have you done to educate yourself in your profession? (A full list of designations is provided at the end of the chapter.)
4. What is your investment process?
5. Do you offer financial planning?
6. Do you offer reviews?
7. Who is your custody firm, and does it offer online access?
8. Does the custody firm calculate and make available investment returns?
9. Do you have any complaints on your CRD? If yes, what for?
10. How old are you?
11. Do you have a website?
12. What is your minimum fee or asset level?

Some of the questions, like the first one, are clear. But some require explanation:

## What Is the Fee Structure?

The fee structure can be commissioned-based, fee-based defined by a percentage fee applied to assets, or an hourly fee.

## What Is Your Investment Process?

The investment process is tricky because most people are not qualified to understand the answers. There are two aspects to the process. The first, is, who does the asset allocation and how much of a role can the client play in the allocation process? Advisors are either using a model supplied by someone else or they are doing it in their office. Usually, it is the latter and, if so, the qualifications of the people doing this are extremely important.

The second part of the investment process is security selection. As mentioned earlier, research shows that this is not as important but advisors often promote their process by showing how impressive the security selection is. That is, they promote the research and professional capabilities of someone else who is doing the security selection. They would normally be promoting mutual funds or separately managed accounts (SMAs). With SMAs, you actually own shares in stocks or directly own the bonds, and you can see them on your statement. The advisor, however, is not choosing the securities, and you have little or no say in which securities will go into the account(s).

The funds and SMAs have their own set of fees, so you have to be sure to ask about those fees, which are different from the advisor's fees.

In either case, I have never seen a fund manager or even an SMA manager that does the allocation for clients. Unless the advisor is using a model, someone else is doing the allocation.

There are two professional duties that you are looking for in an advisor—investment management and financial planning. They are clearly different jobs. Financial planning includes investment management, but planning is done as a way to answer a question. For example, you may ask, "How much do I have to save for retirement?" Or you may ask, "When can I retire to my current standard of living?"

Investment management is the job of finding appropriate investments. Most planners like to do the plan first to help them figure out what the appropriate investments are. There is far more consistency from one financial plan to the next than there is in the investment plan. That is, you will tend to get similar answers to questions about retirement from planners. But when you ask about the investment process, you are likely to get completely different answers from one advisor to the next.

## Do You Offer Reviews?

When advisors follow up with clients, it's called the "review" process. It may be done quarterly, semi-annually, or not at all. For most advisors, the size of the fee determines the frequency of the review, and this is only natural. All businesses provide different levels of service for different levels of fees. In any case, you want to know that someone is going to look at your investments and your plan on a regularly scheduled basis.

No matter what, you want the advisor to have a third party involved, called the custody firm. You don't want your advisor holding your money with the ability to commingle it with their own money or with their firm's money. Ever. Bernie Madoff did not have a third-party custodian for clients of his firm. In fact, any scheming financial advisor will find it far easier to steal your money if they are the custodian of your assets.

## Who Is Your Custody Firm, and Does It Offer Online Access?

The custody firm is the company holding your investments. It usually offers either a monthly or quarterly statement. You should also ask to have online access to your investment holdings. And never, ever, let the advisor change the street address on the account. One of the brokers from the "rogue broker office" got away with churning clients' accounts by switching their addresses to an address that he controlled. The clients were not getting confirmations showing the unauthorized trades.

## Do You Have Any Complaints on Your CRD? If Yes, What For?

All licensed advisors have a regulatory record at the Central Registration Depository, or CRD. The record is available for the public to see, but it would not be rude to ask the advisor at the initial interview if he or she has a record. While an advisor may have had an extraordinary case where a complaint was not fair, you should not do business with any advisor with many complaints, no matter how much you like the person. You can check the information at the Investment Advisor Public Disclosure website.

## How Old Are You?

It is also not rude to ask your advisor how old they are. Or, if you are uncomfortable with that question, you can ask them how many years the person is planning to work until retiring. And while you are on the subject, who would take over your accounts if the advisor retires—or worse, gets seriously ill or dies?

## What Is Your Minimum Fee or Asset Level?

Finally, it will be good to know if the advisor does take your business, how well do you fit in? If you don't meet the minimum, obviously the interview is over, but even if you do meet it, do you want to be in a practice where you barely meet the minimum? And if you are in that situation, is there an advisor assigned to handle smaller relationships?

## MORE THINGS TO CONSIDER WHEN YOU CHOOSE YOUR ADVISOR

Assets are the major consideration for advisors because unless fees are calculated on an hourly basis, there will be a strong correlation between the amount of assets under management (AUM) and fees. Clients with a small amount of assets, less than $200,000, may find it difficult to find an advisor. Their choice may be between an inexperienced advisor or perhaps one with a questionable record. One possible solution would be to work with a junior advisor working under the supervision of a mentor.

Finding an advisor is difficult for people. For me, it is like finding a doctor. I don't know medicine, so what's the best way to figure out the difference between a good doctor and a bad doctor? I mentioned this on my last visit to my dentist, and the hygienist laughed and told me how right I was. She said she often gets new patients who come in after they have moved or maybe when their doctor retires. The new patients will often brag about their dentist, but when she looks inside their mouths, she often sees bad fillings or overlooked issues.

Knowing, then, that people see what they want to see, how can you find an advisor capable of doing a sustainably good job once you've hired him or her? The questions listed earlier should help you get going. And common sense can guide you in determining your satisfaction with the level of service, and probably whether the financial planning issues are answered. But what about the investment advice?

Sadly, the simple answers don't work. Simplest of all is to compare your portfolio returns to a popular stock index like the Dow Jones Industrial Average or the Standard & Poor's 500 (S&P 500). But unless the portfolio is all stocks, this is a mismatch of asset classes. It is not even apples and oranges, it is more like apples and celery. Your portfolio probably has cash, bonds, foreign stocks, and maybe alternative investments such as REITs. Both the Dow Jones and the S&P 500 are pure stock indices.

Less simple and somewhat logical would be to construct a combination of benchmarks to mirror your portfolio. Let's say you have half stocks and half bonds. You could use an average of the S&P 500 and a popular bond index, the Barclays Aggregate Bond Index.

But even this more sophisticated approach has two big flaws. The first is that your portfolio, as noted above, probably has more than just US stocks and US bonds in it, making the approach too geographically simplistic. The second, more important flaw is that this method misses the forest for the trees, and ignores the most important element of the portfolio return—who chose the mix; the allocation of stocks and bonds (and alternatives), and how do you evaluate that decision?

A further problem in mixing benchmarks is that it leads to a moving of the target to match the result. That is, the advisor can find a benchmark that compares well with the results. The advisor can paint the target around the arrow.

Even Warren Buffett has been guilty of this. For many years, Mr. Buffett, the legendary CEO of Berkshire Hathaway, has told investors that for his company, investors should look at the book value to properly evaluate his performance. If the book value goes up more than the stock market, he says he is doing a good job.

After struggling to match the returns of the most commonly used stock market benchmark, the S&P 500, in his most recent annual report, Mr. Buffett has switched the benchmark, suggesting that the return of Berkshire Hathaway stock should be compared to the S&P 500 (Berkshire Hathaway). This is because Berkshire's book value is no longer keeping up with the benchmark, but the stock price, something Berkshire's managers have no control over, is keeping up. Conveniently for him, he switched.

While book value may have been a good measurement for Berkshire Hathaway, for investors, it's a moot point; there is no such measure for the portfolio. Investors need to worry about the returns of their portfolio and should start by demanding the reporting of the returns. If an investor is going to invest in a portfolio that is 100% US stocks, the S&P 500 is not a bad benchmark. But how can investors evaluate their returns if they have a mix of different types of investments?

## A BETTER WAY TO MEASURE RESULTS

There is a simple yet sophisticated solution.

Morningstar is a research firm that evaluates mutual funds. It records the returns of various classes of mutual funds (Morningstar Advisor Workstation). One of the classes is called "asset allocation funds." An asset allocation fund is a fund that invests in various types of investments, including US stocks of all sizes, US bonds, foreign stocks of all sizes, foreign bonds, REITs, and possibly even derivatives, depending on the fund. Such a fund is comparable to a diversified investor's portfolio. And both the manager of the fund and an individual have the same goal: get as much return as possible with as little risk as possible.

To help differentiate between different levels of risk, Morningstar further categorizes asset allocation funds into conservative allocation funds, moderate allocation funds, and aggressive allocation funds. And conveniently, Morningstar calculates the average return for each category.

For example, as of March 23, 2015, according to Morningstar, the average moderate allocation fund returned 0.42% for one month, 2.86% on a year-to-date basis, and 7.87% on a trailing 12-month basis. It even calculates that for the last three years, the average moderate allocation fund returned 9.97% per year and for the trailing five years, the average moderate allocation fund returned 9.14% per year. Morningstar reports that the averages are calculated from data from 952 funds in that category.

An investor with a moderate tolerance for risk could compare himself to the returns of the moderate allocation category. A conservative investor could compare his returns to those of the conservative allocation category, and an aggressive investor could then compare his performance to that of the aggressive category.

If the advisor and the client don't agree on which category is appropriate, then that is the basis for a perfectly healthy debate.

Though clients should expect the advisor to guide them in creating the portfolio, clients should play a large role in selecting the appropriate amount of risk.

These types of conversations between client and advisor should replace the sales conversations. Perhaps there are still people who want to be sold on investment ideas and pay an appropriate commission, but few would consider that to be a relationship between a client and a professional along the lines of a doctor or attorney.

If you are in the market to find the professional advisor instead of a salesperson, how can you tell the difference? For attorneys to call themselves an attorney, they have to pass the bar exam in the state they practice. Unfortunately, it is not so clear for financial advisors. There are, however, a number of designations that can help someone distinguish between financial advisors. Each designation has different requirements, which are laid out in the following table.

The most well-known designation is the CFP® certification. As of Dec. 31, 2014, there are 71,296 CFP® professionals in the United States (CFP Board). I have been a CFP® professional since 1992. The CFP® board does not like us to use the term "Certified Financial Planner" because it implies that we have been specifically certified or approved. Instead, it prefers us to call ourselves CFP® professionals.

The number of certificants has grown steadily since the early 1970s birth of the designation. Since 2009, for example, the number of professionals has grown by 17.6% from 60,634.

To put this in perspective, there are 636,707 registered representatives in the United States as of the end of 2014, according to the website of the Financial Industry Regulatory Authority (FINRA). The organization used to be called the National Association of Securities Dealers (NASD). The self-regulatory organization administers the exams that determine who can call himself a "licensed financial advisor."

Comparing the two numbers, one concludes that a little more than 10% of advisors are CFP® certificants. Deena Katz, whom many consider to be a spokesperson for the financial planning profession, suggests that the CFP® certification is the most appropriate standard of professionalism for advisors. "The designation requires a college degree, professional experience, and a cyclometricly designed board exam based on 72 points from a study of practitioners." In other words, the exam tests skills that will be most useful in practice.[2]

But there are other designations. Most similar to the CFP® certification is the Chartered Financial Consultant®. There are about 46,000 financial planners using the ChFC® designation representing another 7% of the total.

Here is the full list of designations, along with some basic information:

| Designation | Title | Number of Professionals | Specialty | Curriculum |
|---|---|---|---|---|
| CFP® | Certified Financial Planner | 71,296 | Financial Planning | 5 college-level courses—Average study time 350 hours 10-hour board exam |
| ChFC® | Chartered Financial Consultant | 51,875 | Financial Planning | 9 college-level courses—Average study time 400 hours No board exam |
| CIMA® | Certified Investment Management Analyst | 6,895 | Investment Advice | Two exams plus a registered education program at a top business school—Average study time 350 hours |
| CLU® | Chartered Life Underwriter | 104,179 | Insurance | 8 college-level courses—Average study time 400 hours No board exam |
| CFA | Chartered Financial Analyst | More than 100,000 | Investments | 3 six-hour exams taken over at least two years |

Generally, the CLU designation is most popular within the insurance industry; the CFA designation is most popular within the money management business. Insurance skills can be useful for a financial planner and so can money management.

---

[2]In 2013, Katz received the Financial Planning Association's Heart of Financial Planning Award with her husband. She was also selected as one of Investment Advisor's Most Influential People in 2003, 2004, 2006, 2007, and 2008.

While it is impossible to know how many of the CFAs listed above are advising clients as opposed to managing a mutual fund or institutional analysts, it is relatively rare to see a CFA in a client facing position.

There are multiple other designations, but these are certainly the most widely accepted. Some titles draw scrutiny from FINRA, such as anything with the word *senior* in it, which implies an expertise in working with senior citizens. FINRA does not want to see someone call themselves an expert without being an expert, especially if it leads to seniors being taken advantage of.

Of course, both attorneys and accountants have their own set of designations. Many Certified Public Accountants (CPAs) have become financial advisors. The CPA designation commands a great deal of respect, even within the investment business, although the designation relates solely to accounting. While there are no numbers available, experience tells me that only a small number of CPAs are also licensed as financial advisors.

Within the business, the CFP®, ChFC®, CIMA, CFA, and CPA designations carry the most respect because the course requirements are rigorous. It is rare to find financial advisors with the CFA or CPA designation but between the CFP®, CIMA and ChFC® designations, there are over 130,000 financial advisors, enough that one can expect to be able to find a few to pick from. All of the advisors using these designations must meet continuing education requirements or they have to stop using the designations.

It is also encouraging that those wanting to enter the profession can now enroll at a university to become a financial planner. According to *Financial Planning* magazine, a trade publication, "Every recognized profession has its top colleges. Medical and law schools in the U.S. date back to the 18th century. As a much more recent profession, financial planning has spent much of the last four decades developing its own system of education."

There are now six universities with at least 100 enrolled financial planning students: Texas Tech University, Virginia Tech, Boston University, Kansas State, University of Georgia, and San Diego State University, listed in order of size of enrollment.

So, 40 years after May Day, are we a profession? The answer depends on one's experience, which, in turn, depends on the advisor. Scott Adams, author of the Dilbert cartoon, has famously been derisive about the profession.

Not only has he blogged that financial advisors are comparable to palm readers, he went on CNBC to explain why he feels that bad financial advice is such a problem. "What has larger dollar amounts associated with it than personal investing?" Adams said (Navarro 2014). Noting the effectiveness of warning labels on cigarettes, he wondered whether they would be appropriate for financial advisors: "Why not with personal financial advice, when in many cases the biggest risk to the personal investor is the individual giving them advice?"

Soon after, he wrote a Dilbert cartoon. Asok said to his pointy-haired boss "I followed your investment advice and lost all of my savings in the stock market." The boss replied "Did I mention that past performance is not an indication of future returns?" Asok asked, "Then how does 'advice' actually work?'" to which the boss replied "It only works for the people that give it."

Adams's solution is for people to go it alone, to proceed without an advisor. This is a bad idea for most. Two professors, Olivia S. Mitchell of the University of Pennsylvania's Wharton school and Annamaria Lusardi of George Washington University, created a simple three-question financial literacy request (Damato 2015). The questions were very simple. The first question asked,

> "Suppose you had $100 in a savings account and the interest rate was 2% per year. After five years, how much do you think you would have in the account if you left the money to grow?
>
> A. More than $102
> B. Exactly $102
> C. Less than $102"

The next two questions were of similar difficulty.

Less than one-third of Americans answered all three questions correctly.

Most people either don't have the time or the ability to do their own financial planning or manage their own money.

But unfortunately, there is some truth to his Scott Adams's comments. My opinion is that we have made great progress since May Day in 1975 because there are many professionals in the financial advisory business. But I don't think we have reached the point where Scott Adams is more wrong then right.

Some advisors, perhaps more than not, are not professionals, and those advisors should certainly be called "Potholes of Wall Street." But with effort, you can avoid the potholes and find a professional to help you use the advice in this chapter.

# CHAPTER 9

---

# PUTTING INVESTORS FIRST

## THE FUTURE OF FINANCE

Putting Investors First. That was the motivation behind the work that went into this book. The 2008 financial crisis did nothing to improve the already poor reputation of the financial services industry, even though the popular narrative of gambling bankers needing a government bailout is a gross distortion of the causes. While there were certainly bad actors and subsequent penalties that by 2013 had already exceeded $100 billion (Campbell, 2013), the everyday self-seeking advice that is provided to so many individual investors is what really caught our attention. This was happening before the crisis and continued afterward. It's why financial services companies and banks consistently receive low ratings on trust in surveys of public opinion (Harper, 2013).

My own epiphany around this issue occurred during the summer of 2013. After 23 years at JPMorgan spent dealing with institutional clients who generally have the resources to sort good advice from bad, I had set up my own investment firm and began managing money for wealthy individuals as well as institutions. As I reviewed the non-traded REIT investment held by Penelope (described in

Chapter 1), growing incredulity came over me as the prospectus revealed just how abusive the product was. I imagined the guilty laughter of the brokers selling such products after each successful sale drew in another unsuspecting client with little understanding of just how badly their trust was being abused. Frankly, it made me angry. When I was growing up, my grandfather was a bank manager. He ran a local branch of National Provincial Bank (many mergers later, now part of Royal Bank of Scotland). He made loans and took deposits in our suburban community just outside London. It was a very respectable job, and long before computers revolutionized banking it was a respected industry as well. Of course, within financial services there are dozens of very different and specialized subindustries, but most of them ultimately simplify down to providing advice and services around other people's money. The trust clients place in the finance professionals with whom they deal ought to be returned in kind every time. It is not.

The JPMorgan and predecessor firms I worked for operated with integrity, which was manifested in the people who ran them. Well-known names such as Jamie Dimon, Bill Harrison, Walter Shipley, and John McGillicuddy are all current and former CEOs of the lineage from Manufacturers Hanover Trust to Chemical Bank, Chase Manhattan, and JPMorgan. They defined the culture that was built on simply doing the right thing. But the values were propagated throughout the firm by terrific senior managers such as Don Layton. Don is currently CEO of Freddie Mac, one of the two government agencies that underwrite mortgages. America is fortunate to have such an intelligent and highly skilled banker now running a firm whose previous woeful management helped cause the financial crisis. I spent most of my career at JPMorgan working for Don. One of the hallmarks of great management is predictability; if you know how the guy at the top thinks and what questions he would ask if he was in the meeting, the right decision is far more likely to be made without him even being involved. This was the culture that Don Layton instilled. You could hear the questions he'd likely ask and anticipate the expected responses to resolve an issue the way you'd like it to appear on the front page of the *New York Times* (a test that few sales of the products listed in this book could comfortably pass). If the right values are present throughout an organization, the senior manager doesn't need to be everywhere because he *is*, in effect, everywhere already.

I guess I took it for granted that this was the operating protocol in most of financial services. Penelope's experience with non-traded REITs revealed just how far that was from the truth.

As I compared Penelope's experience with those of other new clients, a troubling pattern began to emerge. Moreover, discussions with friends of mine running investment businesses similar to mine began to convince me that these weren't just isolated incidents. We'd all had similar experiences of reviewing past advice and investment products sold that most definitely failed to put the investor first.

It's not that investment recommendations all have to be profitable. Of course it would be nice were it so, but as soon as you move beyond riskless US Treasury bills, the possibility of a higher return naturally comes with the chance of doing worse. The problem is overly expensive, overly complex investment products that render the odds of a successful outcome so poor. And you know what? This is my industry, too. I have spent my professional life in financial services and it will remain my career for the rest of my life. A living made at the expense of clients by selling them inappropriate, expensive products is not a living worth making. The quicker such salespeople switch careers, the better for everyone else. If this book prompts an ethically challenged financial salesperson to move on, or a client to ask more searching questions before committing capital, then we'll have achieved something worthwhile. As long as there are questionable individuals dragging down the reputation of our business, we'll be shining a light in those dark places.

If you strike up a casual conversation with an investment professional and guide the conversation over to non-traded REITs, invariably the response is along the lines of *they're an accident waiting to happen,* a security that ought not to even exist. I once met someone who worked at the firm that had sold Penelope the non-traded REIT in Chapter 1. He had recently joined the training program and hadn't been involved in selling them, at least to that point. I asked him what people inside the firm were saying about American Realty, the REIT in question. He chuckled; commissions had been the driving force behind the recommendation of these and other similar securities to so many clients. With as much as 15% of the investor's money up for grabs through fees, many brokers were able to convince themselves and their clients that even with 85% of your money (i.e., what's left after fees) working for you it was still a good deal.

## UNDERSTAND WHO YOUR ADVISOR WORKS FOR

This and many of the other examples highlight the challenge for the client of identifying the right kind of advisor. As we've discussed, the investment business broadly consists of two types of firm: broker-dealers (B–Ds) and investment advisors (IAs). Confusingly, both employ people calling themselves financial advisors, even though the financial advisors at B–Ds operate differently from those at IAs. It comes down to what is the responsibility of the people you're talking to, or where their loyalties and obligations lie. Investment advisors and the registered people who work for them (called investment advisor representatives, or IARs) have a fiduciary obligation to put the client's interests first. It is required by law, with no exceptions. If you're talking to a financial advisor who works for an IA, he is going to offer advice that is in your best interests or risk losing his license or further sanction. He typically gets paid a fee based on the size of your account, and certainly doesn't share in any transaction fees incurred investing your money. If your financial advisor works for a B–D, he's called a registered representative (RR). He'll still provide you advice, but his fiduciary obligation may be to his employer. He owes his clients a lesser standard of care, that of suitability and disclosure. An important exception to this is the Certified Financial Planner® (CFP), who also owes clients a fiduciary obligation, as John Burke clearly showed in Chapter 8.

It is a confusing structure, and it's unreasonable to expect non–finance people to appreciate the subtle differences, especially when everyone they meet smiles and appears to have only the best of intentions. Think of it like this: an IAR, or a CFP, with their legally binding fiduciary obligation to put your interests first, is sitting at the table alongside of you, contemplating investment choices out there with you. The RR, representing the B–D, is sitting across the table from you. He likely earns his money from transactions, usually commissions on trades but also from mark-up on bond trades he might recommend to you or underwriting fees on newly issued securities (such as non-traded REITs or structured notes). For all of these transactions and indeed, for the advice he offers, he doesn't need to have your best interests at heart. He merely needs to make recommendations that are suitable and properly disclosed.

Recently, there's been attention focused on whether the same fiduciary standard should apply to both types of financial advisor. The Dodd–Frank Wall Street Reform and Consumer Protection Act (known simply as Dodd–Frank) directed the SEC to consider whether everybody advising investors should be a fiduciary. The B-D industry was adamantly opposed. Although such a standard would clearly impede their ability to make money the way they currently do, they argued instead that it would hurt smaller investors, coverage of whom would no longer be profitable and therefore less available. The CFA Institute and others argued in favor of a uniform standard as being in the best interests of clients, reasoning that having some people called financial advisors operating under a different standard than others was confusing. It *is* confusing, and for a while I agreed with the CFA Institute's position. But on reflection, I've come to agree with the B-D industry.

First of all, many financial advisors, or RRs at B-Ds, do offer genuinely good advice. Just because an unscrupulous minority is not acting in the way they should doesn't seem sufficient reason to change how the rest of them work. As long as the nature of the relationship is disclosed, I can't see much wrong with the current setup. I think of the B-D model as similar to a Mercedes dealership. You know when you enter that the friendly salesperson wants to sell you a Mercedes, and will not make any money unless you buy a car. The salesperson is sitting across the table from you, desiring to make a transaction with you. Many people buy cars from Mercedes quite happily in this way. Nobody employs an agent to represent them in negotiating with the car dealer, and even though the sales process emphasizes all the positives of the anticipated purchase while batting away any perceived negatives, it works. Of course, the salesperson genuinely wants you to be happy with your purchase, and probably believes more than anything that this particular Mercedes is the best purchase you can make with your money. However, even if the salesperson doesn't believe all that, you still get the same information, and it doesn't matter. You understand the relationship. You know who represents the car company.

Financial advisors at B-Ds are the equivalent of the Mercedes salesperson in this example. They are generally better educated and the sales process is more sophisticated, but they are nonetheless across the table from you. This works for many clients and crucially, as long as they understand they're not dealing with someone who has a fiduciary obligation to them, I see nothing wrong with this.

Incidentally, some financial advisors at B-Ds will claim they have a fiduciary obligation to their clients at certain times. It depends on the transaction, though, so sometimes they do and sometimes they don't. I would personally dismiss this entirely. You can't have a relationship whose defining quality changes, depending on what is being discussed. You're either a fiduciary 100% of the time or none of the time. There should be no part-time pregnancy in investing when it comes to dealing with clients.

Financial advisors with IAs are more akin to doctors or lawyers, people whose advice is provided with a legal obligation to put your best interests first. This is not to say that doctors and lawyers are flawless, merely to note that the model under which they operate requires them to represent their patient/client wholeheartedly. Conflicts of interest are meant to be disclosed, and if meaningful, the client will be directed to a different professional. To return to the analogy of the table, the financial advisor at an IA is sitting on your side, with you.

As we've seen, both models work, and I don't think the people who work for a B-D should be vilified or forced to overhaul the way they operate. This is one of those issues for which full disclosure can be a sufficient solution. Just as the financial advisor at an IA will inform the client of his obligation to act as a fiduciary, the advisor at a B-D should similarly state that he is not a fiduciary. Sometimes a Realtor will ask you to sign a form acknowledging that the Realtor is bound to put the interests of the seller first, so that if you're a potential buyer you understand the context in which the selling broker's opinions are offered.

I personally think the IA model with its fiduciary obligation is superior, but plenty of people feel differently. The market can decide once accurate information is provided to clients in a plain, easily understood form. I suspect that if every conversation with a broker opened with the admission that the financial advisor is not the type who's a fiduciary, many of them would be clamoring to adopt the same fiduciary standard used by the other half of the industry. Therefore, as long as clients receive accurate information, there's little need to engage in more dramatic change.

This distinction between the two types of financial advisor does raise an interesting point though. If your compensation comes largely through commissions, mark-ups and underwriting fees you are more likely to recommend investments that are laden with those. To use the non-traded REIT example, a careful reading of a prospectus reveals that the fees can reach up to 15% of the investor's capital, leaving only 85% of it to be invested. At the same time, the abuses appear at least anecdotally to be far more prevalent on the B-D side than the IA side. This is because it's virtually impossible for a fiduciary to recommend an investment that results in only 85% of your capital being put to work. It would require the adoption of some fairly heroic and ultimately implausible assumptions on the subsequent return for such a recommendation to really be in the client's best interests. By contrast, the advisor at a B-D isn't burdened by the requirement to put the client's interests first, only by the lesser standard of disclosure and suitability. The clear conflict of interest, in that the advisor stands to benefit from the enormous fees generated by the client's acceptance of the recommended non-traded REIT, need not play a role. They're disclosed and visible to the careful reader. But non-traded REITs are such a poorly designed product that it wouldn't be a bad idea for a new client to inquire of the new advisor whether the advisor had ever sold such a product to a client. It might disqualify the advisor from further consideration by the client, but even if it didn't the knowledge would represent useful information about how that particular individual had balanced his responsibility to clients with his commercial objectives in the past.

## REALLY UNDERSTAND THE FEES

In fact, a common trend at work through many of the chapters concerning investments you should avoid is that they are more frequently recommended by the nonfiduciary type of advisor. It's not a coincidence. It's a bit like hedge funds, in that although the vast majority of hedge fund managers are honest, crooks are attracted to the traditional hedge fund structure because its relative opacity makes it easier to defraud clients than if you're running, say, a mutual fund. To take just one recent example, in January 2015 Magnus Peterson, founder of Weavering Capital, a London-based hedge fund, was sentenced by a London court to 13 years in prison for defrauding his hedge fund investors (Binham, 2015). Weavering had hidden trading losses by executing fictitious derivatives trades between his hedge fund and another entity he controlled. Hedge funds are just easier places in which to engage in such shenanigans. It doesn't mean hedge funds are full of crooks; simply that dishonest financiers find much to like about running hedge funds. Similarly, while the vast majority of advisors at B-Ds are honest, the advantage of the B-D structure for an unscrupulous advisor is that it makes it easier to profit at your client's expense. The absence of a fiduciary standard for B-D advisors is the reason.

The good news is that attention is being focused on the areas we've covered in the book, and daylight is often the best disinfectant. In casual conversations with industry colleagues, the topic of nontraded REITs would typically elicit responses such as, "They're an accident waiting to happen," and similar opinions. In fact, I'd venture that most investment professionals regard these securities quite rightly as overpriced and inappropriate in the vast majority of cases. Their fee structures keep them alive. It's a sorry indictment on the minority who do sell them, and a pity that there aren't more outspoken observers willing to say what they think.

Closed-end funds can be an interesting place to invest. The initial public offerings (IPOs) are generally a bad deal for investors, but there are plenty of smart people who find value for their clients among secondary offerings. A friend of mine, John Cole Scott at CEF Advisors, is someone that can be relied on to navigate the market intelligently on behalf of clients. There are many inefficiencies that clients can exploit; just don't get drawn into participating in IPOs. Most CEF specialists knowingly agree. But once you get beyond that, the discrepancies that occur between net asset value and market price can be worth going after. There just isn't that much liquidity, so although a handful of firms specialize in this area, it requires patience and institutional-sized accounts will need to look elsewhere.

Structured notes are increasingly the target of scrutiny from the regulators. The SEC has an investor alert page that lays out many of the concerns they have about the growth of retail investing in such products. They warn about pricing, poor liquidity, and other impediments to earning an attractive return (SEC, 2015). Jason Zweig is a well-respected writer for the *Wall Street Journal* who has weighed in on the topic. He noted that structured notes, "… are sometimes marketed by less-scrupulous financial advisors" and noted another regulatory warning, from FINRA (FINRA, 2011). At least the regulators are trying to prevent unwitting investors from choosing expensive, poorly constructed products. Generally, the SEC isn't allowed to forbid the sale of an investment just on its merits, and of course, structured notes are compliant with relevant laws and regulations. You can draw your own conclusions as far as what to think of brokers who persist in marketing securities about which regulatory warnings exist. Clearly though, they are highly profitable or firms wouldn't be willing to take the risk. Naturally enough, the brokers that originate and sell structured notes think they're great products. As is often the case, they can point to volumes as proof that they're meeting client demand. Just ask yourself why the buyers are overwhelmingly individuals advised by a salesman rather than institutions who will have greater access to the tools and knowledge with which to figure out how expensive they are.

The hedge fund debate is pretty much over. Today's investors are largely pension funds, reliant on consultants who make money both recommending a chunky hedge fund allocation and then helpfully sourcing individual funds with which to implement it. The smartest people in the business run hedge funds and would never recommend a diversified portfolio. Today's public pension trustees rely on consultants in order to limit their exposure under the Employee Retirement Security Act (ERISA), which governs their activities as well as because many of them don't have sufficient expertise for the role they have. Recommending hedge funds with all their complexity sounds more sophisticated than choosing index funds. Ultimately, the taxpayers who underwrite so many public-sector pension funds will be on the hook to meet the shortfall resulting from poor, self-serving advice provided by the consultants that have been hired.

Because of the economics surrounding how hedge funds are marketed, it's almost certain that if your financial advisor recommends a hedge fund investment he's receiving a lucrative payment if you accept his advice. There are some great hedge funds and happy clients. There always will be. However, the good ones rarely need to pay anyone to find them clients. The people I've met who are happiest with their hedge funds have very few (usually less than five) and often found them informally through a personal recommendation. The best way to use hedge funds is sparingly. You don't need any, but you may come across someone who strikes you as honest and exceptionally smart. Those people are out there, too. If you feel comfortable, go ahead and make a small investment. Don't rely on hedge funds to do much to your overall portfolio, but there are plenty of worthwhile managers, and you may be lucky enough to run into one of them.

The embedded inefficiencies in parts of finance represent a very difficult public policy challenge. The evidence suggests that in some lines of business, banks and brokers are extracting unreasonably high profits, in areas such as investment banking, debt and equity underwriting but also in some transaction areas such as bonds and other more complex products. The year 2008 represented a watershed event in that the government responded to a public outcry over irresponsible Wall Street and moved forward on two fronts: increased regulation and higher capital requirements. Having worked in finance my entire life, I can tell you it was never exactly underregulated. Public opinion demanded a public policy response against Wall Street, but it's not clear to me that lowering the cost of financial services represents a fundamental objective of these initiatives. In fact, the regulatory and capital changes both serve to increase costs as bank CEOs frequently point out. A friend of mine at JPMorgan recently told me that meetings routinely involve at least as many legal and compliance people as business people. It must be a stultifying environment for any business manager trying to navigate a new product through today's complex set of internal approvals and into the marketplace. Of course, financial innovation has only too rarely translated into better ultimate outcomes for clients. However, there have been useful new ideas apart from the ATM, no matter what Paul Volcker may believe. Securitization is one of them; the market for derivatives is another. But the most basic problem is that competition doesn't work as well as it should. The investment potholes described in this book wouldn't be separating nearly as many people from their money if the costs were clearly understood. What's needed is a simpler way of explaining in plain English just what's going on. Instead, financial transactions are documented with densely written prospectuses and contracts that meet the letter of the law in terms of disclosure but fail to explain much that is useful to the non-investment professional. Meaningfully increased transparency can surely only help.

## TRY ASKING THESE QUESTIONS

When choosing your advisor, it can be helpful to have a list of questions ready. The answers will help you decide whether you're making the right choice.

1. *Do you have a fiduciary obligation to me?* If you care about the answer to this question, the only acceptable answer is, "Yes." Nothing else works. "Usually but not in certain cases," or "Sometimes," or, "No but if I was I wouldn't be able to offer you some of our best deals," should all count as a negative response. You can still pursue a relationship with this advisor, but understand that he's sitting across the table from you rather than alongside, and that his compensation will come in part if not entirely from the transactions you do.
2. *How will we assess your performance?* It ought to be such a simple task to figure out whether your advisor's advice has helped you.

After all, investing lends itself to quantitative measures of results more than perhaps any other endeavor. If your advisor plans to rely on qualitative measures such as, "Better than expected," or, "Quite good under the circumstances," then beware. Nobody likes to be benchmarked. When I was investing in hedge funds, I'd often ask a manager how we'd agree after the fact whether he'd done a good job. Although you'd think that evaluating hedge fund performance should be straightforward because they do produce numerical results, every hedge fund manager I ever met insisted that *this* fund couldn't be compared with other similar-looking hedge funds. Although the manager might have sincerely believed that what he was doing was different than anybody else, the absence of a clear benchmark is invariably to the advantage of the one whose responsibility it is to generate the results. My question was receptive to a wide range of answers. The manager could suggest almost any measure of assessing results, as long as it was measurable. He could select comparison with an obscure hedge fund index I'd never heard of, or state a number, such as "at least 10%" (although we'd also have to agree on a risk measure, too, since without it a 10% return target is meaningless). But we had to agree on something that involved the use of numbers. I always found it vaguely amusing that people whose whole life involves analysis with numbers could be so unprepared to submit their own work to the same type of review.

3. *How much will it cost?* You may have to probe a bit on this question to make sure you get a complete answer. For example, in our business we charge a quarterly fee, which is a percentage of assets. When we do trades, the client typically pays a commission of $8.95 per trade to Charles Schwab, where we custody most of our assets. Of course, we don't get the commission and have no incentive to overtrade. Because we run investment strategies that only own equities, there are no other fees. If your advisor works for a B-D, there may be commissions, bond markups, and underwriting fees if you buy new issue securities. Bond markups can quickly add up, and you may be better off owning an ETF or mutual fund because their

transactions costs in the bond market are far lower than those faced by individuals. We pointed this out in Chapter 2. The SEC has published a report identifying the high costs faced by individual bond investors. If your advisor plans to buy bonds for you, make sure you fully understand the transactions costs. Buying new issue securities is invariably expensive and in aggregate not worth the money. We talked about closed-end fund IPOs in Chapter 2 and explained why you should *never* buy a closed-end fund IPO. The same is true of non-traded REITs. Occasionally, there might be a good deal in the secondary market when some poor souls who inadvisedly bought into the IPO finally ditch the disappointing investment at a fire-sale price, but as an individual you're unlikely to see such a transaction and are certainly poorly placed to evaluate it unless you have expertise in the area. Conventional IPOs have in aggregate been shown to dramatically underperform the equity market (Ritter, 2013). Jay Ritter, from the University of Florida, found that the average three-year market adjusted return on IPOs from 1980–2011 was −19.8% (i.e., they underperformed the market by this amount). IPOs are priced to jump on the first day's trading, which is part of the marketing strategy to draw in new buyers. There is a big adverse selection process at work, though, in that you'll get more of the flops while the truly attractive ones are scooped up by the clients who pay the most commissions. You're also buying securities from true insiders who know far more than you possibly could about the company in question. They've selected the time and price at which to sell so as to maximize their own economics, not accommodate your desire for an attractive return. If you forswear all IPOs you'll miss many bad ones to compensate for the odd good one. Especially beware an advisor who claims he'll get you in the latest hot IPOs. One way or another, you'll probably be paying for it. You'll need to go through all of these costs to make sure you have the complete picture.

4. *Do you invest in products that have been the subject of warnings from the regulators?* This is a revealing question, because if the answer's yes, then an explanation has to follow. Indeed, what

is an acceptable response to this question? Most likely, you'll be told that the regulators aren't really that smart, and that they don't appreciate some of the subtle sources of value to be found. Or that his firm only sells the most attractive type of the securities in question. Or maybe that he used to but has since recovered, as if from an addiction. But whatever the answer, you should think pretty carefully before proceeding to do business with someone who has seen fit to promote investments that have drawn such regulatory scrutiny. It's possible there's a good answer, but if you use this question to reject an advisor, you'll probably be better off.

5. *What conflicts of interest do you have?* You want an advisor who puts your interests first 100% of the time. If this isn't going to be the case, you need to understand when, and why, you won't be receiving completely unbiased guidance. The principal–agent problem is fundamental to many of the business relationships that exist in finance. Your advisor is your agent, and whether the advisor is a fiduciary or not, as the principal you need to be prepared to manage that relationship so you get the best possible advice and outcomes.

## WHAT ELSE CAN BE DONE?

The regulatory structure in the United States possesses Byzantine complexity. For example, trading markets are divided between the SEC (for securities) and futures (the CFTC). The fact that an ETF on the S&P 500 is regulated by the SEC while a futures contract on the S&P 500 falls under CFTC jurisdiction is a reflection of the way politicians have put their own interests first. The continued existence of the two regulators traces back to the Senate Committees, which oversee them: finance (for the SEC) and agriculture (for the CFTC, since futures were originally based mostly on agricultural commodities). Even during the overhaul of financial markets regulation that took place following the crisis of 2008, merging the SEC and CFTC was regarded (Vekshin, 2009) by policymakers as a nonstarter, because each committee's members enjoyed campaign contributions from their respective industries. Merging the CFTC into the SEC under the oversight of the Senate Finance Committee would remove an important source of campaign contributions for the members of the agricultural committee, and was regarded at the time by then-Treasury Secretary Tim Geithner as a fight not worth having. The GAO (US Government Accountability Office), a nonpartisan Congressional agency (U.S. GAO, 1995), long ago concluded that such a merger made sense.

Bankers routinely complain about the deadening effect of increasing regulation. JPMorgan's CEO Jamie Dimon notes in the company's 2014 annual report that nowadays when a bank does something wrong, there are multiple regulators, each levying fines that are often set independently of one another. It's not that banks shouldn't be punished when they break the rules, but when multiple regulators all pile on with their own individual punishments, it looks more like an alternative source of tax revenue than part of a carefully considered, investor-oriented regulatory regime.

It would be hard to argue that today's financial services industry is underregulated. Yet we've been able to write a book full of products that in many cases shouldn't be sold to clients in their current form. Although it's tempting to assert that even greater regulation is needed, we believe people in the industry need to take more responsibility for ensuring they do what's right. If the vast majority of the professionals who provide honest advice would speak out more when they see things that reflect poorly on the whole industry, we'd go some way toward restoring reputations and weakening the public policy drift of applying ever-increasing levels of regulation and oversight.

Many of the products we've written about, such as non-traded REITs, structured notes, and annuities, are the subject of investor alerts on FINRA's website. Most people would find it quite extraordinary that even though the agency that regulates broker-dealers provides warnings on certain investment products, some firms continue to sell them. Therefore, do the warnings mean anything? Are they unreasonably cautious, or just wrong? Are investors supposed to heed them and avoid such investments? And on the rare occasion when a client asks of a financial advisor how their firm reconciles its recommendation to buy a non-traded REIT with FINRA's admonitions, how exactly does the advisor respond?

In this respect, we look rather like the tobacco industry, where dangerous products are sold with warning labels. Is that really the limit of the standard to which we aspire? Shouldn't advisors be aiming just a little higher?

## THE ROLE OF CFA INSTITUTE

CFA Institute is a great organization that is well positioned to have a voice on such issues. CFA® charterholders (of which I am one) are required to pass three six-hour exams and conduct themselves in an ethical manner. Chartered Financial Analysts have demonstrated a solid understanding of how to analyze investments, and while continuous learning is a requirement of every charterholder, passing the exams does in my opinion reflect a substantial commitment to personal excellence in the field. CFA Institute doesn't sell anything beyond educational products and membership in its organization. Its Mission statement is:

> "To lead the investment profession globally by promoting the highest standards of ethics, education, and professional excellence for the ultimate benefit of society."

These are lofty goals and yet perfectly appropriate. In fact, the CFA Institute Professional Conduct Program and the Disciplinary Review Committee routinely sanction members it finds have failed in some meaningful way to live up to its Code of Conduct and Standards of Practice. Their names are published in the CFA Institute magazine and on the website along with a description of their misconduct, and applicable sanction which can include permanent revocation of their CFA® charter. Out of the more than 130,000 members worldwide (CFA Institute, 2015), only a very small percentage find themselves subject to the disciplinary process. This is a reflection of the importance that each CFA charterholder places on embodying the Mission Statement. Having invested the typical 300 hours of study recommended to pass each of the three exams few are going to find the possible loss of their CFA® charter a risk worth taking.

CFA Institute launched an initiative called The Future of Finance, part of a "Global effort to shape a trustworthy, forward-thinking financial industry that better serves society." One area of focus is "Putting Investors First." It includes a list of ten "investor rights" that any investor should expect from their financial services provider. Here is the CFA Institute Statement of Investor Rights:

1. Honest, competent, and ethical conduct that complies with applicable law;
2. Independent and objective advice and assistance based on informed analysis, prudent judgment, and diligent effort;
3. My financial interests taking precedence over those of the professional and the organization;
4. Fair treatment with respect to other clients;
5. Disclosure of any existing or potential conflicts of interest in providing products or services to me;
6. Understanding of my circumstances, so that any advice provided is suitable and based on my financial objectives and constraints;
7. Clear, accurate, complete and timely communications that use plain language and are presented in a format that conveys the information effectively;
8. An explanation of all fees and costs charged to me, and information showing these expenses to be fair and reasonable;
9. Confidentiality of my information;
10. Appropriate and complete records to support the work done on my behalf.

#7 in particular would go a long way towards helping clients better understand the investments they're buying. Current standards of disclosure result in documents that run to hundreds of pages being provided. While meeting a legal standard, it doesn't always promote understanding.

CFA Institute is currently finding its voice in this area. Given the preponderance of disadvantageous products still in existence, surely a part of Putting Investors First must include pointing out examples of those interests not being put first. CFA Institute represents much of what's right within the financial services arena. It's fair to say that if everybody in the industry, regardless of whether or not they're a CFA® charterholder, conducted themselves on a daily basis in a way that's consistent with the Statement of Investor Rights listed above, the world would be a better place. Achieving that seems like a worthwhile goal.

CFA Institute also offers an "Integrity List," consisting of 50 more detailed steps Finance professionals can take to promote a better industry. It's promoted as, "Fifty actions you can take to build trust and enhance your firm's reputation." Because while this book is directed at clients, the people that advise them are ultimately the most important part of the solution. The list comprises six categories: committing personally to ethical and honest behavior; inspiring others to do the same; developing trustworthy relationships; transparent communication; continuing learning, and advocacy for a better system.

I won't include all 50 items on the Integrity List here. You can find it at: http://www.cfainstitute.org. Whereas the Statement of Investor Rights tells clients what they should expect, the Integrity List tells the individuals who make up the industry how they can conduct themselves for everybody's benefit. It includes committing to honest and ethical behavior, but also pointing out areas of abuse publicly. Naturally, this book has come about because the writers all believe that more needs to be done. It isn't that hard to provide objective criticism of some things that stand out. If all you know about non-traded REITs is that they charge clients 15% in up-front fees that ought to be enough for anyone striving to live with the Integrity List to disassociate themselves from the product. And it's therefore not hard to write publicly about what you see that's wrong. You don't have to write a book, it can be in your blog or investor letter.

## BIGGER ISN'T ALWAYS BETTER

In finance, size brings with it conflicts of interest. Big firms will usually grab the headlines, but it's harder for big firms to promote all 50 items on the Integrity List. Endorsing ethical behavior is fine, but few large firms are going to tolerate employees practicing #2 on the list of 50, which is to "Name and shame unethical behavior." Large size increases the odds that they'll offend someone who may be a client, and conflicts of interest are an inevitable part of size. Smaller firms with simpler business models are better able to pursue a single-minded focus on providing client-centered service. "Strive for a conflict-free business model" is #3 on the list, and while it's more aspirational than realistic for big firms, it's not an unreasonable objective for smaller ones.

While investing your money through a large firm can inspire confidence that it'll be safely handled, few large firms nowadays can point to an unblemished regulatory record. Often, the point of size is to find synergies across different business units and to exploit "cross-sell" opportunities. Growth demonstrates satisfied clients, but the more important question clients should ask themselves is whether that growth is good for the clients.

Size makes it harder to outperform the market as well. For example, an article in the *New York Times* found that most mutual funds run by large banks underperform the averages. It analyzed data from Morningstar on funds run by Goldman Sachs, Morgan Stanley, Wells Fargo, and my old firm JPMorgan to arrive at this conclusion. In the article (Popper, 2015), Larry Swedroe, director of research at Buckingham Asset Management, commented that, "It's a good business for them—but that doesn't mean it is a good investment."

In this book we've set out to help investors and to provide constructively to the ongoing debate around Wall Street and whether it delivers what it should. The growth in financial services that's taken place over the past 30 years has not obviously coincided with improved economic outcomes. As we've shown, basic measures of the cost of financial intermediation have not changed in spite of the enormous investments in IT that have taken place. Median living standards adjusted for inflation are also roughly where they were at the beginning of the 30-year boom in Finance, as I showed in an earlier book, *Bonds Are Not Forever*. Although the financial sector continues to perform many vital tasks for the economy, the 2008 crisis showed that much was wrong. Investment banks were certainly woefully undercapitalized with as much as \$30 of assets for each \$1 of equity. Approving such wildly risky leverage was frankly stupid by all concerned. Among the many regulatory changes since then has been a steady increase in the levels of equity capital required by banks as well as the creation of the new designation of "Systemically Important Financial Institution," or SIFI. Such companies are deemed "too big to fail," and therefore since they have an implicit public sector guarantee they receive an additional level of regulatory scrutiny as well as heightened capital requirements. Although the patchwork of regulatory agencies in the US represents a great disservice and demonstrates a political inability to put America's interests first, bigger firms do deserve tougher rules. If size is a good thing in banking, it ought to generate a higher return on capital, so higher levels of capital need not be a problem. If it can't do that, it makes sense to shrink.

General Electric (GE) most dramatically demonstrated this in its recent decision to spin off most of GE Capital, their finance arm. There was a time when GE Capital represented almost half of the parent company's profits (Stewart, 2015), although the freezing up of financial markets in 2008 caused them funding problems and led to a steady reduction in GE's reliance on finance to drive its profits. The SIFI designation that GE's size drew was a factor in their decision, and shedding most of GE Capital was expected to free them from being a SIFI along with the increased cost of regulatory scrutiny and capital requirements this entails.

It's hard to see anything bad in this outcome. GE's financial assets will largely wind up in the hands of disparate other firms. GE itself probably becomes marginally less complicated and therefore less risky to the public sector in the event of another crisis. The services GE Capital provided will largely continue to be on offer, just with different owners.

Another consequence of the 2008 crisis has been to make working in financial services a generally more miserable experience.

This is especially so in large firms who bear the brunt of the many changes driven by a strong public desire to avoid a repeat of the public bailouts. Anecdotally, anybody with friends at a large financial institution can recount weary complaints about the internal power of compliance and risk managers. A recent global survey of the industry revealed widespread dissatisfaction about compensation and "dull work" (McLannahan, 2015).

When I worked at JPMorgan, any new investment product had to pass through a rigorous new product approval process. It was necessary to obtain a sign-off from a wide variety of support units covering areas of risk such as market, legal, and reputational. Navigating through this was appropriate and tedious at the same time. Unsurprisingly, reports indicate that substantially more rigorous reviews are now the norm.

Much attention has focused on unreasonably high compensation. It will be obvious to the reader that the authors of this book all make their living in financial services, so one can easily dismiss any views on the topic as lacking objectivity. Any business requires labor and capital to operate. It always seemed to me that in the division of profits in finance between the providers of these two inputs, the providers of capital received the short end of the stick compared to the providers of labor (i.e., the employees). While bankers and brokers can't claim to be poorly paid, there is some evidence that the pendulum is shifting back toward capital; at a minimum, since the industry broadly requires more capital than it used to in order to operate under today's rules, more of the profits are earmarked to provide that capital an acceptable return. This also seems quite appropriate. To my mind, some of the criticism of Wall Street compensation can be traced back to the insufficient levels of capital at which the industry was allowed to operate. Fixing that alters the balance between the two, and while I don't believe there's any merit to a public policy that focuses on compensation in any private sector, compensation critics must at least be drawing some satisfaction from the direction things are moving.

Improved outcomes for clients of the financial services industry will require that the clients become more discerning. It takes homework and effort to find an advisor who will truly put your interests first. Because such things are important but rarely urgent, it's often easy to put off the analysis that will help you find a relationship that's best for you. This book is intended to provide information and tools to allow clients to take greater control of their finances.

There's little doubt that the providers of financial services need to change too, and this book is also addressed at them. Collectively, we need to raise our game. We need to ensure clients are put first, that investments are explained clearly, and that fees are fair. Our industry has been maligned because too many individuals are operating at odds with the CFA Institute's Integrity List or anything similar. The vast majority should take hold of the industry's reputation and ensure the trust so many people place in us is amply repaid.

# ABOUT THE
# CONTRIBUTORS

**Kevin Brolley**
Since 2003 Mr. Brolley has been the managing partner at Oceans Four Development Corporation, a Florida real estate investment company.

Prior to this he spent 16 years in investment banking in London, England. From 1997 through 2002, he was a managing director with JPMorgan Chase and was responsible for the European Credit Sales team covering institutional investors. His team's products covered the full credit spectrum from high grade to high yield, cash and credit derivatives, and structured products. They were a leading player in the development of the CDO business. He also worked seven years with Morgan Stanley and two with Drexel Burnham Lambert.

He received his bachelor of arts degree from the University of Florida, *with high honors*, and his MBA from Trinity College, Dublin, Ireland.

He resides in Delray Beach, Florida, with his wife, and has two daughters recently graduated from college. He is an avid cyclist and fisherman.

## John Burke

John Burke owns and manages Burke Financial Strategies. In 2015, *The Financial Times* listed him as one of the top 400 advisors in the country. He has been a practicing financial advisor since 1983, and during his extensive career has helped thousands of clients with financial planning and investment management. John is also a well-respected strategist; his research was published in the July 2010 issue of the *Journal of Financial Planning*. He has appeared frequently on CNBC and Fox Business News and has been quoted in numerous financial publications.

John's career began at Merrill Lynch, where he was hired as a financial advisor in December 1983. He then joined Smith Barney and later Morgan Stanley, and was named to both firms' President's Clubs. Since joining Raymond James, he has been named to the firm's prestigious 2011, 2012, 2013, and 2014 Chairman's Council.

John received his undergraduate degree in finance from Lehigh University. He went on to earn the Certified Financial Planner™ certification in 1992, and also earned his master's degree in financial planning in 2003.

In addition to Burke Financial Strategies, John owns the Academy for Continuing Professional Education, which provides continuing education classes for accountants in central New Jersey. He is also an active member of his community and church, St. Paul's Episcopal Church in Westfield, New Jersey, where he has served as treasurer.

## Bob Centrella, CFA

Bob Centrella, CFA, is president and managing partner of Forza Investment Advisory, LLC. Bob is a former equity mutual fund portfolio manager with 29 years of experience in the financial services industry, including 23+ years as a professional money manager serving both institutions and private clients. Bob holds the Chartered Financial Analyst® designation (1993), has an MBA in finance from George Mason University (1990) and a bachelor of science in accounting from the University of Scranton (1983). Prior to founding Forza Investment Advisory, Bob spent 14 years at MacKay Shields, where he was a senior managing director ($30 billion total assets) and co-head of all growth equity assets and portfolios. He also served on the Investment

Committee of the Total Return Fund, a balanced mutual fund. During his career, he has worked for several types of financial institutions including banks, a government agency (FNMA), blue-chip insurance companies, and investment management firms. This experience, coupled with his education, provides a unique perspective from which to advise clients and manage investments. (Note: CFA® and Chartered Financial Analyst® are registered trademarks owned by CFA Institute.)

**David Pasi**
Since autumn 2010, David has been the senior portfolio manager for Delta Financial Group, Inc., a registered investment advisor. David began his career in 1982 working as an auditor for national and then international money center banks. From the mid-1980s to 2010, David worked at a number of financial institutions, as well as started and managed a hedge fund (1996–2000). He has an extensive fixed income, portfolio management, and derivatives trading background, as well as experience in risk management, accounting, operations, and audit.

He has been an active member of numerous financial industry organizations and also serves in a leadership capacity with charitable and civic groups.

In May 2011, David Pasi joined the board of Aspen University and is a director on the audit committee. Aspen University is a publicly traded corporation. Aspen is exclusively online education, operating for-profit, primarily seeking students who are enrolling in a graduate-degree programs.

David has a dual degree from Rutgers University in economics and accounting.

# ABOUT THE AUTHOR

**Simon Lack, CFA**

Following 23 years with JPMorgan, Simon Lack founded SL Advisors, LLC, in 2009. Much of Simon Lack's career with JPMorgan was spent in North American Fixed Income Derivatives and Forward FX trading, a business that he ran successfully through several bank mergers, ultimately overseeing 50 professionals and $300 million in annual revenues. Simon Lack sat on JPMorgan's investment committee, allocating over $1 billion to hedge fund managers, and founded the JPMorgan Incubator Funds, two private equity vehicles that took economic stakes in emerging hedge fund managers.

Simon chairs the investment committee for Wardlaw–Hartridge School in Edison, New Jersey, and also chairs the Memorial Endowment Trust Investment Committee of St. Paul's Episcopal Church in Westfield, New Jersey. He is the author of *The Hedge Fund Mirage: The Illusion of Big Money and Why It's Too Good to Be True*, published in 2012 to widespread praise from mainstream financial press, including *The Economist, Financial Times,* and *Wall Street Journal,* and *Bonds Are Not Forever: The Crisis Facing Fixed Income Investors* (September 2013).

Simon is a CFA charterholder and vice-chairman of the New York Society of Security Analysts' Market Integrity Committee. He makes regular appearances on cable TV business shows discussing hedge funds and investing. Simon is also portfolio manager for the Catalyst MLP and Infrastructure Fund.

# BIBLIOGRAPHY

Adams Express Company. *About Adams Express.* n.d. http://www.adamsexpress
.com/about-adams-express (accessed October 17, 2014).

AIMA. *The Way Ahead—Helping Trustees Navigate the Hedge Fund Sector, AIMA,
CAIA.* January 28, 2015. https://caia.org/sites/default/files/documents/news/
caia-aima-paper1-the-way-ahead.pdf.

ALPS. *Alerian MLP ETF.* February 24, 2015. http://www.alpsfunds.com/AMLP
(accessed February 24, 2015).

Baer, Justin, and Andrew Ackerman. "SEC Head: Raise the Bar for Advisers." *The
Wall Street Journal* (March 18, 2015), C5.

Berkshire Hathaway Annual Report, letter by Warren Buffett.

Brandon, Denby E. Jr., and H. Oliver Welch, *The History of Financial Planning*
(2009), 17.

Brinson, Gary P., L. Randolph Hood, and Gilbert Beebower, "Determinants of
Portfolio Performance," *Financial Analysts Journal* (January-February 1995).

Burne, Katy, and Aaron Kuriloff. *Regulators Want Data on Bond-Trade Fees* (January
13, 2015). http://www.wsj.com/articles/regulators-want-data-on-bond-trade-
fees-1421193311.

Buttonwood. *Money to Burn. The Economist* (May 4, 2013). http://www.economist
.com/news/finance-and-economics/21577088-muddle-headed-world-
american-public-pension-accounting-money-burn.

CalPERS. *CalPERS Eliminates Hedge Fund Program in Effort to Reduce Complexity and
Costs in Investment Portfolio.* September 15, 2014. https://www.calpers.ca.gov/
page/newsroom/calpers-news/2014/eliminate-hedge-fund.

CFP © Board website.

CNN Money. "ultimate guide to retirement." n.d. money.cnn.com/retirement/ guide/Annuities/?iid=EL (accessed October 2014).

Cookson, Clive. *Bankers Have Tendency to Lie for Financial Gain, Say Scientists. Financial Times* (November 19, 2014). http://www.ft.com/intl/cms/s/0/21ef6916-6fd8-11e4-90af-00144feabdc0.html?ftcamp=published_links/rss/home_us/ feed//product#axzz3OhvfOq5G.

Dalbar's 12th Annual Quantitative Analysis of Investor Behavior, 2006 Edition.

Damato, Karen, "A Three-Question Test of Financial Literacy," *The Wall Street Journal* (March 28, 2015), B9.

Enrich, David, and Jean Englesham. "Clubby London Trading Scene Fostered Libor Rate-Fixing Scandal." *Wall Street Journal* (May 2, 2013). http://www.wsj.com/ articles/SB10001424127887323296504578396670651342096.

Farrell, Maureen. "For you … anything. Barclays Libor Emails Paint Ugly Picture." CNN Money (July 4, 2012). http://buzz.money.cnn.com/2012/07/04/ barclays-libor-email/.

Ferré, Emily Claire. "The Many Uses of Silver." *Geology* (January 31, 2015). http:// geology.com/articles/uses-of-silver/.

FINRA. *Public Non-Traded REITs—Perform a Careful Review Before Investing.* August 15, 2012. http://www.finra.org/investors/protectyourself/investoralerts/reits/ p124232 (accessed August 25, 2014).

FXCM. *Profitability Analysis.* January 9, 2015. http://docs.fxcorporate.com/ profitability_analysis_en.pdf.

"Government Affairs Regulations Under Federal Securities Law 2013 Fact Book." *Insured Retirement Institute.* 2013. http://www.irionline.org/government-affairs/ annuities-regulation-industry-information/regulations-under-federal-securities-law (accessed November 9, 2014).

Grable, John E., and Swarn Chatterjee. "Reducing Wealth Volatility: The Value of Financial Advice as Measured by Zeta," *Journal of Financial Planning* (August 2014), 45.

Jain, Sameer. The Case for Investing in Non-Traded REITs. WealthManagement.com (November 8, 2013). http://wealthmanagement.com/viewpoints/ case-investing-non-traded-reits.

Kay, John. "Enduring Lessons from the Legend of Rothschild's Carrier Pigeon." *Financial Times* (May 28, 2013). http://www.ft.com/intl/cms/s/0/255b75e0-c77d-11e2-be27-00144feab7de.html#axzz3QPUCpdB4.

Kennon, Joshua. "The Refrigerator Problem." About.com (2015). http:// beginnersinvest.about.com/od/retirementcenter/a/aa110606a.htm (accessed February 24, 2015).

Kelly, Bruce. "Thompson's Former Nontraded REIT Drops Nearly 30%." *InvestmentNews* (July 21, 2014). http://www.investmentnews.com/article/20140721/ FREE/140729997/thompsons-former-nontraded-reit-drops-nearly-30.

Lack, Simon. "Why We're Betting on CDE Management by Buying the Gold Miners ETFs." *Seeking Alpha* (June 29, 2012). http://seekingalpha.com/article/692431-why-were-betting-on-cde-management-by-buying-the-gold-miners-etfs.

Lewis, Michael. *Flash Boys*. New York: W. W. Norton & Company, 2013.

Loomis Jr., Philip A., Remarks at 1975 Annual Conference, The Financial Analysts Federation. From the archives of the Securities Exchange Commission.

Magyar, Mark J. *Christie's $2.4 Billion Cut Triggers Battle over Future of NJ Pension System*. NJ Spotlight (May 21, 2014). http://www.njspotlight.com/stories/14/05/21/christie-s-2-4-billion-cut-triggers-battle-over-future-of-nj-pension-system/?p=all.

Marvin Feldman, CLU, ChFC, RFC, Maria Wood. "Slideshow: The History of Annuities," *LifeHealthPro* (May 8, 2012). http://www.lifehealthpro.com/2012/05/08/slideshow-the-history-of-annuities?page=2.

Mercado, Darla. "Investment News." *investment* news.com. 9 8, 2014. http://www.investmentnews.com/article/20140908/FREE/140909942 (accessed October 1, 2014).

Morningstar Advisor Workstation.

Murphy, Paul. "Death of an FX Punter." *Financial Times* (January 16, 2015). http://ftalphaville.ft.com/2015/01/16/2091772/death-of-an-fx-punter/.

Navarro Bruno J., "Beware Financial Advisors, 'Dilbert' creator says by Bruno J. Navarro," ETCCNBC.com (August 8, 2014).

Pasi, David. "Savings Bond: Little-Known Good Deal." *adviceIQ*, 2012: 1.

Philippon, Thomas. *Finance vs. Wal-Mart: Why are Financial Services so Expensive* (2012). http://www.russellsage.org/sites/all/files/Rethinking-Finance/Philippon_v3.pdf.

S&P Dow Jones. *Unveiling the Hidden Cost of Retail Bond-Buying*. June 30, 2014. https://us.spindices.com/documents/commentary/muni-transaction-costs-june2014.pdf?force_download=true.

Saft, James. "Non-traded REITs Are a Relationship Ender." Reuters (January 23, 2014). http://www.reuters.com/article/2014/01/23/us-saft-reits-idUSBREA0L25720140123 (accessed August 25, 2014).

Salmon, Felix. "Why Investors Should Avoid Hedge Funds." Reuters.com (August 8, 2012). http://blogs.reuters.com/felix-salmon/2012/08/08/why-investors-should-avoid-hedge-funds/.

Schoeff, Mark. *InvestmentNews, The Leading Information Source for Financial Advisors*. 10 24, 2014. http://www.investmentnews.com/article/20141024/FREE/141029947 (accessed November 09, 2014).

SEC.GOV, US Securities and Exchange Commission. *Annuities*. n.d. http://www.sec.gov/answers/annuity.htm (accessed November 11, 2014).

Seides, Ted. "Is CalPERS a Canary in the Coal Mine?" *Enterprising Investor* (November 18, 2014). http://blogs.cfainstitute.org/investor/2014/11/17/is-calpers-a-canary-in-the-coal-mine/.

Shareholders Square Table. *Shareholders Square Table*. April 20, 2015. http://www
.shareholderssquaretable.com/ (accessed April 20, 2015).

Silver Institute. *World Silver Supply and Demand*. Accessed January 31, 2015. https://
www.silverinstitute.org/site/supply-demand/.

Sorkin, Andrew Ross. "Doubts Raised on Value of Investment Consultants to Pensions." *New York Times* (September 30, 2013). http://dealbook.nytimes.com/
2013/09/30/doubts-raised-on-value-of-investment-consultants-to-pensions/?_
r=0.

Timiraos, Nick. "WSJ/NBC Poll: Congress More Unpopular Than Wall Street."
*Wall Street Journal* (August 6, 2014). http://blogs.wsj.com/washwire/2014/08/
06/wsjnbc-poll-congress-more-unpopular-than-wall-street/ Trevedi, Anjani.
"Swiss-Franc Move Crushes Currency Brokers." Wall Street Journal (January
16, 2015). http://www.wsj.com/articles/swiss-franc-move-cripples-currency-
brokers-1421371654?mod=WSJ_hp_LEFTTopStories.

Trugman, Jonathon M. "How NYSE, Nasdaq profit off 'Flash Boys'." *New
York Post* (April 6, 2014). http://nypost.com/2014/04/06/how-nyse-nasdaq-
profit-off-flash-boys/.

Whelan, Robbie. "Nontraded REITs Are Hot, But Have Plenty of Critics." *Wall
Street Journal* (June 15, 2014). http://online.wsj.com/articles/nontraded-reits-
offer-high-returns-but-critics-cite-fees-and-illiquidity-1402670753.

# INDEX